THE REIGN OF
ARTHUR

FROM HISTORY TO LEGEND

CHRISTOPHER GIDLOW

SUTTON PUBLISHING

First published in 2004 by
Sutton Publishing Limited
Phoenix Mill · Thrupp · Stroud
Gloucestershire · GL5 2BU

British Library Cataloguing in Publication Data
A catalogue record for this book is available from the British Library.

ISBN 0-7509-3418-2

To The Oxford Arthurian Society, without which . . .

Typeset in Photina MT 10.5/15pt.
Typesetting and origination by
Sutton Publishing Limited.
Printed and bound in England by
J.H. Haynes & Co. Ltd, Sparkford.

CONTENTS

List of Illustrations

MAPS

PHOTOGRAPHS

1. The earliest reference to Arthur. His name can be seen in the lower right corner. From *Y Gododdin*, in the fourteenth-century Book of Aneirin, Cardiff Public Library Ms 1 (2.81) f37. (Reproduced courtesy of Cardiff Council and the National Library of Wales)

2. Catterick. There are no surface remains of the Roman fort, which stood in the foreground of the picture. (Julie Hudson)

3. Carn Cabal (Carn Gafallt). The cairn itself sits beyond the ridge to the right of the summit. (Julie Hudson)

4. The Arthurian battle-list. From the earliest manuscript of *Historia Brittonum*, Harleian Ms. 3859 f187. (By permission of the British Library)

5. The Arthur Stone, Dorstone, near Hay-on-Wye. Apparently the tomb of Anir from *Historia Brittonum*. (Julie Hudson)

6. Liddington Castle, a frequently suggested site for Mount Badon. (Julie Hudson)

ACKNOWLEDGEMENTS

Many thanks to all those who helped me on the long route to *The Reign of Arthur*. Special thanks must go to Andrew Smith, for his persuasive suggestions, eye for detail and help with tricky translations, and also for permission to use his research on the press coverage of the Artognou stone. Thanks, too, to the numerous members of the Oxford Arthurian Society, especially Peter Ewing, whose thought-provoking talks raised many of the ideas tackled here. Dr Jeremy Catto, Dr Nick Higham and Charles Evans-Günther gave help and support when this book was still in its infancy. I should also like to thank my wife Julie, our son Geheris and my parents Alan and Valerie for, among other things, our intrepid expeditions to most of the obscure Arthurian locations mentioned in this book. Lastly, I should mention my primary school teacher Keith Moxon, who first introduced me to the dark-age historical context of the Arthurian Legends of which I was so fond. It was that encouragement which, ultimately, led to this book being written.

Unless otherwise stated, the images in this book are © Julie Hudson, and are used with permission. The extract on p. 238 is reprinted by permission of Boydell & Brewer Ltd from *King Arthur, Hero and Legend* by Richard Barber (Boydell Press, 1986) p. 135. Extracts from Thorpe, L. (ed. and trans), *Geoffrey of Monmouth, The History of the Kings of Britain* (Harmondsworth, 1966), © Lewis Thorpe 1966 and Thorpe, L. (ed. and trans), *Gerald of Wales: Description of Wales* (Harmondsworth, 1978), pp. 281–8, © the estate of Lewis Thorpe 1978, are reproduced by permission of Penguin Books Ltd.

The quotation from Malory's *Le Morte Darthur* is taken from Vinaver, A., *Malory Works* (OUP, 1971). It is reprinted by permission of Oxford University Press. The quotation from Myres, J.N.L., *The English Settlements* (OUP, 1986), is also reproduced by permission of Oxford University Press.

Unless otherwise noted, extracts from *Historia Brittonum* are reproduced by kind permission from Arthurian Period Sources volume 8, *Nennius* (ed. and trans. by Dr John Morris) published in 1980 by Phillimore, Shopwyke Manor Barn, Chichester, West Sussex, PO20 2BG.

Quotations from *Gildas* are reproduced by kind permission from Arthurian Period Sources, volume 7, *Gildas* (ed. and trans. by Michael Winterbottom), published in 1978 by Phillimore, as above.

INTRODUCTION:
WHO WAS KING ARTHUR?

Arthur was a great king. He ruled a land of knights in armour, damsels in distress, dragons and derring-do, home of Merlin the Magician and Morgan le Fay. He was born in Tintagel, became king by a combination of sword, stone and sorcery, and ruled from the castle of Camelot. At his Round Table sat Sir Lancelot, Sir Gawain and Sir Galahad, seekers of the Holy Grail. Finally, in tragedy, the love of Lancelot and Guenevere brought down the whole kingdom, leaving Arthur sleeping in the Isle of Avalon.

Did this King Arthur really exist? Almost certainly not. He was defined by writers of romance fiction in the twelfth century and refined through the Middle Ages. He inhabited a fabulous world based on that of his medieval audience. It was in this form that Arthur was revived by the Victorians and entered the public imagination.

Could this fantastic king be based on historical reality? By the late twentieth century, scholars reached a consensus. Through the legends, they argued, could be glimpsed a genuine historical Arthur. Perhaps he was not a king but a warlord, a Roman general or Celtic chieftain, leading his armoured cavalry against invading Saxons. He fought battles at such windswept locations as Liddington Castle or Little Solsbury Hill. His capital, a declining Roman city or reclaimed hillfort, remembered by the name of Camelot, could be identified by archaeology. His world, if not exactly one of chivalry, was a last beacon of civilisation against a barbarian wind of change.

This image of the 'historical' Arthur found its way easily into popular history. Professional historians were soon followed by amateur enthusiasts and local antiquarians. Regional partisans still traipse across their local fields, clutching Ordnance Survey maps, seeking names resonant of Camelot and Avalon.

According to the medieval 'Prophecies of Merlin', the deeds of King Arthur would always provide food for storytellers. The number of new Arthurian novels, each longer than all the early Arthurian sources combined, appears to bear this out. Although in the mass media the name of Arthur will always evoke the image of 'knights in armour', most novels since the sixties have cloaked their Arthur in the muddy trappings of the Dark Ages. This new 'fictional' Arthur has become subtly different from his 'historical' counterpart. He emerges from a Celtic twilight into a world where the 'old ways' face the destructive coming of the Church of Rome. While Arthur may be ambivalent in this contest, there is no disguising the 'old' loyalties of the powerful women surrounding him, exponents of a matriarchal tradition stretching back to Boadicea and the Druids. Inevitably, there is love between the Queen and a Lancelot-figure, there is a grail, holy to one tradition or another, an Avalon where Christian and pagan battle for the hearts and minds of Dark Age Britain.

But are these 'Dark Age' Arthurs any more real than the 'medieval' figure which preceded them? Over the last twenty-five years, the academic world has become almost unanimously hostile to the idea of a 'historical Arthur'. It has become scholarly orthodoxy that, although someone called Arthur may have existed at some point in the Dark Ages, even that small admission is best avoided. The first mentions of him were written hundreds of years after he supposedly lived and are so hopelessly entangled in myth and folklore that nothing historical can be gleaned from them. Sources from his own time make no mention of him, archaeology has uncovered no trace of him, so it is best to ignore him completely.

This sea-change in scholarly opinion has taken place largely out of public view. It has hardly entered into popular histories. The public demand for Arthurian books has been fed by reprints of old and discredited works, or poorly researched amateur sleuthing of the 'King Arthur shared my postcode' variety.

The refusal of academic historians to engage with the 'evidence' for Arthur presented in popular works is a great disservice to interested readers. The essential questions remain unanswered. Did King Arthur exist? Was he a significant figure of history and can we learn anything of his reign? If not, how did the legendary image arise?

We shall find out what contemporary sources actually say. We shall use this information to assess how likely later works are to give us a true picture of the enigmatic ruler. We shall see how they came by their information and how reliable they are. Our investigation will take us up to the late twelfth century when romance fiction firmly took hold of the Arthurian genre, obscuring its possible factual content. I will show that the idea of Arthur as a real Dark Age British military leader is very plausible, and goes a long way to making sense of the evidence. On the way, I hope to dismiss some modern prejudices both for and against the 'historical' Arthur.

First, we need to find an approximate date for the reign of Arthur.

 PART ONE

FROM HISTORY

1

IN THE REIGN OF
KING ARTHUR . . .

The popular view of Arthur largely derives from Sir Thomas Malory's *Le Morte Darthur*, written in 1470. Although Malory portrays the king as a medieval ruler, he occasionally reveals the pre-medieval era when his tales are set:

> They com to the Sege Perelous, where they founde lettirs newly wrytten of golde, whyche seyde: Four Hondred wyntir and four and fyffty acomplyssed aftir the Passion of Oure Lorde Jesu Cryst oughte thys syege to be fulfylled , , , 'in the name of God!' seyde Sir Launcelot, and than accounted the terme of the wrytynge, frome the byrthe of oure Lorde unto that day. 'Hit semyth me,' seyd sir Launcelot, 'that thys syge oughte to be fulfylled thys same day, for thys ys the Pentecoste after the four hondred and four and fyffty yere.''

If Sir Lancelot has calculated correctly, the quest for the Holy Grail is about to begin around the year AD 487. Other Arthurian sources give similar dates from the late fifth to the early sixth centuries. However, it is clear that the romances do not give us an accurate picture of those centuries. Malory has an archbishop of Canterbury at least 50 years too early, a Holy Land inhabited by Turks 500 years before they arrived and a siege of the Tower of London (*c.* 1080) using 'grete gunnes' 800 years before they were first seen in England. Not only in such anachronisms is it obvious that we are not reading tales about the fifth century; central images and themes derive from the medieval world, not the Dark Ages. Courtly love and tournaments point us to the twelfth century. Jousting would have been impossible without stirrups, unknown in fifth-century Britain. If Arthur and his companions were real inhabitants of Britain *c.* 487, we must look beyond the romances for evidence of their world.

At the start of the fifth century, Britain had been part of the Roman Empire for almost 400 years. Roman roads, walls and fortifications could be seen all over the country. Although most of the troops had left the island in 409 and the Emperor had formally charged the Britons with their own defence the following year, imperial documents continued to be drafted detailing the military and civil officers of the British provinces. To the bureaucrats in the imperial capitals, normal service would be resumed as soon as possible.

Roman civilisation, by 410, was not that of films such as *Gladiator*. Pagan religion, gladiatorial games and vestal virgins had been outlawed for almost a century. Heavy cavalrymen, not the famous legionaries, dominated the armed forces. In many cases, as imperial authority waned, Christian bishops took over governmental responsibilities. British bishops even ventured across the barbarian-infested seas to attend councils in Europe. The language of the Empire, Latin, continued to be used by the Church. The only British writers whose work has survived from this period were churchmen and wrote in Latin.

Britain, however, was hardly a well-organised Roman province. Angles, Saxons and Jutes had seized control of those parts of the island nearest the continent. We call these people the Anglo-Saxons or the English, though to their enemies they were the Saxons. They later recorded such exploits as that of one of their leaders, Aelle, taking the Roman fort of Anderida and killing all the inhabitants in 491, just four years after the date Malory assigned to the Grail quest.

Archaeology indicates that in the fifth and sixth centuries Saxon settlements were confined to the south and eastern coasts and the river valleys most easily accessible from them. It was many generations before the more remote highlands of Britain were conquered by the English.

Elsewhere in the Empire, barbarians had settled into the structures of the Roman provinces they invaded. They lived in the same cities, used the same titles and eventually, in France, Spain and Italy, came to speak the language of the Romans they conquered. Mostly, these barbarians had come from just beyond the borders of the Empire. They had all been converted to Christianity and those aspects of Roman culture this implied before they crossed the frontiers.

In Britain, the situation was different. The invaders came from areas which had not bordered on the Empire. They retained their pagan religion and culture and did not begin to accept the imperial religion until 597. Inevitably, Roman civilisation, soldiers, bishops and all, disappeared from the lands under their sway. It is English which we speak here today.

Writers referred to two other barbarian groups: the Picts who lived in the north beyond the Antonine Wall and the Scots, invaders of the western shore from Northern Ireland. Between them and the English lay the Britons themselves

Although the word 'British' now covers all the inhabitants of Britain, in the Dark Ages it referred to one specific people. The Saxons knew them as the *Welsh*, or foreigners, but the Britons called themselves the *Combrogi* or fellow-citizens. Although they used Latin on their monuments, they spoke British, the ancestor of modern Welsh and Breton, what we now call a Celtic language.

The leaders of the British came from those areas which had seen the least Romanisation. For example, archaeology and history show the Cornish leaders to have been important, though no major Roman structures have been found west of Exeter. Other British leaders came from Wales, Cumbria (still bearing the name of the *Combrogi*) and, north of Hadrian's Wall, land which had barely been under Roman control at all. Some British rulers held Roman cities. Most preferred to refortify the ancient hillforts deserted since the Roman Conquest. The massive South Cadbury Castle, often said to be the original Camelot, is one of the most famous.

There seemed to be little trace of Roman culture among these Britons. St Patrick wrote of some that they were 'not Citizens of the holy Romans, but of the devil, living in the enemy ways of the barbarians'.

It was among the Britons that the legends of Arthur were preserved. History, archaeology and, perhaps, their legends provide clues to these, the darkest of the British Dark Ages. Somewhere in the gloom, if the medieval romances are to be believed, we should find the evidence for the reign of Arthur.

ANCIENT MANUSCRIPTS

The main historical texts relating to the years 400–550, with the approximate dates they were written, are:

Gildas's *De Excidio Britanniae* ('On the Destruction of Britain') (*c.* 500)
Bede's Ecclesiastical History of the English People (731)
Historia Brittonum ('History of the Britons') (829)
The Anglo-Saxon Chronicle (early part 891)
Annales Cambriae ('Annals of Wales') (977)

All except Gildas are from long after the time they describe. This is a common feature of most history books and does not necessarily imply that they are untrustworthy. To investigate the real Arthur, we must discover how reliable and internally consistent these texts are, how plausible are their accounts, and how they compare to what can be deduced from archaeology.

Historians used to place great reliance on written sources. These provided the names, dates, kings and battles from which conventional history was constructed. Writers tended to accept that the sources covering the Dark Ages were a close approximation of the truth. Even later sources were sometimes used, on the grounds that they probably contained material from oral tradition or lost written sources. Archaeological remains were largely interpreted on the basis of these written sources.

Where historians were critical, they were inclined to favour the English over the British material. The first English historian, Bede, a congenial and deceptively modern scholar, provided a reassuring framework of AD dates and recognisable kingdoms. The apogee of almost uncritical acceptance of written material came in 1973 with John Morris's *The Age of Arthur*. Sources of disparate periods and genres were combined by Morris into a highly imaginative story of Arthur as Emperor of Britain. This was challenged four years later, in the rather more obscure pages of the journal *History*, by David Dumville. An expert in the ancient languages of the British sources, he argued that all of them were very late and so infected with legendary material that no reliance could be placed on them. Academics have, generally, accepted Dumville's thesis. It is assumed, rather than argued, that the ninth- and tenth-century material dealing with Arthur is 'inadmissible evidence' (Dark 2000).

Archaeologists have effectively been given *carte blanche* to disregard the written sources. No longer fettered by the prejudices of ancient Britons, they treat sub-Roman Britain to all intents and purposes as prehistoric. Finds can be interpreted according to the prevailing fashion. Gildas can be used selectively to bolster a case, as where he says that Britons retreated to fortified hills, but ignored when he says that they were fleeing Saxons intent on destroying their cities and massacring them. Because all written sources are equally suspect, they are all equally useful if they reinforce or attract publicity for an archaeologist's latest finds. Thus, experts who would dismiss any notion that Arthur was a Dark Age king will happily connect the name 'Artognou' on a slate from Tintagel with the twelfth-century legend that Arthur was conceived there by magic.

As noted, this change in academic opinion is unknown to the general public. Morris's *Age of Arthur*, discredited by reputable historians, is still in print and available in all good bookshops. Books by Dumville are harder to find. Readers with a general interest in King Arthur, spurred on by authors such as Morris, are surprised to find few academic works ready to debate the points.

The 'evidence' deserves to be analysed, not simply dismissed. For this reason, I will deal with the written sources in some detail. I will show why they are not used as uncritically as once they were, while re-examining whether they have anything plausible to say about the reign of Arthur.

All Dark Age sources were written to serve particular interests, especially the Catholic Church and the dominant dynasties of Wessex and Gwynedd. They derive from eras when literacy was confined to the elite. There were no sources composed by 'ordinary' people. Moreover, the written sources only survived because elite groups had them copied and preserved. This is just as true of the sixth-century 'admissible' evidence as it is for the ninth-century 'inadmissible' evidence. The work of Gildas survived because it contained a message which it was useful for tenth-century ecclesiastics to perpetuate.

If a history book is written to support particular circumstances, this does not by itself prove it is false. Current circumstances might exist because of those past events. Conversely, knowing that these sources were written and preserved to serve particular interests is also useful. When the material supports those interests, attention should be drawn to it. When it has nothing to do with, or indeed contradicts, them, this provides very useful evidence indeed.

HE WAS NOT ARTHUR

Apart from the odd monument inscribed with names such as Voteporix or Drustanus (Sir Tristan?) the sixth-century British left practically no written records. Instead, Gildas tells us, they loved to hear their deeds recited by bards, men with 'mouths stuffed with lies and liable to bedew bystanders with their foaming phlegm'.

Bardic poems were passed on from generation to generation, surviving to be written down in the Middle Ages. The oldest of the poems, *Y Gododdin*, gives detailed insight into the lives of the Britons. It includes this verse referring to Arthur himself.

More than three hundred of the finest killed.
In the middle and on the flanks he laid them low
Splendid before the host, most generous willed,
Bestowing horses from his own herd every winter's snow.
He brought down black crows to feed before the wall
Of the city, though he was no Arthur.
Of men he was amongst the mightiest of all,
Before the fence of alderwood stood Guaurthur.

The poem was written down in the thirteenth century, but scholars agree that many of its verses are much earlier in origin. The most recent work concludes, on grounds of language and content, that this verse is among the oldest, possibly from as early as 570 (Koch 1997). Not only is Arthur the rhyme for the hero's name, but in the original Welsh all the four last lines rhyme, making it unlikely that Arthur was inserted by a later scribe.

Guaurthur was one of the heroes of the Gododdin, the tribe living around Edinburgh, who took part in an expedition against Catraeth (modern Catterick). This is probably where he provided the crows with carrion, since the word used, *Cair*, refers specifically to a *Roman* city, as Catraeth was. The Gododdin were fighting against the Saxons of Deira some time in living memory before 570. In some way, Guaurthur was comparable to Arthur. Arthur was not said to be among the Gododdin. The best explanation is that he was a famous figure the poet expected his audience to recognise.

Keep this in mind when we confront arguments against Arthur being a historical figure. If *Y Gododdin* were the only source mentioning Arthur, no one would doubt that he was historical, famous as a warrior, from a period sometime before the expedition to Catraeth. No one else in *Y Gododdin* is a mythical superman, a composite character pieced together from scattered legends. Another verse includes the comparison 'what Bratwen would do, you would do, you would kill, you would burn'. Bratwen is not a rhyme for the hero's name, or anything else in the verse. No one, however, has written articles suggesting Bratwen's name was intruded into the text close to the thirteenth-century date of the manuscript. Bratwen is accepted by all commentators as a genuine character familiar to the listeners.

The *Gododdin* reference to Arthur ought to be uncontroversial. Unfortunately, the weight of medieval tales is always set in the balance against such simple conclusions. This seems most unfair. If being the stuff of medieval legends is a good enough reason for being banished from genuine history, Alexander, Charlemagne and Richard the Lionheart would be discounted as historical.

It is crucial to know whether *Y Gododdin* is genuinely early. Like most works from the ancient and early modern world, it survives only in a copy from a much later period. Historians must judge the content, not the physical age of the book. There are three main reasons for dating it to the late sixth century. In its current form, it has verses attributing it to Neirin. The *Historia Brittonum* says that Neirin was a famous poet soon after Arthur, apparently in the sixth century. This argument is circular, as either of the references could have influenced the other. Moreover, the name Neirin does not appear in the earliest verses.

To fight at Catraeth, the Gododdin would have had to pass through the land of Berneich (Bernicia). Various sources describe a Saxon takeover of Berneich in the mid-sixth century. The earliest version of *Y Gododdin* only speaks of the Deor (Deirans), the English in the Catraeth area, with no mention of Berneich. It is therefore reasonable to assume that the expedition took place before the Saxon conquest of the more northerly region.

Most compellingly, the language of *Y Gododdin* is an incredibly old version of Welsh. The manuscript preserves two versions of the text, the first (A) being a more recent and expanded version than the second (B). Many pre-Old Welsh spellings are preserved in both texts, a fact which can be checked from established linguistic theory, place-names and contemporary Irish material. These forms predominate in the B text, which includes the Arthur verse. Koch argues that the B text is itself a composite, with some parts, including the Arthur verse, of sixth-century vintage. His hypothesis is not universally accepted, but all authorities agree that the B text is earlier than the A. The idea that the Arthur reference was inserted when the manuscript was written does not explain why the inserter would put it into the more difficult older text while not carrying it through into the easier A text, where Guaurthur is also named.

Since the nineteenth century, philologists have demonstrated the regular and predictable rules by which languages have evolved. It is now relatively simple to trace how the name 'Maglocunus' found in Gildas became 'Mailcunus' in *Historia Brittonum*, later emerging as 'Malgo' in Geoffrey of Monmouth and 'Maelgwn' in the Triads. However, this process was not understood by Dark Age or medieval writers. It is thus easy for modern historians to deduce the age of the sources by the form of language used, irrespective of the age of the manuscript or any chronological claims within it. At its most simple level, we know that Geoffrey of Monmouth's source for the exploits of Urien Rheged must be later than that used by the *Historia Brittonum*, as he calls the king Urianus, while the *Historia* preserves the name in the earlier form of Urbgen. By studying their language, we can deduce that poems like *Y Gododdin* are much earlier than the late thirteenth- or fourteenth-century manuscripts in which they survive.

All the evidence suggests that the reference to Arthur was an original part of a mid-to-late sixth-century poem. He was a famous warrior, with whose deeds those of one of the Gododdin men were comparable. To suggest anything other than this straightforward explanation is utterly illogical. The probability is that the reference is to a real warrior of the recent past.

This is a plausible and reasonable inference from the evidence. There is nothing to suggest that Guaurthur was not a real British warrior of the sixth century. There is likewise no reason to think any differently of Arthur. Arthur's existence rests on exactly the same source. If Koch is right, then Arthur was known to have existed before the late sixth century, when the first verses of *Y Gododdin* were composed. His fame as a warrior made him a fitting subject for comparison to a similarly named Gododdin hero.

This plausible and reasonable hypothesis forms the basis of the rest of the book. There was an Arthur. His deeds were known to a sixth-century poet and his audience. He was comparable to and better than Guaurthur. Like everyone else in the poem, he is not a mythological demi-god. He is not a composite character formed from various stories of men of the same name. For the *Gododdin* poet there is obviously one recognisable Arthur. We know, in short, that Arthur existed in so far as it is possible to know that any named Briton of the fifth or sixth century existed. There is no reason why he alone should have to demonstrate his existence beyond reasonable doubt, rather than on the balance of probability.

Asserting that Arthur was a real person, however, is not the same as proving that 'King Arthur' existed. Though the poem has given us reason to believe that Arthur was real, we will have to look at other Dark Age sources to see what light they shed on the enigmatic comparison. If Guaurthur was not Arthur, then who was?

2

ARTHUR FOUGHT AGAINST THEM IN THOSE DAYS

Then Arthur fought against them in those days, with the kings of the Britons, but he himself was the leader in the battles. The first battle was towards the mouth of the river which is called Glein. The second and third and fourth and fifth were on another river, which is called Dubglas and is in the Linnuis region. The sixth battle was on the river which is called Bassas. The seventh battle was in the wood of Celidon, that is Cat Coit Celidon. The eighth battle was in Castellum Guinnion, in which Arthur carried the image of Saint Mary ever Virgin upon his shoulders, and the pagans were put to flight on that day and there was great slaughter upon them through the virtue of our Lord Jesus Christ and through the virtue of St. Mary the Virgin His Mother. The ninth battle was waged in the City of the Legion. He waged the tenth battle on the shore of the river which is called Tribuit. The eleventh battle was made on the hill which is called Agned. The twelfth battle was on the hill of Badon, in which 960 men fell in one day in one charge by Arthur. And no-one laid them low save he himself. And in all the battles he emerged the victor.

Historia Brittonum

The source which first gives the military career of Arthur is *Historia Brittonum* (The History of the Britons). The earliest version is found in Harleian Manuscript 3859, so called because it once belonged to the eighteenth-century collector, Edward Harley, Earl of Oxford. In the Harleian Manuscript, the *Historia* is anonymous, but other versions give its author as, variously, Nennius, a son of Urbacen, Mark the Anchorite or Gildas, a much earlier writer.

The Arthurian material in the *Historia* is of vital importance, since it is the earliest record of the actual deeds of Arthur. Whether this material is historical or legendary is crucial to any argument about the reign of Arthur. We must therefore consider what kind of document the *Historia* is.

Dumville, the current editor of the *Historia*, is adamant that it is overwhelmingly of a legendary or 'synthetic' character. The ninth-century author has heavily edited his sources to fit them into a preconceived framework. Unfortunately, Dumville has yet to complete his publication of the work, meaning that for the past twenty-three years we have simply had to take his word for this. Historians have consciously avoided making any comments but have generally taken his assertions as full permission to ignore the *Historia*'s Arthurian material. It is academic received wisdom that the *Historia* is valueless as a historical source for the fifth/sixth centuries.

Popular works on the historical Arthur usually make no reference to this. In them it is generally assumed that the *Historia* was written by a ninth-century Welsh monk called Nennius and that much of the material is presented at one remove, for instance by translating Welsh poems into Latin, from lost primary sources. This gulf of understanding is compounded by the version of 'Nennius' most accessible to amateur historians. This version (Morris 1980) is so inaccurate and inconsistent that it must be used with extreme caution. Its editor, John Morris (author of *The Age of Arthur*), died before completing his work. What was published was the Harleian Recension, augmented with excerpts from other texts and with no indication as to the criteria used for selection. Other additions, such as a section identifying Badon as Bath, are not found here in any text whatever.

Historia Brittonum was copied numerous times in the Middle Ages. Its disjointed style made it easy for scribes to omit or add sections and update the material. These produced many variants, which we can group together in families called 'recensions'. The recensions follow, more or less faithfully, a particular exemplar. The Harleian Recension, represented by the oldest surviving text, is generally considered the closest to the original. Whether this is actually true must await Dumville's full publication. For the purposes of this book, we assume it is.

The Nennian Recension claims to be written by a certain Nennius. Its prologue continues: 'I have undertaken to write down some of the extracts that the stupidity of the British cast out; for the scholars of the island of Britain had no skill, and set down no record in books. I have therefore made a heap of all that I have found, both from the annals of the Romans and from the chronicles of the Holy Fathers, and from the writings of the Irish and the English and out of the traditions of our elders.'

Unfortunately, it is unlikely that the Nennian prologue was part of the original *Historia*. If it had been, we might expect it to be reproduced in the other recensions as well. There is no reason to believe that the writer, although he may be passing down a true tradition of authorship, had any genuine knowledge of the author's sources or intentions. Nevertheless, the name 'Nennius' is now conventional for the otherwise anonymous author. I use 'Nennius' when discussing the methods and intentions of the author, without committing myself to his actual identity.

Most commentators follow the Nennian prologue in assuming that the author simply gathered together excerpts from various books, mixed them with oral traditions and regurgitated them almost undigested in the *Historia*. The ancient sources are therefore preserved at only one remove in a sort of historical scrapbook. Dumville, however, is convinced that the writer had worked over his sources in a comprehensive way to fit a chronological framework, leaving little material unaltered. This understanding is crucial to an appreciation of the *Historia*.

Historia Brittonum covers a broad sweep of time, from the legendary founding of Britain after the Trojan War, through to the seventh century. About two-thirds of the book deal with the most recent 300 years of history. The author provides the approximate date of the book. At the start, he gives the present as AD 831. Later, he calculates that Patrick went to Ireland in AD 405, 421 years before the present (i.e. AD 826). In the same section, he gives Patrick's date as 438, giving a date for the present of 859. Either an authorial or scribal error has resulted in two different dates for the same event, or the manuscript has been updated. Dumville suggests that Nennius intended a date of AD 829 for the present (IV in Dumville 1990).

WONDERS OF BRITAIN

After the end of the *Historia*, there is a gazetteer of Wonders of Britain, the *Mirabilia*. It is not clear whether this originally formed part of the work. The author seems to be a contemporary of Nennius and to share an interest in the same area of Britain. The wonders have been associated with the *Historia* from early in the manuscript tradition, passing together into different recensions. I will treat them as the work of the same author, although if they

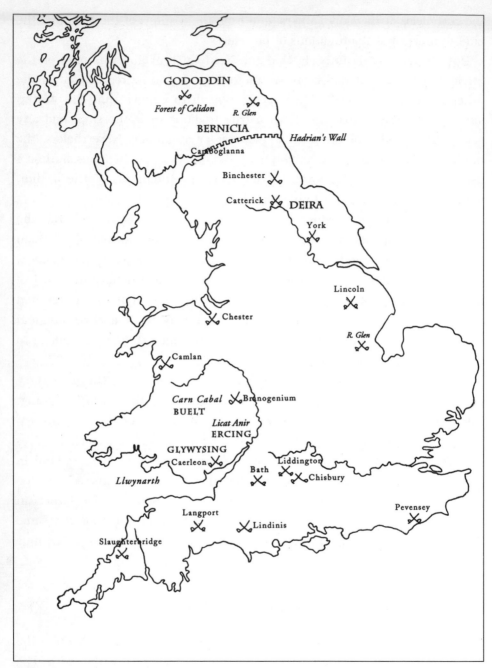

'Arthur's Britain'.

are not, the fact that two ninth-century writers give supporting material on Arthur would strengthen my case.

Although the scope of the wonders is national, the fact that most of them are actually to be found in South Wales and the Severn Estuary points firmly to the author's home area. In Buelt (Builth), he tells us, there is a pile of stones called Carn Cabal built by Arthur the Soldier. The topmost stone bears the footprint of Arthur's dog Cabal, made when he was hunting the boar Troynt. In Ercing, 35 miles away in modern Herefordshire, is the wonder of Licat Anir. This Anir was the son of Arthur the Soldier, who killed him and built a tomb there. The author has personally tried to measure the tomb and found it impossible to obtain the same measurement twice. (The name of Arthur's son is frequently given as Amr. I follow the reading of the current editor.) The only other wonder the author connects to a named individual is a tomb in a church built by St Illtud in Llwynarth, on the Gower peninsula, 50 miles away from the two Arthur wonders.

These wonders are important pieces of information. They tell us Arthur was a soldier, as we might have expected from *Y Gododdin*, but locate him in South Wales. We know that, as *Y Gododdin* was transmitted through the early Middle Ages, it acquired verses linking it to Welsh heroes. However, these emphasised the North Welsh Kingdom of Gwynedd, not Builth or Ercing. Moreover, we also know that the verse referring to Arthur pre-dated those interpolations.

Although the wonders are folkloric in character, this gives no reason to doubt that Arthur was real, any more than that Illtud was a real Dark Age cleric. Folklore and legend linked to real characters and events were in the idiom of even the most sober Dark Age historian. The wonders attributed to Arthur are no more than would be expected from a writer of Dark Age Britain. No one doubts Bede's account of Oswald of Northumbria's death at the battle of Maserfelth. Yet Bede devotes most of this account to describing wonders such as the cure of a sick horse which rolled onto the spot where Oswald was killed or the man whose house burnt down save for the beam where his cloak, touched by the mud from the site, had hung (EH IV 2). Even tombs of varying length were not considered impossible. The stone sarcophagus made for King Sebbi of the East Saxons was too short. 'In the presence of the Bishop and of Sighard, son of the monk king . . . and a considerable number of men, the sarcophagus was suddenly found to be the correct length for the body.' By contrast, although Anir's tomb and the footprint of Cabal are wonders to the contemporary writer, they derive from less than wonderful events in Arthur's life, hunting a boar at Builth and killing his son in Ercing.

What they do lack is any sense of a historical context. The reason for this is perhaps that one had already been provided by the *Historia*. Here, Arthur is one of three named leaders of the British in their wars against the Saxons. The *Historia* says these wars began after a British ruler, Vortigern, invited the Saxons to settle in the island in return for military service against the Picts. This was in the consulship of Felix and Taurus, i.e. AD 428.

Nennius treats Vortigern as ruler of Britain, but his own regional bias is obvious. Most of Vortigern's deeds are located in central and southern Wales. The writer tells us that Fernmail, contemporary ruler of Buelt and Guorthigirniaun, is a descendant of Vortigern. He traces his genealogy back through ten generations to that king.

The Saxons were led by two brothers, Hengist and Horsa. The Saxons settled peacefully in Kent, but soon broke into revolt. Although Vortigern is shown as weak and helpless, other Britons are ready to take up the fight. The three successive leaders are Vortimer, son of Vortigern, Arthur and Outigirn.

Nennius writes in the same way about all three resistance leaders. Either their exploits derived from a single source or the author has worked different sources into a unified style. At first sight, this seems not to be the case. The passages dealing with them are not sequential, but crudely interwoven with material from apparently different sources. King Ida appears after Arthur and then again, just before Outigirn, though several English genealogies have been inserted between the two mentions.

The first resistance leader is Vortimer, who won four battles against the Saxons, three named and apparently located in Kent. 'The second battle was fought at a ford called Episford in their language and Rithergabail in our language, and there fell Horsa with a son of Vortigern whose name was Categirn.'

Vortimer died soon after his victories. The Saxons were once again resurgent. We are told about St Germanus and St Patrick. 'At that time [we still seem to be in the fifth century] the English increased their numbers and grew in Britain. On Hengist's death, his son Octha came down from the north of Britain to the Kingdom of the Men of Kent, and from him are sprung the kings of the Men of Kent.'

This is followed by the Arthurian battle-list which begins this chapter. This has been examined countless times. Current opinion favours the idea that the list is a composite of battles from various periods ascribed to one legendary leader. It is sometimes said that the battles have been multiplied to bring them up to the 'legendary' number twelve. There is nothing to show that Nennius saw any significance in this number. He was happy to give other leaders different numbers of battles.

Most of Arthur's battles are probably unidentifiable, irretrievably hidden behind modern English place-names or British ones too common to be pinpointed. Only two can be located with certainty. It seems clear that the Caledonian wood was somewhere in Scotland. In the Dark Ages, the name was applied to the forests of lowland Scotland.

There were two cities called 'the City of the Legion', Chester and Caerleon-on-Usk. Special pleading could be made for York, which had been a city of the (Sixth) legion though it is never given that name in Dark Age sources. We can be certain which of these the author of the *Historia* had in mind – Chester. He includes between the historical section and the wonders a list of the cities of Britain. These include York, as Cair Ebrauc, Caerleon as Cair Legeion guar Uisc and Chester simply as Cair Legion. *Annales Cambriae* mention Chester twice, once as the City of the Legion, in Latin exactly as in the battle-list and once as Cair Legion, site of a battle which also figures in Bede. He gives the Latin and Welsh forms of the name, as well as the English Legacestir, from which our word Chester derives.

The other battles are more problematic. The Linnuis region is usually taken to be the Lincoln area. Castellum Guinnion ought to be a Roman fort. The *Historia* refers to Britain having 'innumerable *castella*, made from stone and brick' which can only be Roman buildings. Unless named after an unknown man called Guinnion, it seems most likely to be the British version of Vinovium, Binchester in County Durham (Rivet and Smith 1979).

Every writer on Arthur has his theory about the location of Mount Badon. Liddington Castle, on the Ridgeway between Badbury and Baydon, is a favourite. Other Badburys, like the hillfort in Dorset, are also frequently cited. The earliest medieval idea placed it at Bath, perhaps at one of the hills like Little Solsbury outside the city. We will return to the location of the battles again later, but it is important to see that the battle-list implies that Arthur fought wide-ranging campaigns against the Saxons.

After Arthur's victories, the English invited more settlers and leaders over from Germany. This continued until the time of Ida, who became first King of Bernicia. Working backwards from the reign dates for the Northumbrian kings given in the *Historia*, we can calculate that the author was thinking of this event as taking place shortly before 560. (Bede placed Ida's arrival in 547.) The flow of the narrative is broken by some Saxon genealogies, but it soon returns to Ida. 'At that time, Outigirn then fought bravely against the English nation. Then Talhearn Tataguen was famous for his poetry and Neirin and Taliessin and Bluchbard and Cian, who is called Gueinth Guaut, were at the same time famous in British poetry.'

We know nothing more about Outigirn from any sources. Possibly he was celebrated by some of the poets mentioned. The fact that he has no wonders attributed to him, no famous victories or adversaries and no dynasty, all convince that the *Historia* had no ulterior motive for mentioning him, except a tradition that he had fought the English. Few historians doubt that he was a real figure from this obscure period. Unlike Arthur, he was not burdened by a weight of medieval legends.

As mentioned, later verses added to *Y Gododdin* claim that it was written by Neirin. Whether Neirin composed the poem or not, the early verses give a view consistent with the *Historia*, that the expedition took place before Ida's arrival in Bernicia.

The *Historia* thus provides a story covering the period *c.* 450 to *c.* 550, with the career of Arthur perhaps somewhere in the middle. Arthur seems to be connected to central or south-eastern Wales and to have fought, in the north, with the kings of the Britons against the Saxons. This background is perfectly consistent with *Y Gododdin*. We can see how Guaurthur was like Arthur: they both fight the Saxons, in the north, at a Roman fortified city. Guaurthur has fought at an encounter where three hundred were slain, but he is not up to the standard of Arthur, who won twelve battles and overthrew three times as many. The obvious conclusion is that the *Gododdin* poet knew the same story of Arthur as Nennius; that Arthur was credited with similar feats as early as the sixth century. It is highly unlikely that both authors coincidentally linked an Arthur to wars against the Saxons at the same time in similar locations. Although Nennius knew of the Gododdin tribe, he shows no knowledge of the poem. In short, the story of Arthur recorded in the *Historia* seems to be just what the *Gododdin* poet had in mind when he made his comparison in the late sixth century.

THE COMING OF THE SAXONS

The basic story of the Saxon settlement, revolt and British resistance did not originate with the *Historia*. It is only the name of Arthur as resistance leader which is not found in the earlier sources.

Bede gives the most detail on names and dates. He uses Gildas's *De Excidio* as a primary source, but adds English materials. Bede supplies the name Vortigern for the British ruler who invites in the Saxons, and is followed by all later versions. Gildas simply called this ruler *Superbus Tyrannus* (the Proud Tyrant). Most commentators see this as a pun on the name Vortigern, which means 'foremost prince'. There is a convincing case that Gildas specifically uses the Latin term *tyrannus* because of its similarity to the title *tigern* actually used by the rulers (Snyder 1998). Some writers argue that Vortigern was not the ruler's name, but a title, similar to 'high king'. There is no evidence for this. Many Dark Age men had names incorporating royal or noble titles. 'Vortigern' is treated as a proper name by all subsequent writers, and was never used as a title by anyone else.

Gildas may even have named his Proud Tyrant as Vortigern. The name appears in the Avranches family of Gildas manuscripts, from which the earliest excerpts are taken, but not the earliest complete text (I in Dumville 1990). It seems more likely, however, that this name was inserted by a later copyist. Gildas was generally very sparing of proper names. Given the near unanimity that the tyrant's name was Vortigern, I will use it as a shorthand for the Proud Tyrant when comparing Gildas to the other sources. Whatever his actual name, all sources agree that he existed.

Bede more or less introduced the AD dating system to England. Using it, he established a fifth-century date for the arrival of the Saxons. Gildas states only that the first settlement of the Saxons took place at some undefined time after the Britons had appealed to a Roman leader on the continent, one called Agitius, 'three times consul', for help against the Picts and Scots.

The appeal to Agitius can be dated in various ways. At its earliest, the appeal would be made to Aetius, Roman military commander in Gaul from 425, at its latest to Aegidius, sub-Roman ruler of northern Gaul from 457 to 462. The balance of scholarly opinion favours Aetius in the period 446–54 when he was actually consul for the third time. Dark Age writers often used the Latin letter 'g' to stand for the 'y' sound, meaning Gildas may have pronounced the name as 'Ayitius', very close to Aetius. Here the *Historia* shows its independence from Gildas. If Nennius knew about the appeal to Aetius, consul for the third time, he could have dated it from the consul lists he was using.

The idea that the Saxons were given lands specifically in Kent originates with Bede as well. Bede's book is called *The Ecclesiastical History of the English People*. It traces the spread of Catholic Christianity through the kingdoms of the Angles and the Saxons. Bede's concept of the kingdom of Kent being the first Saxon kingdom to be established in Britain is closely linked to the fact that it was the first to be converted to Christianity. Gildas tells us only that the Saxons settled in 'the eastern part of the island'. Archaeologists have found Saxon settlements over most of eastern England, although whether this directly corresponds to the extent of their political control is not certain. The Saxon revolt did not lead to the massacre of all Britons in the east of the island. Gildas says that some Britons remained there as slaves.

Both Bede and Nennius see Vortigern's government as being taken over by the Saxons. This would follow the pattern of contemporary events in the rest of the western Roman Empire. Germanic peoples settling in the Roman Empire in return for military service, followed by their violent takeover of these lands, is common in the fifth century. Modern scholars seem to be keen to dismiss Hengist and Horsa themselves as legendary. Archaeology seems to show Saxons infiltrating the island for over a century. The Roman coastal defences were already known officially as the 'Saxon Shore'. This was paralleled elsewhere in the western Roman Empire, where Germanic barbarians had settled gradually during the fourth century. Universally, however, the Germans took over the western provinces during the fifth century, under named rulers. No one doubts the historicity of Alaric the Visigoth or Clovis the Frank. They led their people in these wars, establishing dynasties which continued to rule in the areas they conquered. Hengist and Horsa are not therefore implausible

What is unique is the idea that the Britons organised their own resistance. This was no wishful thinking by later Welsh writers. Gildas tells us that he is living in a period of peace which has followed the British resistance. The sixth-century Byzantine historian Zosimus says that the Britons, 'fighting for themselves, freed their cities from the attacking barbarians'. He dates this to the period immediately following the defeat of usurper Constantine III in 409.

If Nennius was harking back to a mythical golden age, it is hard to see why he named Vortimer, Arthur and Outigirn as the leaders. They were not remembered as the founders of Welsh dynasties nor were they used to explain contemporary place-names, as both Saxon and British leaders are used in the Anglo-Saxon Chronicle. There seems to be no ulterior motive for ascribing the victories to them.

The details of the wars from the British side are first found in the *Historia*. Unsurprisingly, Bede and the Anglo-Saxon Chronicle concentrate on the English side of the picture. Gildas confirms that, up to the battle of Badon, both sides scored victories. Bede knew that Horsa had been killed in battle against the Britons and was buried in east Kent. His principal authority on the area was Albinus, an eminent scholar and Abbot of Canterbury from 709. None of Bede's English sources passed on the names of the Britons who opposed them until Brocmail, a leader killed at the Battle of Chester, the City of the Legions, in 603. The *Historia* had no knowledge of Brocmail.

The Anglo-Saxon Chronicle says that Horsa was killed in 455 at the battle of Aegelesthrep (Aylesford in Kent?). In this version, Vortigern himself was the British commander, though this might have been a guess. Battle after battle under various Saxon leaders is recorded in the Chronicle. The British commanders are nearly all unnamed. In 501, Port, Bieda and Maegla fought at Portsmouth and 'slew a young Briton, a very noble man'. Seven years later, Cerdic and Cynic slew 'a Welsh King, whose name was Natanleod, and five thousand men with him. The district was known afterwards as Natanleag [Netley].' Natanleod was not remembered by the Britons, and his name may have been concocted, as indeed Port's might have been, to explain the place-name. The next Welsh leaders named are the Kings Coinmail, Condidan and Farinmail, killed at the battle of Dyrham in 577. Being remembered after these wars seems to be a fairly unpredictable occurrence!

It is thus unlikely that the *Historia* had one source naming both Arthur and Octha as adversaries in these battles. The author had a genealogy, reproduced later in the work, of the kings of Kent naming Hengist's son as Octha. He probably deduced that, if Hengist was the leader in the first generation of the revolt, his son would have followed in the second wave. Bede had heard of Octha too, in the genealogy of Ethelbert, King of Kent, where he is given as Hengist's grandson, son of Oisc, Hengist's son. Oisc appears in the Anglo-Saxon Chronicle under the more modern spelling *Aesc*. He is said to have become co-ruler with Hengist in 455 after the death of Horsa. Thereafter, the two are always reported together until 488: 'In this year Aesc succeeded to the Kingdom and was king of the people of Kent for twenty-four years.' There is nothing at all of what he did in those twenty-four years, by which time he would be in his late seventies at least. Thereafter none of the dynasty is mentioned until 565 when Ethelbert succeeded. Three years later, he is recorded as being defeated in battle by the West Saxons.

If Arthur indeed fought against the kings of Kent, they seem to have taken a severe beating. It is even possible that the line of Hengist and Horsa had really died out. The kings of Kent were in Bede's time called the Oiscings after their ancestor, Oisc, whom they simply linked to the existing traditions about Hengist. Moreover, in Bede's time, the inhabitants of Kent were said to be Jutes, though no source describes Hengist's mercenaries as anything other than Saxons.

The *Historia*'s assumption that the kings of Kent were always the leaders of the Saxons during these wars may be based on lack of evidence about any other potential adversaries. According to Bede, before the time of Ethelbert of Kent, two Saxon kings had ruled over all the provinces south of the River Humber. The first was Aelle, King of the South Saxons; the second, Caelin, King of the West Saxons. Considering that Bede's interest lay in tracing the ecclesiastical history of the English – starting first in Kent, then moving to his own land of Northumbria – this tradition of the Great Kings, serving no political purpose at the time it was recorded, is extremely valuable. The Anglo-Saxon Chronicle preserves a title for these great Kings, the *Bretwaldas*, 'Rulers of Britain'. The chroniclers, although their primary purpose was to celebrate the exploits of their West Saxon dynasty founder, Cerdic, faithfully recorded victories of Aelle, Bretwalda from the (by then) politically moribund South Saxons. In 491, for instance, he besieged the Roman Saxon shore fort of Pevensey, and took it, killing all the British inside. This was the first time the conquest of a Roman fortification by the Saxons was recorded.

Even the Anglo-Saxon Chronicle cannot disguise the fact that Saxon victories did not continue unabated. Aelle is never mentioned after his capture of Pevensey. The next Bretwalda, Ceawlin (Bede's Caelin), fights against the Welsh in 556 and becomes king of the West Saxons in 560. Before his time, there had been a period of twenty-five years (527–52) in which not a single victory against the Britons was reported.

I do not imagine that these dates have any absolute value. The compilers of the Anglo-Saxon Chronicle faced the same problems as the author of *Historia Brittonum*. They had traditions from various Saxon kingdoms with no means of fixing them until the histories of the West Saxons and men of Kent shared a common event just before the arrival of St Augustine. Only the conversion of the king of Kent brought their traditions within the ambit of literate Christian historians.

We know that one of the sources used to compile the history of the Anglo-Saxons, their kings' lists, were not completely reliable. Bede reports that the disastrous rules of two Northumbrian kings, killed fighting the Britons, were omitted by the men who kept the kings' lists. We have a glimpse of what might be something similar in some of the versions of the Anglo-Saxon Chronicle. In one of the West Saxon genealogies, Creoda, son of Cerdic, is given as the grandfather of Ceawlin and father of Cynric. In all the other genealogies he is omitted and Cerdic, founder of the dynasty, is given as father of Cynric. In the actual entries of the Chronicle, Cynric rather implausibly accompanies his 'father' Cerdic, throughout the early conquest of Wessex, then rules through the victoryless period of 527–52 before appearing again for a victory at Old Sarum. Creoda has evidently been written out of the official history, and a period of defeat by the Britons provides a convincing reason. In spite of the best propagandist efforts of its compilers, the Anglo-Saxon Chronicle seems to tell the same story of British victory as the *Historia*.

The *Historia*, therefore, gives us a picture of Saxon settlement and revolt, followed by British resistance, which accords with the other sources. The *Historia*'s unique contribution is naming the warleader of the main wars as Arthur.

THE WAR OF RESISTANCE

Historians fall into two main camps over the Arthurian battle-list. Most see it as almost mythological in its hyperbole, and unworthy of consideration. The others, particularly before Dumville, saw it as preserving almost intact an ancient Welsh praise-poem, translated into Latin. Let us consider the charge of mythologising first.

At the Battle of Mount Badon, Arthur is said to have overthrown 960 men in a single charge 'and no-one laid them low save he alone'. This is supposed to set up Arthur as a mythical superman who could destroy whole armies in single combat. Even given the tendency for exaggeration by Dark Age writers, I cannot believe this is how Nennius intended his comment to be read. It was a commonplace, then as now, to ascribe the feats of an army to its commander. The Anglo-Saxon Chronicle, on the battle of Chester, says:

'Aethelfrith led his levies to Chester and there slew a countless number of Welsh.' In the report of the death of Natanleod, a literal reading would suggest that Cerdic and Cynric had killed all 5,000 Welsh. Only Aelle and his son Cissa are said to have captured Pevensey and slain all the inhabitants. The absurdity of suggesting that the battle-list means that Arthur in person had killed all the 960 men is obvious. The presence of armies with the leader is implicit. If Arthur was leading a charge in which 960 men were overthrown, the claim is modest compared with the totals recorded by the Saxon leaders.

If we look at the report of Mount Badon in context, it is plain that the statement 'and no one overthrew them save him alone' is not meant to exclude Arthur's troops (they have never been mentioned), but his partners, the kings of the Britons. In previous battles, they fought together, but in this final charge at the last battle, the glory went to Arthur alone.

The alternative explanation of the list, repeated since the 1930s (Chadwick and Chadwick 1932), is that it is a translation of a Welsh praise-poem. The implication is that we are reading a genuinely ancient source, composed close to Arthur's time, in which his exploits were celebrated.

Fortunately, we can compare the list with an actual surviving praise-poem, that of Cadwallon of Gwynedd. Bede recorded the death of King Edwin of Northumbria at the battle called in English Haethfelth in 633. The victor was 'Cadwalla', king of the Britons. The *Historia* knew this too, giving the battle its Welsh name, Meicen, and identifying its victor, 'Catguollaun', as the King of Gwynedd. Here is the praise-poem celebrating the campaign:

Cadwallon, before his coming waged them for our good fortune: fourteen *chief battles of fair Britain and sixty encounters.*

The camp of Cadwallon on the Don: fierce the affliction of his foe. A lion of hosts over the Saxons.

The camp of Cadwallon the famous on the upland of Mount Digoll: seven months and seven days each battle.

The camp of Cadwallon on the Severn, and on the other side of the River Dygen, almost burning Meigen.

(translation by Bromwich in Barber 1972)

The other eleven battles follow. Most give the King's camp on a riverbank. Two were on hills, one was at a Caer (usually a Roman city), where there was

'A besieging army and one hundred zealous men'. At one waterside camp, Cadwallon 'satiated eagles after battle'.

Arthur's battle-list has twelve battles, most on rivers, two on hills, one at a Roman city, quite convincing correspondences. Unfortunately, Cadwallon's praise-poem is itself a late document. It appears in the late fourteenth-century *Red Book of Hergest*, and is written in language suggesting a date of composition in the ninth or tenth century (Bromwich 1961). It could, therefore, post-date the *Historia* battle-list, and even have borrowed features from it.

In all other respects, Arthur's battle-list does not read like the poem. Arthur's battles are in a numbered sequence, a feature not found in the praise-poems, and only two have incidents linked to their names. The main thrust of the 'praise-poem' argument does not relate to style, however. It is argued that certain linguistic features are only explicable if they derive from a Welsh original. The names Guinnion, Celidon and Badon, for instance, rhyme, as do Dubglas and Bassas, which might indicate a poetic source.

The most widely cited 'proof' of a Welsh original is the description of the battle at Castellum Guinnion. Here, Arthur carried the image of the Virgin Mary on his *shoulders*. This is supposed to be explicable only if Nennius mistook the Welsh word for shield as the similar word for a shoulder and then put it into the plural.

This argument is so weak it is surprising to find it as a given in every book on the historical Arthur. Even if the design was on his shield, a writer could justifiably have said this was being carried on his shoulders, whatever his language. Medieval guesses put the image on Arthur's shield, on a banner, or made it a three-dimensional image carried for piety. The same phrase occurs in *Annales Cambriae*, where, at the battle of Badon, Arthur carried the cross of our Lord Jesus Christ on his shoulders for three days and nights. It seems highly unlikely that this terse entry was a snippet from a Welsh praise-poem, and unlikelier still that its author should have made exactly the same mistake in translation. This is especially true if, as the proponents would have it, the phrase 'on his shoulders' was meaningless to a reader of Latin.

An ivory carving thought to be of the Roman *Magister Militum* Stilicho, from the early fifth century, shows a variety of ways in which the reference can be understood without resorting to a lost source in another language. He has on his shoulder an embroidered patch decorated with crosses. These shoulder-patches were standard in the late Roman army. His shoulder-slung cloak is embroidered with images of saints or perhaps his imperial commander and his shield has an inset cameo of a mother and child, who could be seen as the Virgin and Jesus.

Concentration on the shield/shoulder confusion has obscured a much more fruitful line of enquiry. When Dark Age and medieval writers needed to explain or translate material they were copying, they would usually add a 'gloss', a short phrase usually beginning 'that is . . .'. The battle in the Caledonian wood is given first in Latin, then glossed in Welsh. If the lists were composed in Welsh, then translated into Latin, we would expect to find the opposite e.g. 'the battle of Cat Coit Celidon, that is [in Latin] the Celidonian Wood'. Elsewhere, in instances such as Vortimer's battles or the English-derived genealogies of the northern dynasties, Nennius's glosses follow this same pattern, giving the information in Latin, then adding glosses giving Welsh translations. For example: (HB 57) 'the battle called Gueith Lin Garan'; (HB 61) 'He is Eata Glinmaur'. The conclusion is inescapable. Nennius had the entry relating to the Caledonian wood, if not the whole list, from a source which was not Welsh. It could only have been in Latin or even English material of some kind pre-dating the early ninth century.

Although the details are different, the basic framework of the Saxon wars in *Historia Brittonum* accords with that presented by Bede and derived from Gildas. There is one striking area in which they differ: the role played by one of the major figures of the period.

As Gildas tells it, after the Saxon revolt, the Britons banded together under Ambrosius Aurelianus and challenged the Saxons to battle. 'From then on the victory went now to our countrymen, now to their enemies . . . This lasted right up till the year of the siege of Badon Hill, pretty well the last defeat of the villains and certainly not the least.' Bede took Gildas as saying that Ambrosius Aurelianus was the victor of Mount Badon.

The *Historia* says much more about Ambrosius than Arthur. He is known both by his Latin name and as Embreis Guletic, showing he figured in Welsh tradition. He appears as a fatherless child about to be sacrificed by Vortigern and as the son of one of the consuls of the Roman people. He is a native of Mais Elleti in Gleguissing, the region of South Wales between the Gower and Gwent. His prophecies to Vortigern, revealing two fighting worms under his fortress, are the key point to a story with more in common with the legends of the Mabinogion than sober history. After Vortigern's death, Ambrosius rules in western Britain and is described as 'King among all the Kings of the

British nation'. It is by his permission that Fernmail of Builth's ancestor is given his lands to rule. Just about the only thing we are not told about Ambrosius is that he fought the Saxons. On the contrary, he is said to be an adversary of Vortigern, who lived in dread of him. It is implied that this is one of the factors which impelled Vortigern to employ the Saxons in the first place. The warfare, sometimes in favour of the Britons, sometimes against them, is instigated by Vortimer and carried on by Arthur and Outigirn.

For Nennius, Arthur is famous as a leader in battles, but nothing else is revealed about him. In contrast to the obviously fictitious material attached to Ambrosius, Arthur's role does not strain credulity nor smell of folklore. Yet, despite the legendary accretions, historians accept Ambrosius as a real character, while Arthur is now treated as all but entirely mythical.

WHAT IS *HISTORIA BRITTONUM*?

On the Saxon invasions and British Resistance, *Historia Brittonum* merely supplements available earlier material. With Ambrosius, it seems to part company entirely. We will have to establish how acceptable the *Historia*'s version is, by examining the author's sources and how he incorporated them into his work, before analysing his picture of Arthur and his age.

The major issue is how far the *Historia* is the work of a single author, in the sense that Bede or Gildas are the authors of their work, or, as the 'Nennius' prologue suggests, a barely edited collection of historical materials. We can begin by asking where 'Nennius' might have got his facts from.

Certain areas of Britain are given more attention in the *Historia* than others. This could be an indication of the location of the author, or of his sources, or both. As a comparison, Bede's Ecclesiastical History gives prominence to both Northumbria (Bede's home kingdom) and Kent, where his earliest and most reliable sources are found.

The main geographical areas covered by the *Historia* are:

1. South Wales, the lower Severn Valley and estuary and marches of England. A striking example is the inclusion of the full genealogy of Fernmail of Builth 'who now rules', an unparalleled reference to a contemporary British ruler, and one so minor he can only be included for local interest.
2. Kent. Much material, especially relating to the first settlement of the Saxons, focuses exclusively on Kent.

3. North-east England/south-east Scotland. In particular, the *Historia* includes lists of Kings of the area, as well as the origins and British equivalents of place-names there.

4. Ireland. The *Historia* presents foundation legends of Ireland, such as are found in the Irish *Lebor Gabala* (the Book of Invasions). There is also a major section on the life of St Patrick.

Of equal importance are the areas about which the *Historia* knows little or nothing. Beyond Kent, there is nothing about lowland England. Aside from the list of twenty-eight cities at the end of the *Historia*, there are no place-names in the south between the Isle of Wight and Gloucester and the Severn Valley. The Isle of Wight is mentioned once, as one of the three adjacent islands of Britain. Sussex is the only named region of southern England beyond Kent.

While we might expect a 'History of the Britons' to say little about English areas, it is striking how limited its interest is in the British areas. There is nothing about Devon and Cornwall. North Wales and the north-west (Gwynedd and Rheged) are hardly mentioned. Apart from references to Snowdon and Caernarfon, North Wales features only as the homeland of great British kings such as Mailcunus and Catgablaun. These do not appear in a North Welsh context, but as adversaries of the English kings of Northumbria or descendants of the Gododdin. Urbgen (Urien of Rheged) is not located by Nennius. He, too, is only important as an opponent of the Northumbrians.

It is difficult to imagine an author with such disparate geographical interests. The only convincing explanation is that Nennius follows sources from discrete geographical regions.

The South Welsh, Kentish, north-eastern and Irish elements of the *Historia* are of different styles and content, linked only by Nennius, interweaving them in his book. This interweaving between passages is generally not smooth. One moment we might be reading about how St Germanus prophesies about Catel, whose descendents 'rule Powys even to this day', then find ourselves moving immediately on to 'And it came to pass, after the English were encamped in the aforesaid Island of Thanet', aforesaid, that is, in that it was mentioned four chapters earlier before the St Germanus material which knows nothing of Thanet, Kent or the Saxons and seems to be taking place a generation earlier.

The knowledge that Nennius uses geographically discrete sources is of crucial importance now we come to examine the Arthurian battle-list. It might be that Arthur's battles derive from areas not elsewhere represented in the *Historia,* but it is most plausible to assume that it conforms to the general pattern of Nennius's sources.

IRELAND

We can swiftly dismiss the Irish material as the origin of the battle-list. Nennius always presents Irish historical sections as discrete from the British history. In the Harleian, it is only linked to the fifth/sixth-century British material at the beginning by the phrase 'And St Patrick was, at that time, a captive' and at the end, six chapters later, by 'at that time, the Saxons increased in number'. The sources are two late seventh-century Irish lives of St Patrick, with some later additions (VII Dumville 1990). The previous reference to Ireland was forty chapters earlier, a prehistoric origin legend. Ireland is never mentioned again in the *Historia.*

KENT

The Arthurian battle-list is placed firmly by the author in a Kentish context. It begins with an introduction on the kingdom and kings of the men of Kent, continuing: 'Then Arthur fought against them in those days . . . .' The style of the list is similar to the Vortimer section, which is indisputably set in Kent, including identifiable Kentish place-names, and is clearly of Saxon and, presumably, Kentish origin. It includes the genealogy of Hengist back to Geta 'one of their idols, which they worshipped'. Place-names in the Vortimer section are given first in English (Thanet, Canturguolralen, Episford), then glossed as 'in British Ruoihm' 'in our language Chent' 'in our language, on the other hand, Rithergabail'. The same feature is found in the Arthur battle-list: a non-British place-name is glossed into British: 'That is Cat Coit Celidon.'

The title *Dux* applied to Arthur is only found elsewhere in the *Historia* in Roman material linked to the Kent sources. The Roman and Kentish material is not only linked stylistically. They share a common dating system based on consular years. The two Roman consuls were elected annually. Although they played an almost entirely honorary role in the late Roman Empire, their names were used as a system of dating: 'In the year of the consulship of A and B.' Nennius himself misunderstands this system, thinking that the consuls are in some way synonymous with Emperors. In the time of the Emperor Maximus, we are told, 'the consuls began, and they were never again called Caesars'. This was presumably the date from which his Consuls'

List started. Thereafter Nennius uses *Consul* for 'Roman ruler'. Nennius's lack of understanding of the difference between emperors and consuls ('Gratian ruled for the second time, with Equitius') is a clear indication that it is his source, not he, which originates the consular system of dating. The *Historia* links a dating system based on the Passion to the Kentish material, but it is less clear where this derives from. This system, used in the opening quotation from Malory, took as its starting date the death, rather than the birth, of Jesus. It was the work of enthusiasts like Bede which caused it to be superseded.

Dumville suggests that our author, 'Nennius' himself, has the Pascal tables of Victorius, which synchronise post-Passion and consul dates, in front of him (IV Dumville 1990). I think this is unlikely, given that these synchronisms are only applied to particular material, rather than throughout the *Historia*. The Paschal tables lead back to Jesus's time, and do not explain Nennius's belief that the consuls were a late feature of Roman history, synonymous with the earlier Caesars. These features can only be explained by their incorporation in particular sources used by Nennius.

The counter-arguments, that the Arthur battle-list is not exclusively Kentish, are all exterior to the text itself. We *know* that the Caledonian wood cannot be in Kent. It must be in the north. Gildas refers to the City of the Legions and the siege of Mount Badon, but shows no knowledge of Kent.

SOUTH WALES

I use this term to mean medieval Wales excluding Gwynedd, but including the adjacent marches in what is now England. In general, the *Historia* concentrates on south-eastern and central eastern Wales, Gwent, Glywysing and Powys.

The South Welsh material is recognisably of two types. The first is a *Life* of St Germanus, said in the *Historia* to be a 'Book of the Blessed Germanus'. It seems to have no internal dates. It includes an origin legend of the Kingdom of Powys, probably where it came from, and locates Vortigern in Gwerthrynion and on the Teifi in the land of the Demetians, Dyfed.

The second consists of legendary material of local interest. It is dominated by the story of Ambrosius, who comes from Mais Elleti in Glywysing. He subsequently rules 'all the kingdoms of the western part of Britain', including Builth and Gwerthrynion (which Vortigern's descendant still rules). Although it has a strong South Welsh flavour, the Ambrosius material has a scope encompassing 'the whole of Britain' and the fate of the British people. It starts in Gwynedd in Snowdonia and sees Vortigern consigned to Caer Gurtheyrn in the region called Gwynessi, somewhere in the north.

Surprisingly, Arthur in the *Historia* shows more affinity to St Germanus than to Ambrosius. The legendary, magical and prophetic features of Ambrosius's story are completely absent from the battle-list and only slightly more apparent in the *Mirabilia*. The battle-list has a strong Christian tone. Arthur carries an image of Holy Mary and by her power and that of 'our Lord Jesus Christ' overcomes the 'pagans' at Castellum Guinnion. Germanus uses the power of prayer to destroy fortresses. There are other similarities of language, too.

The *Mirabilia* support a South Welsh location for Arthur. The writer, although supposedly covering the whole British Isles, shows his parochial vision by locating his wonders mostly between Builth in the north, Ceredigion in the west, Wye and Hwicce in the east and the Severn in the south. We cannot be absolutely sure that the writer of the *Mirabilia* and the *Historia* are the same person (Arthur is the only figure common to both works), but even if they are different, there is no doubt the works were combined at an early stage of the manuscript tradition. A shared interest in south-east Wales is one of the most likely reasons for the works, if distinct, to have been combined.

The alternative, that the *Mirabilia* were written later, by an author mining the *Historia* for an interesting name to attach to a wonderful cairn and tomb in his own land, is untenable. There is no reason for him to latch arbitrarily on Arthur the Saxon-killer. The figure of Ambrosius, already associated with magical landscape phenomena and located in South Wales, would have been an obvious candidate. The ruler of Builth's own ancestors, named in the *Historia*, could have been the magical huntsmen who left the dog's footprint at Carn Cabal. There is absolutely nothing in the *Historia* to lead a writer to think that Arthur had hunted a famous boar or killed his own son. There is only one conceivable reason for reporting that Arthur the soldier was responsible for the wonders of Carn Cabal and Licat Anir – local traditions that said that he was.

Gildas was familiar with the broad area. He knew of the ruler of Dyfed, for instance. His Mons Badonicus could well be within the horizons of a South Welsh writer. Both Gildas and the battle-list refer to the city of the Legion/Legions. One possible location, Caerleon, is in South Wales. The more plausible contender, Chester, is not far away. It may even, as some historians argue, have been part of the kingdom of Powys at the time.

What, then, of those stylistic features which made a connection between the Arthurian and Kentish materials so plausible? If the author knew that Arthur came from South Wales, seemingly his own home area, why did he not mention this? On the contrary, while Vortigern and Ambrosius are linked specifically to South Welsh locations, the Arthurian material is clearly written as if it is linked to Kent.

INTEGRATING REGIONAL MATERIALS –
NENNIUS AND VORTIGERN

It is quite possible that 'Nennius' found Arthur in sources from both areas. He knew of Vortigern from separate sources and tried to integrate the information into a single story. Vortigern was a character in at least three of the sources used, the Kentish material (paralleling his role in Bede), the Life of St Germanus and the legend of Ambrosius the prophetic child. Vortigern probably also appeared independently in other minor sources, such as the family tree of Fernmail of Builth. Evidence of other material comes in a later passage, where the *Historia* calculates there were twelve years from the reign of Vortigern to the discord between Ambrosius and Guitolin, a discord known as Guolloppum or Catguoloph (the battle of Wallop in Welsh). The genealogy of Vortigern has Guitolin as his grandfather, though this contradicts the story that Ambrosius was a child in Vortigern's reign.

The contrary position, that Nennius took Vortigern from one source (the Kentish, Bede-influenced one) but inserted him in unrelated material about tyrants, cannot be supported. If that were the case, we would expect to find a single narrative thread, based on Bede, with no need for contradictory stories to be reconciled with it. Instead, we find that each source supplies a similar, but not identical, story of wicked fifth-century tyrant, Vortigern.

Nennius links the stories in two framing passages. At the start, all Vortigern's major enemies, Scots, Picts, Romans and Ambrosius, are listed together. At the end, all his sons are given in a single list.

It is just as plausible that Nennius knew Arthur from both a South Welsh and a Kentish source and linked the two strands in a similar way. But what of the Caledonian wood, which is no more in Wales than it was in Kent? The starting point for our investigation of Arthur as a historical figure was the reference to him in a north-eastern source, the *Gododdin*.

	KENTISH SOURCE	BOOK OF GERMANUS	AMBROSIUS SOURCE
VORTIGERN RULED:	Britain, including Kent as overlord, Essex and Sussex.	Gwerthrynion, Demetia, the valley of the Teifi.	Britain, Snowdonia, Gwynessi and Caer Gwrtheyrn.
HE WAS WICKED BECAUSE:	he let the Saxons into Britain.	he was not a Christian, and was incestuous.	he received the Saxons into the country.
HE HAD A NOTORIOUS UNION:	with Hengist's daughter.	with his own daughter.	
HE FATHERED:	Vortimer and Categirn, who fought the Saxons in Kent.	St Faustus, brought up and baptised by St Germanus.	Pascent, whose family were later permitted to rule in Builth and Gwerthrynion by Ambrosius.
HE WAS ASSOCIATED WITH A COUNCIL:	which tried to make peace with Saxons but was massacred by them.	which convened to condemn his wicked incest.	of wizards who advised him on how to seek security.
HE FEARED:	Picts and Scots.	British clergy and St Germanus (Romans?).	Ambrosius. Romans? The Saxons.
HE WAS PUNISHED BY BEING:	made a prisoner of the Saxons.	burned in his fortress on the Teifi.	driven out of Wales and into the north by Ambrosius.
AND HIS MISERABLE FATE WAS TO BE:	a hated wanderer dying of a broken heart without mourners.	swallowed up at night in his fortress.	

THE NORTH-EAST

Rather than being linked to the southern material which precedes it, Arthur's battle-list could be linked to the paragraph which follows: 'When they were defeated in all these battles [the Saxons] sought help from Germany . . . until the time when Ida reigned, who was the son of Eobba. He was the first King in Bernicia, that is Berneich.'

Although I have followed modern editors in imagining a new paragraph after Arthur's victory at Badon, Alcock points out (Alcock 1971) that this is not the case in the Harleian Manuscript. Although the initial letters of each section, intended to be filled in later in red, are not present, it is easy to see where the section breaks were intended. One was at the start of the renewed wars with the Kentish kings. The next begins 'Then Arthur . . .', running through without a break to the end of the first Ida passage.

If the scribe was faithfully following his original, this clearly links Arthur to the Northumbrian wars. Unfortunately, we cannot be certain of this. Arthur was a more famous figure at the time the manuscript was copied, and the scribe might well think his introduction merited a section break and decorated capital letter. After the Ida section quoted, the narrative flow ends abruptly and a scribe could reasonably decide on stylistic grounds to start a new section there.

In fact, at this point in the text, the Irish, Kentish and South Welsh material previously used in the *Historia* run out. Nennius uses different sources to continue his work. The new material, of northern English origin, continues the history to the reign of Egfrith of Northumbria, who died *c.* 678 or 682. This northern material covers the same ground as Bede and could derive from a commentary on his work. It consists of English genealogies and Northumbrian material based on kings' lists. Incomplete chronographical material, tying Ambrosius, the battle of Wallop, Vortigern and the coming of the English to Roman Consul lists, follows this but is not connected to it.

Although the genealogical material is English, it has been annotated by a British speaker. A battle with the Picts is called Gueith Lin Garan, King Penda's rich gifts to the British Kings is recalled as 'Atbret Iudeu'(the distribution of Iudeu). A British pun is made on the name of Welsh King Catgabail ('and so he was called Catgabail Catguommed [the Battle-shirker]'). The passages concerning Outigirn, Mailcunus and the British poets, must be British in origin. These additions are from a very late stage in compilation. It is simplest to see them as the work of the author himself.

Even when the British material in this section is not about the north-east: a synchronism with 'Mailcunus, Great King among the British, that is in Gwynedd', it is taken as an opportunity to tell the story of how his ancestors came from the Gododdin region. None of Outigirn's battles is named, but it is unlikely that his exploits alone in this section derive from a Kentish or South Welsh rather than a north-eastern source. And, as we have seen, the style makes a link to the Arthur battle-list almost inevitable.

This northern milieu is exactly where the *Gododdin* leads us to expect to find sources dealing with Arthur. Neirin, its supposed author, is one of the bards named in this section. Arthur's victory in the Caledonian wood must be somewhere in the region of Bernicia and Gododdin. Binchester in Deira could be Castellum Guinnion. There is a river Glen in Bernicia. It flows by Yeavering, a sub-Roman location which was a home of the Northumbrian Kings by the time of Bede, who mentions the river by name.

On the other hand, we have equally compelling arguments for Kentish and South Welsh sources for the battle-list. Gildas knows nothing of the north after the building of the Roman walls, but makes the siege of Mount Badon the crucial event of the British resistance. If Mount Badon was actually in the north, it would be the only northern location named in the whole of Gildas's work. We might also wonder how a campaign against the Saxons waged exclusively in the north would have decisively turned back the invaders and secured peace for a generation. All Saxon sources saw the southern kings as spearheading the attack and archaeology bears out that this was the most heavily settled area.

MULTIPLE SOURCES, ONE ARTHUR?

The only explanation which fits the facts is that Nennius has blended material from different sources to create a single Arthurian chapter in his chronological scheme. We can see the same method in chapter 38 or at the beginning of chapter 56 of the *Historia* where Hengist's sons Octha and Ebissa, from the Kentish source, are linked to northern events and localities.

Two possible situations could have led Nennius to create a composite chapter on Arthur:

1. He found widespread traditions of British victories before the coming of Ida, but the name of Arthur in only one area, and attributed all the battles to him.

2. He found Arthurian material in all his source areas (South Wales, the north-east and Kent) and forged them into a single narrative

The first alternative has the advantage of caution. In this theory, for instance, Arthur could be a South Welsh hero credited by Nennius with victories at Badon Hill or the Caledonian wood. He might alternatively be a warrior of the Gododdin, relocated to the south to reflect Nennius's geographical interests.

This limited explanation is less plausible. It does not explain why Nennius chose Arthur for this role. He was quite capable of writing about more than one character. He knew of Vortimer and Outigirn as anti-Saxon leaders. Both are included in the *Historia* without the need to fuse their battles in a single list. He has no difficulty recording Vortimer and Ambrosius or Outigirn and Mailcunus as contemporaries without combining them into a single character.

If Nennius was just searching for a name to attach to a list of battles, he had plenty to choose from. He knew the names of the famous kings Urbgen and Mailcunus. Embreis Guletic was a local South Welsh hero with a historiographical tradition, from Bede, that he fought the Saxons at Badon. If Nennius was concerned that his chronology involved a large gap between Hengist and Ida, he could have mined the genealogies for Fernmail's ancestors or Catel's descendants of the right period. He did not even need a name to link to the battles, which could just as easily be ascribed to the anonymous 'Kings of the Britons'.

If Arthur was a significant local figure in any one of the source areas, we can hardly imagine why Nennius did not make this explicit in the text. The battle-list gives no idea of Arthur's 'home ground'. There is no mention of his descendants or ancestors, or his native land. Yet Nennius often links the figures of the fifth/sixth centuries to contemporary locations and dynasties. If he could make these links for Vortigern and Ambrosius, why not Arthur? In particular, why are the majority of the battles at obscure locations, rather than at local sites or ones already mentioned in the *Historia*?

The creation of the figure of Arthur to link previously unconnected traditions of the British resistance is motiveless and implausible. Elsewhere in the *Historia*, Nennius is happy to eke out sparse materials, including named individuals with only one incident connected to them, or events without named participants. If he had in mind the idea that a legendary superman must have led the Britons, his imagination has failed in the case of Arthur. The most legendary material in the whole work, with prophetic worms, fatherless boys and councils of wizards, concerns the undoubtedly historical Ambrosius. Similarly, the very real Germanus of Auxerre is shown destroying whole fortresses with fire from heaven. To turn an incredibly famous, non-historical Welsh culture-hero into a mundane Saxon-fighter is simply bathetic. The idea that Nennius did not have the inventiveness to parcel out victories in Kent to, say, Pascent son of Vortigern, near South Wales to Ambrosius and in the north-east to Urbgen or anyone else mentioned in his sources, beggars belief. There is no reason to ascribe all the victories to a single Arthur the Warleader, unless they were already ascribed to Arthur in his sources.

This leaves us with just one plausible explanation: Nennius found material relating to Arthur as a warleader in all three of his source areas. Just as he had with Vortigern, he worked these sources together into a single story. That he meant his readers to understand that Arthur had a wide-ranging military career is implicit in his 'kings [plural] of the Britons'. Furthermore, Nennius used the exploits of Arthur across the country as a centrepiece to hold the clearly regional Vortimer and probably regional Outigirn into a framework of an extended pan-British war against the Saxons.

The evidence of *Historia Brittonum* is that sources referring to Arthur across Britain already existed before 830. The story, that Arthur was famous for fighting against the Saxons, that he fought at a Roman fortification and overthrew a large number of men in a single charge, is the same in both the *Historia* and the sixth-century *Gododdin*. The *Gododdin* is not one of Nennius's sources, so the story must have been arrived at independently.

There is no need for a single Arthurian battle-list to be Nennius's source. It is more likely that Nennius created his list by blending widespread material on Arthur the Warleader. This increases the value of the *Historia*, rather than diminishing it. It would clearly be more valuable to know that several sources contributed to Nennius's picture of Arthur the fifth/sixth-century Warleader, than to imagine that he picked an old Welsh poem out of his heap of sources and set it, barely altered, in an historical scrapbook between St Patrick and Ida of Bernicia.

WARS ACROSS BRITAIN

There are two possible ways that sources from different areas preserved accounts of the wars of Arthur:

1. Arthur fought widespread campaigns, winning battles across the country. These left memories of his exploits in various regions

or

2. Arthur fought in just one area, but stories of his exploits spread to other regions. Perhaps British exiles had physically moved to another area taking the stories with them. Alternatively, Arthur was perhaps such a famous character that other areas wished to claim association with him.

The first suggestion is the most straightforward. There is nothing implausible about Arthur fighting Saxons across the country. Writers often lose sight of the fact that Britain is a relatively small area. Many theories about Arthur have limited his activities to what are in fact tiny regions, as if a military commander were restricted to the range of a committed rambler. Hence we find Arthur's campaigns located in, say, Somerset or Gwent. In reality, from the Roman conquest onwards, large conflicts have turned the whole country into a war zone. Gildas reports the Saxon invasion and British resistance as extending across the island.

Other writers have concocted ideas of Arthur as a cavalry leader to explain his 'extraordinary mobility'. As we have no idea over what period these battles were fought, we have no idea how swift his forces would have to be to reach them. Even if they were fought in rapid succession, armies reliant on infantry, such as those of the Roman Agricola or the Saxon Harold in 1066, show us how easily they could move from one part of the country to another.

The Anglo-Saxon Chronicle provides numerous cases of wide-ranging conflict. Ceolwulf of Wessex is said to have made war against the Angles, the Welsh, the Picts and the Scots. His reign, beginning in 597, could be classed as belonging to the same 'legendary' era as Arthur's, but there are many examples from the later and undeniably historical portions of the Chronicle. The Vikings invaded the areas which had seen the first English settlements. They ravaged the island and were confronted by various English kings. These campaigns show what was possible in the Dark Ages. Between 872 and 877, the Viking 'great army' sallied out of East Anglia to camp at Torksey in Lincolnshire, on the Tyne, at Dumbarton, then down to Exeter and Gloucester. In 892 another great army landed in Kent. Three years later they were retreating from Chester, sweeping through Wales, then returning to East

Anglia via York. In this campaign, they faced a united English defence under King Alfred. Arthur's battle-list is thus not inherently implausible as a series of campaigns against the earlier invaders.

The alternative, that Arthur was a regional warleader whose fame spread to other areas, raises the question 'why?' This could only have happened if Arthur was already famous as a leader of battles, more famous than the 'real' leaders of the resistance. The story of the British resistance is not a legend. It is attested by the contemporary Gildas. It was brought about by the united efforts of the Britons. We would expect that, if all the kingdoms had different traditions, they would each have been able to name a local king who joined in the fight. As it is, none of these kings is named by Nennius. They are completely overshadowed by the warlord himself, Arthur.

Even if Arthur was a battle leader whose fame spread beyond his home area, he must still have been famous before the early ninth century. This is fundamental to understanding the *Gododdin* verse which began this investigation. In the *Historia*, Arthur is only famous for fighting the Saxons. The battle of Mount Badon was *the* memorable victory against them, as Gildas put it. If Arthur was not the commander at the battle, then the real victor of Mount Badon has been replaced by an even more famous Arthur. But what could Arthur possibly have done to become more famous than the victor in the greatest battle against the Saxons? In truth, there is only one thing Arthur can reasonably have been famous for. He must have been the victor at Mount Badon.

Someone led the Britons to victory at Badon. Aside from Bede's speculation, no other name has ever been applied to the victor. If Arthur was not his name, we have to accept that an Arthur who did not lead the Britons, nor found a dynasty, give his name to a prominent place nor have anything else to distinguish him, somehow supplanted the real victor in the memory of all British peoples. Frankly, it stretches credulity to the limit to believe that the victor of Mount Badon was not Arthur.

3

THE STRIFE OF CAMLANN

*H*istoria Brittonum paints a picture of Arthur, warleader in the campaigns culminating in the battle of Mount Badon, which is consistent with known sources and not obviously influenced by legendary or dynastic considerations. Although composed in the early ninth century, it clearly draws on earlier sources. So far, we have seen nothing in it to predispose us to reject its information. Some historians and archaeologists consistently reject all of *Historia Brittonum* as late and inadmissible. Most, though, while rejecting the Arthur material, are happy to mine the rest for names and dates to suit their purposes.

An example can be found in *The English Settlements*, the volume of the Oxford History of England covering this period. 'There are just enough casual references in later Welsh Legend . . . to suggest that a man with this [name] may have won repute at some ill-defined point of time and place during the struggle. But if we add anything to the bare statement that Arthur may have lived and fought the Saxons, we pass at once from history to romance' (Myres 1986).

Contrast this with Myres' treatment of another figure from the *Historia*, Soemil. All we know of him comes from the *Historia*, where we are told he was the ancestor of the Northumbrian king killed at Meicen and 'first separated Deira from Bernicia'. Yet Myres is happy to write: 'He could therefore have been a prominent figure among the Yorkshire Laeti in the early years of the fifth century. It looks as if he was remembered for the leading part he played in making his people independent of whatever sub-Roman authority had succeeded to the military command once held by the Dux Britanniarum in the northern frontier lands that were eventually to become Bernicia' (Myres 1986).

This is clearly every bit as speculative as saying that Arthur was a late fifth- or early sixth-century British leader who led the Britons to victory at Badon Hill, and has far less evidence to support it. Although Myres cites

Gildas as one reason for rejecting Arthur, his main prejudice is summed up in the word 'romance'. There is nothing romantic or legendary about the *Historia*'s treatment of Arthur, and the fact that medieval writers embellished the story is no reason to reject it.

While the Harleian Recension is the earliest reference to Arthur's battles, it does not stand in isolation. The later recensions add new information and clarify, as far as their authors understand it, some difficulties in 'Nennius's' text.

The Vatican Recension has been through two processes separating it from the Harleian (Dumville 1985). An English writer in the mid-tenth century brought the synchronisms up to the date of the fifth year of the reign of King Edmund of the English. Some time before this, between 830 and 944 (Dumville estimates between 875 and 925) the text was updated by a Welsh scribe. His home region becomes clearer when we examine his version of the *Historia*'s list of twenty-eight cities. The new scribe misread XXVIII as XXXIII, and had to add five more cities. The ones he chose were Cair Guroc (Worcester?), Cair Merdin (Carmarthen), Cair Ceri (Cirencester), Cair Gloiu (Gloucester) and Cair Teim (Llandaff), clearly signalling his interest in South Wales and adjoining England.

This writer added glosses, giving the Welsh names of some of Arthur's battles. According to him, *urbs leogis* (*sic*) was in British Cair Lion. In the list of cities, he uses this exact form to replace the Harleian's 'Cair Legeion Guar Usc' – Caerleon. He is the only writer in all the recensions to locate this battle at Caerleon rather than Chester, and it is likely that the similarly named city in his local area caused him to make this addition rather than real knowledge of where the battle was fought.

The battle of Tribuit is glossed as 'Which we call Traht Treuroit'. If this, too, is familiar to a South Welsh writer, it seems likely that it originally came to Nennius from his South Welsh source, rather than the north-eastern or Kentish ones. If it was actually in South Wales, we would expect the place-name to exist still. Logically, therefore, Tribuit was in an adjacent area which has since become English-speaking: the lower Severn Valley of Gloucestershire, which Nennius knew as the country of the Hwicce, or Herefordshire, which includes some of what was Ercing.

The eleventh battle is more intriguing. Where the Harleian listed the battle of Mount Agned, the Vatican has: 'The eleventh battle was on the mountain called Breguoin where they [the Saxons] were put to flight, which we call Cat Bregion [Battle of Bregion in Welsh].' Another recension, the Gildasian, provides the link in the development. It simply glosses the battle of Mount Agned as 'that is 'Cat Bregomion' [the battle of Bregomion in Welsh].

Breguoin/Bregomion could have several explanations:

1. Mount Agned is the English version of the battle the Welsh call Bregomion.
2. The writers did not know where Mount Agned was, but they did know that Arthur fought the Saxons at Bregomion and equated it with Mons Agned. Mons Agned could then be either an English name or a now lost Welsh name.
3. The writers did not know anything about Mons Agned, but to keep the number of battles up to twelve they inserted a famous battle of Urien Rheged, which a poem about him calls Brewyn.

Perversely, this last suggestion is the one most favoured by scholars. Quite why a writer who did not know where Agned was did not just leave it in the current text is baffling. No other unknown places in the text have been replaced in this way. If the writer wanted, for whatever reason, to mention one of Urien Rheged's battles, he had a perfect place to put it: in the part of the *Historia* where Urien himself appears.

This option is plainly far-fetched, given that there is no indication in either of the recensions that the writers knew anything different about Urien Rheged than the original author did. It is often suggested that Brewyn or Bregomion is Bremenium, the northern Roman fort of High Rochester. A battle at this location, in the north-east, not far from the Caledonian wood or the Northumbrian River Glen, is in one of the areas we would expect. However, it is difficult to see why a South Welsh writer should use the name of this battle to replace that of Mount Agned.

The only place around the South Wales area which might give rise to a battle of Bregomion is Branogenium, now Leintwardine in Herefordshire. On the borders of Ercing, this would be within what we have already established as a key area for the survival of Arthurian traditions. There is nowhere in the area which preserves the name Mount Agned, leaving the question of why one name replaces the other unanswered.

ARTHUR DUX

Instead of the introduction with which we are familiar from the Harleian, the Vatican begins straight after St Germanus with the arrival of Octha from the north to establish the Kingdom of Kent. 'Then warlike Arthur, with the soldiers of Britain and the kings, fought against them. And, although many were more noble than him, he was twelve times *Dux Belli* [warleader] and victor in the battles [the list of twelve battles follows] . . . but as much as the Saxons were laid low in the battles, so they were reinforced continually from Germany and by other Saxons, and they invited kings and *duces* with many soldiers from nearly all provinces to come to them. And this was done up to the time when Ida reigned.'

The writer clarifies what he sees as the original intended meaning, that Arthur was not himself one of the 'kings of the Britons'. Furthermore, he makes it explicit that Arthur is lower in rank and that his position as *Dux Belli* was informal. The Harleian uses the plural form *Dux Bellorum* (Leader of Battles). The slightly altered title *Dux Belli* is used by Bede of St Germanus.

The understanding that Arthur was not a king did not survive beyond the tenth century. Later sources were determined that Arthur had been a king. We will examine ranks and titles later, but for the moment we should note that it is far from clear what constituted a 'proper' king in early Dark Age Britain. Gildas calls the leaders of his time tyrants, kings, judges, governors and leaders (*Duces*, the plural of *Dux*). The rulers themselves use a variety of titles. Vortiporius appears on his memorial stone as 'Protector'. One of the leaders in *Y Gododdin*, Uruei, has the title 'Ut Eidin' (Judge of Eidin), derived from the word *Iudex* which Gildas uses. The poet tells us that 'his father was no *Guledic*'. That is the title the *Historia* knew for Ambrosius, in Latin 'King among all the kings of the British nation'. Either Uruei's father is not as high up as a *Guledic*, or Urei had not inherited his position.

It is conceivable that Arthur may have borne a royal title. The *Annales* often leave out the titles, whether bishop or king, of the characters referred to. Pantha, slain *c.* 657, can only be recognised as 'King Penda' of the Mercians from Bede, or the *Historia*'s notice that he 'reigned for ten years'. Cadwallon is called King in only one of his three entries. He is never given a title in his praise-poem. We could also speculate that Arthur was not a king at the time of his victories, but became one subsequently, perhaps as a result of them.

It is possible that the inference that Arthur *Dux* is not a king is brought to the battle-list by the Vatican redactor or even by the original author, misreading his source. While Gildas used *dux* and *rex* as synonyms, by the ninth century, they had become distinct. An original description of Arthur as the leader of the (other) British kings in battle could have been misunderstood as assigning a particular and lower rank to him.

Discussion on the subject of Arthur's rank in the *Historia* has been clouded by the idea that the work is a mélange of different sources, each using its own terminology. If, on the contrary, the battle-list only achieved its current form when Nennius combined Arthurian material from various sources, it is legitimate to compare the language used in it with that in the rest of the *Historia*.

Nennius uses titles in a systematic way. The Roman emperors are Caesars, emperors or consuls, usurping emperors are tyrants. The principal rulers of Britain are *reges*, 'kings', and their junior colleagues are *reguli*, 'minor kings' (HB 22). He is also aware of *Iudex* 'Judge' as a synonym for king: (HB 8) when *iudices* or *reges* are spoken of, people say 'he judged Britain with its three islands'. *Dux* and its plural *duces* mean only one thing to Nennius – generals or governors subordinate to the Roman emperors (HB 28). 'The Romans did not dare to come to Britain because the Britons had killed their *duces*' (HB 30). 'The *duces* of the Romans were killed three times by the Britons.' 'The Romans had come to Britain with a great army, established the emperor with his *duces*.' 'The *duces* of the Romans were killed by the Britons – three times.' That is the only sense of the word which Nennius uses. He makes the distinction absolutely clear in chapter 24, which seems to be related to the Kentish material. In this, Karitius becomes 'Emperor and tyrant' by killing Severus with 'all the *duces* of the Roman people . . . and struck down all the *reguli* of Britain'. This shows us that when Nennius writes that Arthur is a *dux*, he means something specific. His use of the word *dux* contrasts the nature and status of Arthur's power with the *reges Brittonum*, the kings of the Britons. He is in some sense acting as a Roman general or governor.

Historians have tried to fit Arthur into the framework of late Roman government. Some of the words used by Gildas and the *Historia* were technical terms in the Roman administration. The offices most cited in connection with Arthur are military ones. The *Comes Britanniarum* was the commander of the mobile, mainly cavalry, forces. The title *Comes* was never used of Arthur, and the idea that he was a cavalry leader owes more to medieval romances than to contemporary evidence. The *Dux Britanniarum* – Leader of the Britains, has a title tantalisingly similar to *Dux Bellorum* (Leader of Battles) which the *Historia* gives to Arthur. There is no reason, however, to think that *Dux Bellorum* is a misremembered Roman title. Comparable Welsh titles *Llywiaudir llawur* (Battle

Ruler) and *Tywyssawc Cat* (Battle Leader) are used in early poems. The first is used of Arthur himself, in conjunction with 'Emperor'.

The phrase 'then Arthur fought against them in those days, with the kings of the Britons', in the context of the Vatican Recension, is used to mean that he is not one of those kings. The writer says this specifically, and reinforces it with the connection between the kings and *duces* of the Saxons. The Vatican Recension also clears up the possible inference that Arthur is a superman, by adding the *milites*, the soldiers, to the British forces. As a man from South Wales, the writer might be influenced by the local description of Arthur (in the *Mirabilia*) as *miles* (singular of *milites*) – the soldier.

Although it is most plausible that Nennius intended us to understand that Arthur held a different type of rank to the kings, there is another possible reading. By writing that Arthur fought the Saxons 'with the Kings of the *Britons*', Nennius may have meant that Arthur was not himself a Briton. The first historical character known to have borne the name Arthur is the son of the Irish/Scottish King of Dalriada Aedan mac Gabran, mentioned in a book written *c.* 700. It was common practice for the late Romans to employ barbarians as military commanders.

Dumville comments rather unfairly that the Vatican's Welsh editor 'had access to Welsh legend', to make his amendments. There is no Welsh legend about Traht Treuroit or Cat Breguoin, or about Arthur being a less than royal elected warleader. We might rather say that the writer had access to Welsh historical material focusing particularly on his area of interest, South Wales and the lower Severn.

These issues will have to remain unresolved for the time being, while we turn to the next Dark Age references to Arthur, in *Annales Cambriae*.

ANNALS OF WALES

A later British source, the so-called *Annales Cambriae* or Annals of Wales, is nearly always treated in conjunction with *Historia Brittonum*. This is because the earliest surviving versions of both happen to be found in the same manuscript, Harleian 3859. The two texts are not related, in that the authors of each did not use or even seem to know of the other. There are some thirty-six later versions of the *Historia* and two of the *Annales*, but these are always found separately. In the period we are covering, they have only one incident in common. Both report Arthur fighting at the battle of Badon.

The *Annales* are simple in form. They are a sequence of years, each marked with the abbreviation *an*, for Latin *Annus*, 'year'. Every tenth year is marked with a roman numeral, counting from year 1 at the beginning of the cycle. The basic framework is found in Irish manuscripts, and probably has its origin in a system for calculating Easter. Most years are blank, but occasionally some memorable event is listed. *Annales Cambriae* take the Irish entries, but add events from British history. The end result is a sequence of 'dated' historical events which, in published form, look deceptively similar to the Anglo-Saxon Chronicle. We will examine their structure in a moment, but first let us look specifically at what the *Annales* say about Arthur.

'The battle of Badon, in which Arthur carried the cross of our Lord Jesus Christ for three days and three nights on his shoulders, and the Britons were the victors.' Arthur is the only named participant, so presumably, as in the *Historia*, he was the victorious commander. Here we have an independent source stating that Arthur was at Badon. It seems unlikely that both the *Annales* and the *Historia* arbitrarily decided to link the name of the same famous battle to the same legendary Welsh folk hero.

The only alternative to each source independently recording the same tradition is that they are not independent, specifically that the later *Annales* have been influenced by the *Historia*. The scribe who copied both texts around 1100 is often said to have expanded a terse reference to Badon to include the legendary figure of Arthur. If so, it is odd that he did not use material from the *Historia* he had just copied. In other early twelfth-century material, Arthur was seen as a foil of the saints, making it strange the scribe invented him carrying the cross of Christ.

Even if he had wanted to, it is doubtful how competent the scribe would have been inventing an *Annales* entry. In the entry relating to Gabran, son of Dungart, he mechanically transcribed 'an. Gabr. an. Fillius Dungart moritur', as if there was a year characterised by a meaningless 'Gabr' followed by one in which an anonymous son of Dungart died. All the evidence is that he is faithfully transcribing a mid-tenth-century document with no regard to the content. His exemplar must therefore have already included this reference to Arthur.

In the unlikely event that the reference to Badon has been contaminated, the *Annales* give an independent witness to one of Arthur's other battles. Twenty-one years after Badon, we read: 'Gueith Camlann in which Arthur and Medraut were slain and there was a plague in Britain and Ireland.'

'*Gueith*' is a Welsh word meaning strife, used elsewhere in the *Annales* in the names of battles: the battle of Chester is 'Gueith Cair Legion'. Perhaps this indicates Camlann was from a Welsh source and Badon from a Latin one. Medieval versions of the story were unanimous that Medraut was Arthur's adversary in this battle. 'Modred', the name by which he is better known, is possibly derived from a Breton or Cornish version. That they are indeed opponents seems the most sensible inference here.

Arthur is a figure of unparalleled importance in the *Annales*. No other secular figures or events are recorded in the first hundred years of entries. The entries in this section, excepting the first about Pope Leo changing Easter, refer to the births and deaths of Irish ecclesiastics, derived from the framework the Annalist was using at this point. In the later entries, northern Wales and North Britain become more prominent, but South and Central Wales are sparsely dealt with. Here we seem to have a confirmation of the *Historia*, that Arthur's fame was not confined to South Wales.

There is absolutely nothing objectionable about the references to Arthur in the *Annales*. Everyone else in the *Annales* is a real historical character. The style of the entries about Arthur is no different from those, for example, concerning the wars of Cadwallon. One cannot help thinking that, if the *Annales* were the only source other than Bede and Gildas, his existence as the victor of Badon would be taken for granted.

Received wisdom has it that the *Annales* had their origin in marginal notes in a table of Easter dates based on a great cycle of 532 years. As we have it, scribal defects would make any such computations impossible. Although the years are marked out in decades from the beginning of the cycle, in their current form some decades have eleven years, some nine and some ten. Easter is mentioned in the first entry and again, 220 or so years later, when it is first celebrated among the Saxons. In this year, a second battle of Badon was fought. Some entries are in the nature of 'St Columba born' (five years after the first battle of Badon), showing that they were not compiled, diary fashion, in the back of some monk's service book, but constructed after the events, like the early entries of the Anglo-Saxon Chronicle. As the entries approach better-recorded times, we can fix the otherwise unlocated chronology at various points. These are not always what we expect, and are in some cases very defective. The battle of Chester, which we would have expected to find *c.* 603, seems to be given ten years later. This is an easy mistake to explain away, caused by placing the event in the next numbered decade. What, however, are we to make of entries like the first Saxon Easter, apparently in 665, or the conversion of Constantine to the Lord in *c.* 587?

The battle of Badon is noted around 516. It is placed fifty-nine years after the death of St Patrick, drawn from the Irish Annals. This shows once again the *Annales'* independence from the *Historia.* Nennius had used the phrase 'At that time' linking St Patrick's story to Arthur's. By the time the *Annales* were composed, some versions of the *Historia,* including the Vatican Recension, had moved the St Patrick section to after the battle of Badon. Equally, there is nothing at all about the Saxon wars leading up to Badon, nor about Ambrosius or Vortigern. As the *Annales* stand in the Harleian Manuscript, it is possible to read the unfinished chronographical material at the end of the *Historia,* covering for instance Ambrosius and Guitolin, as being connected with them. If so, the writer was unable, despite these computations, to work out a position for Ambrosius relative to the other annals. There are no mentions of the Saxons at all until a hundred years after Arthur's time.

Modern translations of the *Annales* give the impression that dates such as Badon 516 or Camlann 537 are actually to be found there. In fact, there is quite a lot of variation between possible dates for those events. We could start with one of the later dates, such as the death of King Edmund (year 503), reported in the various Anglo-Saxon Chronicle manuscripts to 947, give or take a year, then count backwards. This would indeed place the battle of Badon (year 72) in 516, again give or take a year. Over this span of time, six phantom years have crept into the *Annales,* due to some decades being given eleven years. If the decade counts are wrong, but the number of individual years is right, then Badon would be dated 510.

If, however, Badon is 516, then the battle of Chester (169) is placed ten years later than expected from Bede. If we fixed the early *Annales* by making the battle of Chester AD 603 as Bede does, this would put Badon at 506. On the other hand, if the Death of Edwin in year 186 is linked to Bede's AD 633, Badon would have been fought in 519. Alternatively, we could work forward from Pope Leo's changing of Easter in 455, bringing us to a battle of Badon in 518.

All the possible *Annales* dates seem later than we would expect from the *Historia,* where Arthur fights Hengist's son soon after the time of St Patrick. They fit better with the idea that he was an adversary of Octha, Hengist's grandson, and that his career ended just before the arrival of Ida of Bernicia in the mid-sixth century.

The Arthur entries are two of three in the early part of the *Annales* which relate to secular events in Britain. These three entries were placed at ten- or twenty-year intervals. The slight misplacing of Badon relative to Camlann (21 instead of 20) is explained by the fact that the previous decade has been given eleven years by accident. These regular spacings suggest how the Annalist fixed them to the rest of the chronology. The link is the beginning of the reign of King Edwin of Deira. This comes '101' years (which without the phantom year is exactly 100 years) after the battle of Badon. North-eastern Arthurian material could have passed on this synchronism, or it could just be a rough estimate ('one hundred years before the reign of Edwin') originating with the Annalist. The reign of Edwin, when Christianity was first brought to Northumbria, starts the historical material with which we are familiar from Bede, which in turn links to the career of Edwin's North Welsh opponent, Cadwallon, who figures prominently in the *Annales*.

The link with the reign of Edwin is easy for the Annalist to set down. He simply noted the related British events two years after the numbered decade counts. This in itself led to scribal confusion, where the copyist was inconsistent as to whether the numbered decade counts should themselves be counted as years.

The third of the secular entries in the Badon–Camlann sequence is recorded ten years after Camlann *c.* 547 (537 at the earliest and 550 at the latest): 'There was a great plague, in which Mailcun King of Genedota (Gwynedd/North Wales) passed away'. This king appears twice more in the Harleian Manuscript. In the *Historia*, immediately after the passage on Outigirn and the British poets, Neirin, Taliessin and the others, we read 'Mailcunus reigned as great king among the Britons, that is in the Guenedota region'. His descent from Cunedag of the Gododdin tribe is then given.

Included in the Harleian Manuscript is a series of genealogies. These date from the same period as the *Annales*, and may be related to them, though they do not appear together in any other manuscripts. The first of the genealogies is of Ouen, tracing his descent through his father Higuel (Hywel the Good) and the Kings of Gwynedd, back to Mailcun, Cuneda(g) and beyond. In the *Annales*, Higuel's death is recorded three years after Edmund of England, that is in 950. Mailcun is shown as the ancestor, five generations back, of the King Catgollaun (Cadwallon) of Gwynedd, the adversary of the Northumbrian kings. In the *Annales*, his death is recorded as *c.* 631, and is dated by Bede to 634. This seems a plausible span of time.

The linkage of these characters to Higuel's dynastic line is uncertain. Our first impression is that there are too many generations. Death dates for Higuel's ancestors are given in the *Annales* six generations back to Rotri, who died 196 years previously – a reasonable average of 32.66 years per generation. Rotri, however, is given as the great-grandson of Cadwallon. If the same average is continued back seven generations beyond Rotri to Mailcun, we would expect to find Mailcun dying around 470, much earlier than his position in the *Historia* or *Annales*.

The genealogy of Higuel seems to have been constructed by combining his well-attested ancestors back to Rotri with some famous early figures from the *Annales*: Cadwallon and Catgualart, Iacob son of Beli and Mailcun. Where there is a long gap between *Annales* records, another figure (Iutguaul, Catman and Run) not mentioned in the *Annales* is inserted in the genealogy, a process which has apparently inflated the number of generations. The genealogy creates the illusion that a single hereditary dynasty has been ruling Gwynedd since at least the time of Mailcun and that Higuel and Ouen are its lineal descendants. We know this is not actually true. After the death of Rotri, a Caratauc was king of the region. A different genealogy is given for him, tracing his lineage back to Mailcun's grandfather.

Disjunctures like this make it difficult to place too much value on the genealogies. Some are demonstrably false. It is extremely unlikely that Hywel's wife was descended from an unattested Dimet ('Dyfed man'), son of the Emperor Maximus, and totally untrue that Maximus was the descendant in eight generations from Constantine the Great.

Much weight has been put on them, because of the importance of genealogy in medieval Wales. Then, Welshmen were usually named with their father's name used as a surname. However, this does not seem to have happened in the sixth century. None of the tyrants Gildas denounces are given patronymics, nor does one feature on Voteporix's memorial stone. In the *Gododdin*, many of the warriors do not have patronymics. In the *Historia* only Vortimer, 'son of Vortigern', is named in this way. In the *Annales*, the first Briton to be given a patronymic is Selim, son of Cinan, in year 169. Before him only the two Irish leaders, Gabran, son of Dungart, and Aidan map Gabran have them. Even the seventh-century Cadwallon's father's name is not given in early sources.

The genealogies of Higuel, his wife Elen and Caratauc have similar plans. Mailcun is given in the same generation as Cincar son of Guortepir

(Vortiporius) and of Cinglas (Cuneglassus). This information, that Mailcun and Cuneglassus are contemporaries and that Vortiporius is a generation older, harmonises with what is recorded by Gildas, and could derive from him. The names 'Arthur' and 'Outigirn' do appear in the genealogies, but in contexts which make it clear that these are not the same as the warleaders of the late fifth and sixth centuries. Arthur is listed much more recently than Mailcun, and Outigirn much earlier.

The importance of this information is that Mailcun was indisputably a real person from the generation following Mount Badon. He was a contemporary denounced by Gildas, using the sixth-century version of his name, Maglocunus.

MAGLOCUNUS AND MAELGWN GWYNEDD –
DOUBLE STANDARDS IN THE DARK AGES

Practically every historian studying the period, no matter how sceptical about Arthur, takes it for granted that Maglocunus is Mailcun or (in modern Welsh) Maelgwn Gwynedd. That is, they accept that Gildas's Maglocunus was the sixth-century ruler of Gwynedd, and probably an ancestor of the Gwynedd dynasty. Even the most sober historian is prepared to construct complex arguments about Gildas's location or the government of sub-Roman Britain based on that equation.

Unequivocally, Maelgwn Gwynedd is a figure of ninth- and tenth-century historical writing, exactly as Arthur the warleader is. He is found in exactly the same sources, *Historia Brittonum* and *Annales Cambriae*, with all their limitations. Gildas does not mention the Kingdom of Gwynedd at all; still less does he say that Maglocunus is its king. That information is derived from exactly the same sources that tell us Arthur was the leader of the Britons at Mount Badon. In the case of one, Gildas names the man, Maglocunus, without naming the place, in the other he names the place, Mons Badonicus, without naming the man. The logic – that Maglocunus must have been king of somewhere, and that Gwynedd must have had a king, therefore there is no reason not to accept the ninth-century tradition that Maelgwn was king of Gwynedd – can be applied with equal force to Arthur. Somebody led the united Britons at the siege of Mons Badonicus. The only person the Britons said was the leader was Arthur, and we have no reason not to accept that tradition either. On the contrary, the arguments in favour of Arthur leading the victorious Britons are far stronger than those which make Maelgwn Gwynedd Maglocunus.

The fact that Maglocunus is named in Gildas while the leader at Badon is not adds nothing to the force of the argument. Ambrosius is named by Gildas too, but that does not allow us to infer that he really was a fatherless prophetic boy who predicted magical worms beneath Vortigern's fortress. Although Gildas has much to say about Maglocunus, that material does not appear in the *Historia* or the *Annales*. It is simply his name which is used in those later sources.

In the ninth and tenth centuries, Arthur served no obvious political purpose beyond offering Britons the comforting idea that one of their leaders had fought successfully against the English. No contemporary dynasty claimed to be descended from him, or acknowledged him as part of a collateral line. No Welsh state of the period owned him as a native son or used him to justify their territorial claims. His status and battle-sites bore no relationship to the political realities of the time.

Not so Maelgwn Gwynedd. By the time of the *Historia,* and even more so the *Annales* and Harleian Genealogies, the rulers of Gwynedd were undeniably the most important British rulers. It is hardly surprising they should adopt Gildas's foremost tyrant, Maglocunus, as their ancestor. After all, the crimes Gildas accused him of – fighting rivals, listening to praise singers and rewarding his warriors – were likely to endear him to a Dark Age audience.

It is quite conceivable that references to Maelgwn might have been altered to fit a contemporary North Welsh agenda. It is clear that Nennius tries rather awkwardly to place Maelgwn in a North Welsh context. While providing British synchronisms for the reign of Ida, he writes 'Then at that time Outigirn was fighting bravely . . . then Talhearn Father of Inspiration was famous for poetry and Neirin and Taliessin and Bluchbard and Cian at the same time were famous for British poetry, Maelgwn, Great King of the Britons was reigning.' Then is tacked on the transparent gloss 'that is in the Gwynedd region'. It is transparently an addition not just because it is clumsy, but because it is immediately contradicted by the rest of the passage. Maelgwn is a descendant of Cunedag who 146 years earlier had come down from the lands of the Gododdin to expel the Irish from 'these regions'. What regions were these? 'The sons of Liathan prevailed in the country of the Demetians and in other regions, that is Guir Cetgueli (Gower Kidwelly), until they were expelled by Cuneda and by his sons from all the British Regions'; South Wales, that is, not North Wales at all.

That is *the* evidence for Maelgwn Gwynedd – hardly compelling. The *Historia* later deals with the deeds of Cadwallon, King of Gwynedd, with no indication that he is a descendant of Mailcun. That information is only given in the Harleian Genealogies, where not just those two kings but also Cuneglassus, Vortiporius, Magnus Maximus, Constantine the Great and many other figures of history are recruited to the family trees of Higuel the Good and the royal family of Gwynedd.

The *Annales* reinforce the view that Maelgwn is King of Gwynedd: 'Great Plague, in which Mailcun King of Gwynedd passed away.' It is hardly surprising to find him here, given the prominence of the kings of Gwynedd in the other entries. Once again, an identical source is used by historians to confirm that 'Maelgwn Gwynedd' is the tyrant Maglocunus, to that we are using to identify Arthur as the leader of the Britons at Mons Badonicus. While the evidence for Maelgwn Gwynedd is equivocal, that relating to Arthur gives useful and plausible evidence supporting what we know from Gildas. After the *Annales*, Welsh legends and Saints' *Lives* would give similar treatment to Maelgwn Gwynedd as to Arthur, which should not lessen our belief in the historicity of either.

I do not argue that the *Historia* is wrong in connecting Maglocunus with North Wales. I believe, rather, that the case for ascribing the victory of Mount Badon to Arthur is much stronger, not being tainted by obvious dynastic interests. There is no reason why both pieces of information should not have surfaced in the written record of the ninth-century *Historia Brittonum* after having been preserved since the sixth century. However, historians cannot have it both ways. If Arthur must face blanket challenges to his existence, then so should Maelgwn Gwynedd, and if Maelgwn Gwynedd can be accepted on a balance of probabilities, then so should Arthur.

THE BATTLE-LIST

The list seems intended to show that Arthur fought across Britain. We can infer that it combines locations in the north-east, the Kent area and in the Severn Valley and adjacent regions at least. Most of the battle sites are unknown, suggesting that they are now in England, with English names. Some clues can, however, be drawn from the little information given.

Many of the battles are on rivers. Logically, the battles would either have the rivers across them as a barrier, or they would follow the line of the river as an invasion route. In either case, Arthur and the Britons could be attackers or defenders. If the campaign is attempting to cross the river, then Arthur would either be attacking into Saxon territory or holding the river to prevent a Saxon crossing. Alternatively, he could be using the river valley as a line of advance downstream into Saxon territory, or blocking the Saxon advance upstream. The Saxon presence in coastal areas, with Britons in the highlands, makes it inevitable the rivers were used in this way.

The battle on the River Glein is fought near its 'mouth'. The Welsh used the same word for mouth or confluence, making the latter a possible reading. It is unlikely that either side is trying to force a crossing at such a site, so this must be a battle along the line of the river, hence a thrust into Saxon territory on the east coast. There are two existing River Glens in England, one in Northumberland, one in Lincolnshire. Both are in plausible war zones, with the balance in favour of the Northumbrian Glen, which is named by Bede and runs by the formerly British and then Anglian royal centre at Yeavering. Neither Glen has a mouth, being tributaries of larger rivers. Perhaps the Glen name was originally carried by the main branch down to the sea, or the confluence was indeed intended.

The case for the Lincolnshire Glen is bolstered by the description of the next battles as being 'in the Linnuis region'. This is taken, on the slight similarity of names, as the Lindsey region of Lincolnshire, although no river Dubglas can be found there. Since Arthur was victorious in all his battles, the four battles on the Dubglas must have been defensive, preventing a Saxon crossing, or part of a campaign downstream. If Arthur was trying to cross the river, then by definition all the battles could not have been victorious. A slightly better location, the Lindinis region of Somerset, is examined below.

The sixth battle was on the River Bassas which, like the Dubglas, is unknown. The two names rhyme, which might suggest Nennius found them together in a verse source. This in turn might imply that they are in the same area. Beyond that, we can only guess which of the riverine scenarios it represented.

The seventh battle was in the Wood of Celidon. This is the only battle of whose general location we can be sure. It was somewhere just north of Hadrian's Wall. We assume that the Britons are on the defensive here, as the wood is inland from any potential Saxon settlements. Such lack of settlement is good evidence for a British victory against the Saxons. The area was the focus of English activity from the mid-sixth century and there is no reason to think they simply avoided the area fifty years previously.

The next battle gives us unequivocal evidence that Arthur was a Christian. He carries the image of the Virgin Mary on his shoulders. The scene of the battle, Castellum Guinnion, is assumed to be a Roman fortification. As the result of the battle is that the pagans are put to flight, we have to understand that the Britons are defenders. If the Saxons were in the *castellum*, they had nowhere to flee. The best guess is that Guinnion is Vinovium (Binchester, Country Durham) hence part of the north-eastern milieu. It is close to Catterick/Catraeth.

The ninth battle, in the City of the Legion, must also be interpreted as a British defence. On the evidence of the city list, this was most likely Chester, which only fell to the Saxons in the seventh century. Caerleon is a viable alternative. Either would derive from a South Welsh source. None of the rest of the battles is demonstrably in the north, and it may be that Nennius has eight named battles from a north-eastern source, followed by four from southern sources. The tenth battle, on the shore of the river which is called Tribuit, and the eleventh, on the hill which is called Agned are, with the City of the Legion, the only ones which a tenth-century South Welsh writer felt confident to name in Welsh.

Agned may or may not have been the same as Bregomion. A northern location for this has been suggested, although Branogenium (Leintwardine in Herefordshire) would fit a South Welsh pattern better. If Agned is in the South Welsh area, we assume that the Britons are defending it. Unless Arthur made a habit of being trapped in such situations, the most sensible inference is that he led relieving forces to rescue the besieged Britons.

None of the battles has a demonstrably Kentish location. We could assign the unknown locations to Kent, but that would be sheer guesswork. On the evidence, the Kentish source may have done no more than refer to the wars of Octha, without giving the battle names.

The twelfth battle was on the hill of Badon, a famous victory remembered as having secured peace and a virtual end to Saxon attacks. The *Annales* use this battle to report Arthur's Christian affiliation. Here we are told that Arthur carried the cross three days and nights, so a siege seems intended, as described by Gildas.

This story of Arthur, Warleader of the united Britons *c*. 500, is internally consistent and consistent with other sources. There is nothing inherently implausible about it. Someone led the British at the real siege of Mons Badonicus. *Historia Brittonum* and *Annales Cambriae* both independently said his name was Arthur. We have to assume that Arthur did not perform this as a one-off feat, but that he had a military career in the wars between Britons and Saxons which preceded it. The battles ascribed to him are not (apart from Badon) famous ones in search of a named leader.

The *Historia* and the *Annales* both tell us that Arthur was at the British victory at Mount Badon. They have nothing else in common. There is every reason to suppose that they were composed independently. Neither the *Annales* nor the *Historia* has detailed knowledge of Gildas. They are most unlikely to have derived their versions of Badon from it. They were both probably loosely familiar with Bede's History, but Bede thought that Ambrosius was the victor. The *Annales* had not even heard of Ambrosius, at least in any context after 455. The *Historia* had and, logically if Bede was the only source for Badon, would have linked the great battle to Ambrosius. That Nennius did not is a powerful argument in favour of his independent use of a pre-existing tradition.

WHERE WAS MONS BADONIS?

Is Gildas's siege of Mons Badonicus really the same as the battle of (Mons) Badonis in the *Historia* and *Annales*? We need to tackle this question directly, as it is the touchstone for the existence of Arthur as a historical character. We will look at Gildas's description of the Saxon Wars later. Suffice for the moment that he says they culminated in the siege of Mons Badonicus. *Mons* means a hill or mountain. Gildas uses *Collis* which specifically means hill in other contexts, so is probably thinking of *Mons* as something on a larger scale. Some writers, usually with special pleading for a favoured location, translate it 'hill-country'. On its own, this might be so, but it is hard to imagine how someone might besiege a hill-country!

Badonicus is an adjective describing what kind of mountain it is – a Badonic, Badonish or Badonian mountain. Gildas uses this adjectival form only once elsewhere, when he describes the area across the seas from Britain as *Gallia Belgica* – Belgic Gaul. The reasonable understanding is that this hill is in a region called Badon or at a place called Badon. It is a highly unusual construction if the name of the hill itself is 'Badon'.

More inferences can be drawn from Gildas's text. He has previously told us how the Britons had fled to the hills (using the form *colles*). We understand, therefore, that the Britons are those being besieged at the Badonic Hill.

Although it is possible that an unsuccessful siege was the undoing of the Saxons, it is unlikely that this would have the catastrophic results Gildas describes. Given that Gildas thought that retreating to the fortifications was in itself misguided, we have to conclude it was not a tactic used by the victorious Britons in this case. The obvious inference is that the victors were a relieving force which broke the siege of a strategic British position in the Badonian area.

It is unlikely that Gildas expected us to infer that the hill at/in Badon was itself an important centre or fortification. He had a range of words such as *urbs* (town/city), *castellum* or *receptaculum* (fortress) which he could have used if that had been his intention, rather than the neutral *mons*. Archaeological evidence shows that the refortified hillforts of the period had usually stood without residential or military use for centuries. They might no longer have had names of their own.

In *Historia Brittonum*, *Bellum* means a battle, rather than its classical meaning of war. *Badonis* means of Bado or of Badon, understood as the name of a person or place. Compare it with *Celidonis* earlier in the list – the forest of Celidon. The writer is not telling that the hill was called Badon, any more than that the forest was called Celidon. He was perfectly capable of describing what a hill was actually called. The previous battle was 'on the hill which is called Agned'.

The final piece of evidence that the hill is at Badon not called Badon comes in the *Annales*, where the engagement is 'Bellum Badonis' – the battle of Badon, with no mention of its hill. This battle seems to take three days and nights, indicating it is most likely a siege, as Gildas said. There is nothing to make us think that the sources are not all referring to the same battle.

As for its actual location, probably we should look in the south-western part of Britain, east of Dumnonia and where Gildas and Nennius share a geographical interest. Nennius is likely to have found information on the battle either in a South Welsh source, which would come within Gildas's area of interest, or in the Kentish material, essentially a romanticised version of the story given by Gildas.

Within these areas, we are looking for a place or region called Badon with a hill, probably a large hill, fortifiable if not with a fifth/sixth-century fortification present. We are not looking for a hill called Badbury. Badbury does not mean a hill near Badon. It means a fortification named after (for argument's sake) Badon. It would be the English translation of a British Din Badon or a Latin Castellum Badon, not Mons Badonis/Badonicus.

We do have one significant pointer to the location of the battle of Badon, or at least where the writer of *Annales Cambriae* believed it to be. Approximately 150 years after the Arthur victory (the round figure may be the result of a deliberate synchronism) *c.* 665, is recorded 'Bellum Badonis Secundo' – the second battle of Badon. The battles at this period in the *Annales* are fought by the North Welsh and the Mercians, and the Northumbrians.

Bede presents the circumstances of these battles. His people, the Northumbrian Angles, were struggling against the Mercians who had not yet converted to Christianity, and their North Welsh allies. Although there is much confusion about the names of the battles and how those in Bede relate to those in the *Historia* and the *Annales*, Bede records nothing which would equate to a second battle of Badon around 665. Bede knew from Gildas that there had been a first battle of Badon, and might have mentioned if he knew about a second. The *Annales* record the first Saxon Easter in the same year as Badon II. This could be a mistaken impression of the Synod of Whitby, on the Easter controversy, in 664.

This suggests that we must look outside Bede's area of interest for this second battle. The Anglo-Saxon Chronicle covers wars of which Bede had little or no knowledge, those of the West Saxons. Bede reports how Wulfhere of Mercia established his hegemony over the South Saxons and the Isle of Wight. The Anglo-Saxon Chronicle continues the story with Wulfhere's battle with Aescwine, King of Wessex. It dates this to 675, the year that Wulfhere died according to Bede. However, these early dates for West Saxon history can hardly be treated with precision. The Chronicle spreads them out regularly, perhaps to give the West Saxons a more consistent presence in the early entries. It could be that Wulfhere's battle with the West Saxons was actually part of his southern campaign ten years before this.

The Mercians fought the West Saxons at Bedanheafod, meaning Bedan-head. This seems more than coincidentally similar to the *Annales* second battle of Badon. 'Head' could convincingly refer to a hill or mountain. Could we in this entry be looking at the English name for Mons Badonicus?

Where then was Bedanheafod? Logic dictates it was somewhere on the borders of the Mercians or the West Saxons, or within Wessex, given the circumstances of the battle. Furthermore, for the battle between two Saxon kings to be at the same place as a previous battle between the Saxons and the Britons, it would have to be somewhere which in 500 was in British or disputed territory, but by 675 was outside the British sphere.

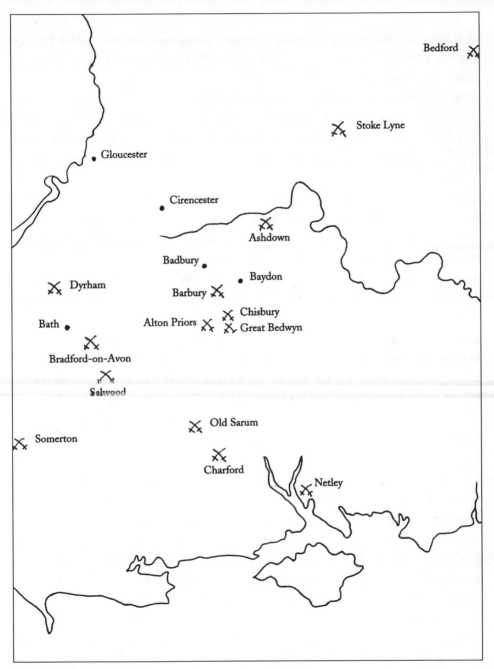

Searching for Mount Badon.

In Bede's time, the West Saxons bordered on the Hwicce in Gloucestershire and Somerset in the west, but that is all the evidence we have. The Hwicce did not found a kingdom lasting into the eighth century, and their history is thus unknown.

As the Anglo-Saxon Chronicle relays it, during the first half of the sixth century, West Saxons had spread as far as Netley and Charford. In 552 they were fighting the Britons west of this frontier, taking first Old Sarum, then Barbury in Wiltshire. Next they moved north to Bedford, moving into the Thames Valley in 571. Then, 577 saw the momentous victory at Dyrham which secured Gloucester, Cirencester and Bath. The frontier was further defined by battles at Alton Priors in Wiltshire and Stoke Lyne in Oxfordshire.

Approaching our date (665/675) we see the 614 battle at Beandun (unknown), 648 hegemony over Ashdown (Berkshire), and 652 fighting at Bradford-on-Avon. In 658 victory over the Welsh gave the West Saxons Penselwood as far as the Parret in Somerset. By 709, their westward expansion had led to the creation of two dioceses among them, divided east–west by the Selwood forest. Selwood has Barbury and Old Sarum on one side and all the post-Dyrham expansion sites on the other. It is tempting to see it as marking a division between old and new West Saxon territories. Britons held on to the rest of Somerset until the fall of Somerton in 733.

There is nothing absolutely certain about this chronology or even the identity of the belligerents. We would expect other Saxon peoples such as the Hwicce to be those extending the frontiers, not the West Saxons. The impression, however, is that the area which changed from British to Saxon control over the 150 years is Wiltshire, north Somerset, Gloucestershire, as well as the Thames Valley from Berkshire to Oxfordshire. This is very much where we would expect to find Mons Badonicus, as we shall see from Gildas. It is not unlikely that Mons Badonis and Bedanheafod were fought in the same place. Plummer suggested (1892–9) that Bedanheafod was (Great) Bedwyn, Wiltshire. Although there is no continuity of names – Bedanheafod is not found anywhere other than in this chronicle entry – the site is a surprisingly good one. Bedwyn itself is in the river valley, but its head or hill is immediately to the north and west of it, capped by the hillfort now called Chisbury. Chisbury dominates all approach routes and would, for instance, constitute a barrier to Saxon expansion. It is, moreover, on the extreme east of the Savernake Forest, an obstacle to movement into modern times. Fortified hills and dense forests are exactly the defensive positions Gildas tells us the

Britons adopted. Great Bedwyn also happens to be extremely close to the cluster of those Bad- names, Badbury and Baydon, used to support the case for Liddington.

THE DEATH OF ARTHUR

It is rather too much to expect that Arthur the Warleader would die in his bed. Gildas does not say what happened to the victor of Badon, but we can imagine a likely scenario. Although the external wars ceased, civil wars continued to be waged down to Gildas's own time. *Historia Brittonum* hints that Arthur was involved in civil strife, relaying the tradition in Ercing that he had slain his own son.

Annales Cambriae say that Arthur was slain at *Gueith Camlann* twenty or twenty-one years after Badon, enough time for him to have a grown son to fight against. Alongside Arthur fell Medraut. All subsequent versions of the death of Arthur have made the two adversaries. It seems likely that this is what the annalist intended.

Where was this Camlann? We would expect it to be in a British area. Although we have used the grave of Anir in Ercing to locate Arthur, we have to acknowledge that civil strife need not be carried out in either of the participants' backyard. The tyrants pursued thieves all over the country, if need be, as Gildas tells us.

Camlann could be in one of the South Welsh, north-eastern or Kentish areas where Arthur's Saxon-fighting activities have been placed. I am more inclined to think that the battle was fought elsewhere, precisely because Nennius does not know about it. Its name, *Gueith Camlann*, as opposed to *Bellum Badonis*, might indicate a Welsh/British source of continuing tradition. While Mount Badon was more or less unknown in Welsh tradition, there is a rich vein of legendary material relating to the battle of Camlann. Badon, most probably, passed out of British control by 665. We can suppose that Camlann, on the other hand, was still a living British location at this time.

Although the name Camlann actually means 'crooked enclosure', there is a consensus that it really derives from the British 'Camboglanna' – crooked stream/valley (Alcock 1971). There is one place known to have borne that name in Roman times, the fort of Castlesteads by Hadrian's Wall. Camboglanna was, in fact, maintained during the sixth century. It is possible that Arthur's heroic *death* at a Roman fort in the north is one of the features which he had in common with Guaurthur of the Gododdin. The northern Camboglanna is thus a distinct possibility for Arthur's last battle.

There are, though, some alternatives. There is a Camlan in modern Wales, the side of the valley above a sharp bend in the River Dyfi. This lies on the main route between Gwynedd and Powys. Above it is a second hillside Camlan and tributary Afon Gamlan (River Camlan), a suggestive cluster of names. Gildas testifies to the civil wars raging beyond Dyfed, presumably either in North Wales or Powys, in which the tyrant Maglocunus took the leading part. It is also close enough to Ercing to consider that it was part of the Welsh conflict which had previously seen Arthur kill his son, and is just beyond Carn Cabal. There is a distinct North Welsh predominance in the *Annales*, which would add to the plausibility of this suggestion.

There are plenty of other Cam/Camel streams to support regional theories. Geoffrey of Monmouth was the first to specify a location for Camlann, as a stream in Cornwall, the modern Camel. Tradition places the battle at Slaughter Bridge, Camelford. This is the first suggestion that Arthur might have fought in Dumnonia. Another suggestion is the Camel by South Cadbury hillfort, one reason why Leland identified it with Camelot. Clearly, this method, based on the similarity of names, is too imprecise. More precision can be gained by re-examining the *Annales* entries.

The early annals are based on Irish Annals composed in 741. Eleven British entries are added to these annals, giving events up to *c.* 613, the first of which are the two Arthurian ones. After this, the focus of the *Annales* is obvious. The entries concentrate first on the wars of Cadwallon of North Wales and the Northumbrians, before shifting to South Wales. From the early ninth century, at least, the *Annales* seem to be written in St David's. Kathleen Hughes (1973) identified the first stage of composition as being between 741 and 769. If the Arthurian entries date from that phase, they would be earlier than *Historia Brittonum*. Unfortunately, their early placing in the *Annales* is not necessarily indicative of their early composition.

The eleven entries are located as follows: two unlocated (Arthurian), four northern, three or four North Welsh and two or three South Welsh (depending on whether we consider Urbs Legion (Chester) a northern outpost of Powys or part of Gwynedd). One of the South Welsh entries, on the death of Bishop Dubric, actually seems to derive from the St David's phase, grafted on to an originally North British entry.

The balance is, therefore, in favour of Camlann being in North Wales or the north, but assigning the Arthurian locations to any of the three regions would create an imbalance in its favour. We need another form of analysis to be certain.

Another approach is to look at verbal similarities between the entries. Most of the entries are very terse. The Arthur entries leap out because of their sentence structure and detail. If their particular linguistic features occur in other entries, this may give a pattern pointing to a common origin. The diagnostic features on which we can make the comparisons are: explanations of events as being ones *in quo/in qua* (in which) something happened; use of *Gueith* to mean battle; and the results of battle being *corruit/corruerunt* (he/they were slain) or *victor fuit/victores fuerunt* (he was the victor/they were the victors).

Those features occur, with their approximate dates, in these entries:

516	Bellum Badonis, in quo Arthur . . . et Britones victores fuerunt	Unlocated
537	Gueith Camlann, in qua Arthur et Medraut corruerunt	Unlocated
547	Mortalitas magna in qua pausat Mailcun	North Wales
613	Gueith Cair Legion . . .	North Wales
630	Gueith Meicen. . . . Catguollaun autem victor fuit	North Wales
631	Bellum Cantscaul in quo Catguollaun corruit	North Wales
644	Bellum cocboy in quo Oswald . . . et Eoba . . . corruerunt	North Britain
682	Mortalitas magna . . . in qua Catgualart . . . obiit	North Wales
722	Bellum Hehil apud Cornuenses, Geuith Gartmailauc . . . et Brittones victores fuerunt	Cornish
750	Id est Gueith Mocetauc	North Britain
760	Id est Gueith Hirford	South Wales
813	Bellum . . . Higuel victor fuit	North Wales
844	Gueith Cetill	Unlocated?
873	Gueith Bannguolou	Unlocated?

The pattern is strikingly clear. It refutes the charge that the Arthur entries are late additions based on their complexity and structure. The majority of those of similar length and construction refer to the seventh/eighth centuries and the style is not continued beyond 873. Four of the last battle entries are similar only in their use of the word Gueith, twice as a gloss for entries which probably originally did not include it.

As is readily apparent they are features of a North Welsh phase of writing up to 813. All except one are about the North Welsh or (once) the Mercian and Northumbrian participants in the North Welsh wars. The only exception is the detailed description of the wars in Cornwall in 722.

Badon we have assumed to be a southern location, but for Camlann, with no other information to guide us, we should consider that it fits the rest of the pattern. Although a Cornish location is not out of the question, the balance of probability is that Camlann is a North Welsh battle. As there is a perfectly plausibly North Welsh Camlan, on the Dyfi, we should assume that is the battle-site the writer meant. Camlann continued to be a focus of Welsh tradition long after memories of the other battles, including Badon, faded, adding to the likelihood that it was a known location in Wales..

A later scribe did not expand a terse entry in the *Annales* reading 'Bellum Badonis' to incorporate the now famous figure of Arthur. This new analysis demonstrates the exact reverse. The description of Arthur's victory is perfectly in accordance with the seventh- and eighth-century North Welsh entries. It is the location, *Bellum Badonis*, which is the anomaly. If any doctoring has taken place, it would be a replacement of an original obscure (North Welsh?) battle name with that of the more famous Badon, possibly derived from the *Historia* battle-list. If the battle at which Arthur carried the cross thirty years before the death of Mailcun was not originally equated with Badon, then a major discrepancy between the *Annales* and Gildas on their dating would be removed.

BRIDGING THE GAP

We have focused on the *Historia* and *Annales* as the major battleground in the fight to prove the existence of a historical Arthur. If these accounts derive from the fifth and sixth centuries in any way, there is good reason for believing in him. If they are later fabrications, then the concept of Arthur as a real leader falls to pieces.

These sources impress because they are consistent, both with each other and well-established facts; they are plausible and they derive from sources which are independent and which existed before the works in which they appear. Information about the historical Arthur could only have been passed down between the sixth and the ninth centuries orally or in writing.

ORAL TRANSMISSION?

There are two main categories of oral evidence. The first is local hearsay and legend, subject to the vagaries of memory and changing perception of the past. Only two pieces of the early Arthur material fall into this category: the wonders of Carn Cabal and Licat Anir. The author gives no indication that the wonders derive from anything but current observation and local tradition. The very fact of their existence is important for us. If Arthur was known to be a fighter only in the north-east and Kent, it would be odd for his name to be attached to wonders in South Wales. Only he and St Illtud have wonders attributed to them and no one would argue that the saint was just a generally famous cleric capriciously attached to a South Welsh site. The idea that Arthur was a soldier is another believable piece of information. Whether Arthur had actually killed his son Anir or hunted a boar called Troynt with his dog Cabal is another matter. It is unlikely that either of these pieces of information were supported by reliable sources.

The second is deliberate oral preservation. The British maintained an oral tradition, based on bardic poetry and genealogies, which was professional and systematic. This lasted deep into the Middle Ages and certainly was to be found between AD 500 and 800.

Genealogy is easy to dismiss. No genealogical links are provided for Arthur, nor is he placed in a sequential list of kings. There is no evidence for oral chronicle-style material in Wales. That leaves elegies and praise-poems as potential sources.

The *Historia* places the career of Arthur in the generation preceding the era of famous Welsh poets. It may be that Nennius implicitly claims these poets as his sources. Talhearn Tataguen stands out, with the others included more as an afterthought. Only Neirin and Taliessin have left their names attached to surviving works of poetry. In the 'Book of Aneirin' (the later Welsh version of his name) we find 'Neirin's' poem *Y Gododdin*. We will look at some of the poetry attributed to Taliessin later.

Arthur's mention in the *Gododdin* shows poetry is indeed a possible source. Arthurian poems would be composed in South Wales or the north-east, but are unlikely to survive in Kent. Arthur's battle-list is no elegy for a fallen hero. There is no indication that he has died at Badon and the *Annales* flatly contradict this. We are then, perforce, thrown back on the concept of a praise-poem.

The arguments for a praise-poem are briefly summed up. The battle-list either comes from before Arthur's death or derives from a poet writing in the persona of someone from before Arthur's death. Welsh poets were quite capable of such imaginative writing. Two words, *ostium* and *humeros*, are said to point to Welsh originals meaning confluence or shield, respectively. Welsh poets were, however, equally able to refer to river mouths and men's shoulders, the literal meanings of the Latin, and the list is not difficult to understand without altering these words. Finally, some of the battle names would rhyme in a putative Welsh source.

The Arthur material does not read like any surviving Welsh poetry. It is light on poetic imagery, has little repetition or other indication of verse structure. Most importantly, why are so few Welsh names preserved? Every battle in the source would have its Welsh name. Nennius translated *Silva Celidonis* for his British readers, but did not think to offer glosses for *Castellum Guinnion*, *Urbs Legionis* or *Linnuis Regio*, none of which is self-explanatory.

In truth, the reign of Arthur lies at the extreme limit of the period from which Welsh poetry could derive. In the fifth century, the British language had yet to become recognisably 'Welsh'. Words still maintained their changeable endings, which altered depending on their role in the sentence. These forms still occur in Gildas's time, but would shortly disappear in favour of words whose function, as in modern Welsh and English, was determined by their position in a sentence.

This change would have rendered early poetry unpoetic and even unin-telligible. Rhymes dependent on case endings would disappear in updated versions. This means that the mid-sixth-century poetry of Neirin and Taliessin is probably the earliest that could have survived to be appreciated by medieval Welsh audiences.

None of the comparable Welsh poems provide the all-important element of context. We hear of the battles of Catraeth and Meigen, for instance, but not the era when they were fought. For this we have to turn to written sources, as surely the author of *Historia Brittonum* must have done.

WRITTEN SOURCES?

Though the Nennian prologue condemns the Britons as preliterate fools, the *Historia* proper contradicts this. For instance, the descent of Brutus from Noah is said to be preserved in 'old books of our elders' (HB 17). One written source, a *Life of St Germanus*, is specifically referred to in the text. This linked

Germanus to the Powys dynasty, and was written before 820 when Powys was devastated by the English. A real fifth-century *Life of St Germanus* survives, and was used by Bede. It included victories over the Saxons with Germanus in the position of elected warleader (*Dux Belli*, as Bede phrases it). If the version of this used by Nennius included Arthurian material, it would have been as a continuation of the main story. Germanus had visited Britain in the 420s, and although both Bede and Nennius stretch the chronology of the story as far as possible, it still does not reach the next generation after Vortigern, where Arthur is placed.

Nennius had access to British material, dealing with the wars against the Northumbrians, down to Cadwallader in about 682. This is used as a source after the Arthur battle-list. It covers much the same ground as Bede's *Ecclesiastical History* and may be a commentary on it. A more intriguing possibility is that it might pre-date Bede, since it does not continue into the early eighth century as Bede does. This source seems likely to be the principal 'north-eastern' source for the Arthurian material.

The northern material is interlinked with English genealogies, extending down to about 796 with Offa's son in the genealogy of the Mercians. Most of the other genealogies end in the seventh century. Dumville rejects a more convoluted theory, that the northern British and English materials had already been merged by an early eighth-century historian, perhaps the 'son of Urbagen' given as the author in the Chartres Recension. It is safest to conclude that there is only one author responsible for linking together the sources of *Historia Brittonum*, the early ninth-century 'Nennius'.

The last source, which seems to have been responsible for the framework in which the battle-list fits, is an English chronicle relating to the settlement of Kent. The material in this goes no further than the late sixth century, but it would be wrong to deduce it was written then. When the terms 'late sixth century' and 'Kent' are linked, the subject matter becomes obvious: the chronicle covered the origins of the Kingdom of Kent down to its conversion to Christianity in 597. If all the Saxon-fighters are linked within this frame, then Outigirn would be no later than this date, which accords with the other synchronisms. In its current form, the romanticised Kentish Chronicle seems to post-date Bede's similar version of the story, and is therefore mid- to late eighth century, but its sources may be earlier.

A shared feature of the Arthur and Vortimer battle-lists is that they appear to have been composed in a language other than Welsh. *Episford* is glossed as '*in nostra lingua Rithergabail*' (in our [Welsh] language Rithergabail) and '*bellum in silva Celidonis*' as '*id est Cat Coit Celidon*' (that is [in Welsh] battle of the wood of Celidon). If the lists were composed in Welsh, then translated into Latin, we would expect to find the opposite, e.g. 'the battle of Cat Coit Celidon, that is [in Latin] the Celidonian Wood'. This points us towards a potential English source.

It is conceivable that the framing for the Arthurian battle-list and Outigirn entry, which are identical in style to the Vortimer/Hengist passages, might derive from the same 'Kentish Chronicle'. Arthur's battles are specifically said to be happening in the same area, against the same people. An English history would have its own limitations. The Anglo-Saxons had no written records of the fifth century, neither did they have a well-developed oral tradition.

The Anglo-Saxon Chronicle shows how Saxon historians worked. It is written to celebrate the West Saxon kings. The compilers have Bede, place-names, probably the kings' lists and genealogies, and 'traditions'. These are worked rather crudely into an analytic frame using Bede's AD dating system, crudely, we can say, because some of the methods remain obvious. For instance, the chronological frame is almost certainly one in which leap years were marked out, probably for liturgical reasons. Many of the events of early Saxon history are set down as happening in leap years. The events of different dynasties are not interwoven. The entries of Kent are followed by those of the South Saxons, then the West Saxons. It is surely more likely that periods of Saxon expansion saw activities by all groups, rather than baton-passing between them. Bede's story of Hengist and Horsa has resulted in the foundations of other kingdoms being presented as small groups, often under pairs of leaders, arriving on the south coast and then fighting their way to dominance over the local Britons. Finally, nothing is said of any peoples who were not 'kingdoms' in the ninth century.

In spite of these limitations, the Chronicle gives a useful illustration of how ninth-century writers imagined the sixth century. Of great importance are entries like those of Aelle which do not reinforce the West Saxon case. Saxon sources agree that this period saw reversals in their fortunes, though their adversaries' names were rarely preserved.

We have an archaeological check on the Chronicle. Myres (1969) noted a break in the archaeological pottery sequence between the early and mid-sixth centuries in Kent, Essex, Hertfordshire, East Suffolk and Buckinghamshire. This would confirm the impression from the written sources that there was a real period of Saxon reversal around this time, and that the wars of Arthur had been synchronised to a very plausible period.

How does this compare with possible English sources for *Historia Brittonum?* One indication that their origins, at least, pre-date Bede, is that they lack Bede's most important innovation, the AD dating system. Other accounts of the conquest, like the Anglo-Saxon Chronicle, eagerly latched on to this system to give legitimacy to the origin legends. The difference can be seen in, for example, the assigning of an AD date to the death of Horsa in the Chronicle, where none is even hinted at in the *Historia.* After Bede, AD dates became ubiquitous and this gives us the strongest hint that the Kentish Chronicle and the north-eastern kings' lists use sources older than the early years of the eighth century.

The sources for the Arthurian section seem to be something like this: Nennius provides contemporary early ninth-century folk material on local wonders and activities of Arthur in regions adjoining South Wales. Some historical framing is given to the start of the period by the *Book of the Blessed Germanus*, a work from Powys before 820. Material relating to the north comes from British and English sources, combined by Nennius. Both these sources extend to the end of the seventh century, but have been revised, to bring some of the genealogical material to the late eighth century and to update British material. The sources are unknown, but include written English and British material, and possibly poetry from the named poets. Some of the Kentish material comes from an essentially pre-Bede (late seventh-century) source. Are these sources inadmissible?

Dark uses a generation count of thirty years to estimate the extent of time over which oral traditions might have been preserved (Dark 2000). Working on the supposition of a historian writing down the words of the oldest person available, recording what they had been told by, for example, a grandparent when they were a child, he deduces that 200 years is the maximum time one can reasonably expect oral tradition to survive without serious distortion. On this assumption, all we need is for the Arthurian material to be written down *c.* 740, less than 100 years before its incorporation into the *Historia.* As we can see, there is every reason to suppose that the author drew on both British and Saxon written sources of at least this age. This, combined with the *Gododdin* reference, suggests that, far from being inadmissible, the first historical sources to mention Arthur deserve serious consideration.

Taken together, the sources we have studied so far have produced a plausible and consistent picture of Arthur the Warleader. For those historians who affirm that this gives us no reason to accept it, we can reply that it gives us no reason to reject it either. To make that decision, we must look directly at the evidence from the turn of the sixth century. Only if we can find no trace of the reign of Arthur here can we be confident in dismissing it.

4

THE DESTRUCTION OF BRITAIN

Gildas was a man of God who believed he was watching the imminent destruction of Britain. Although he thought he could discern both the pattern leading to its destruction and the only way to avert it, he waited for ten years, uncertain that he was worthy to pronounce on the matter. Britain, after all, had leaders enough to deal with the situation.

At last, Gildas could wait no longer. He wrote the book which we call *de Excidio Britanniae*, 'On the Destruction of Britain'. In it, he denounces his contemporaries, both religious and secular, named and unnamed, for not just being oblivious to the destruction of Britain, but actively bringing it about. Gildas's view of history, based on his close study of the prophetic books of the Bible, was that there were obvious cycles. When patterns – either in the time of the Israelites or in the recent history of the British, God's 'latter-day Israel' – could be seen repeating themselves, then it was only a small step to deduce what the future was likely to hold.

Most clearly, Gildas could see the fate of his homeland reflected in the fate of the Kingdom of Israel. When the Israelites turned from God and fell into disobedience and civil strife, God gave forewarning through the prophets and then the destruction of the northern kingdom by the Assyrians. In spite of this, the southern kingdom, Judah, persisted in its old ways. The result was the conquest of the Holy Land by the Babylonians and the exile of the Jews. This story is told in the historical and prophetic books of the Bible. The analogy was quite clear for Gildas – his own homeland was poised between two calamities and only a wholesale repentance by the leaders of Britain could avert its final destruction.

It is most unfair to say, as many modern writers do, that Gildas was not a historian. Historical analysis was a crucial part of his work and he was considered a historian by later generations. He analysed the past for clues about the present, examining trends and patterns rather than individual episodes. As such, he has rather more in common with modern historians, particularly those studying the early Dark Ages, than writers like Bede and Nennius. Unlike

Gildas, the historians of the eighth and ninth centuries were happy to string together historical anecdotes and details from royal family trees, with little critical evaluation of their material. For Gildas, the analysis was everything. This makes his work very different from theirs. We should not expect to find exact dates, regnal lists or genealogies, any more than those elements figure in modern social or economic histories. It is historical trends which are important to Gildas, and the model he uses to analyse them is a religious one.

That is not to say that we do not see many deficiencies and errors in his analysis. Gildas himself confirms that he cannot rely on any British literary sources, these having been burnt by the invaders or carried overseas by exiles. This lack of sources is literally true. We can only, for instance, correct Gildas's impression that Hadrian's Wall was built after 388 (actually *c.* AD 120) by reference to continental sources. We can check this with archaeology, another resource unavailable to Gildas, although he did speculate about the various Roman remains visible in the island, their origins and fate.

In the earlier part of *de Excidio Britanniae*, especially up to the arrival of the Saxons, facts are distorted for didactic effect. Things which Gildas knew, but were not part of a repeating pattern, are ignored as incidental to his message.

As the narrative approaches Gildas's time, our confidence in it increases. He assumed a great deal of prior knowledge on the part of his readers which we unfortunately do not possess. There was no need for him to repeat common knowledge. His job was to present a reasoned analysis of the immediate situation and a remedy to improve it.

The climax of the work is a denunciation of his contemporary rulers and priests, some of whom are addressed directly by name. The Saxon revolt and its attendant calamities were only a few generations in the past. As Gildas intended to convince his readers to turn from their wicked ways by his interpretation of recent history, every error they could pick up would weaken his argument. Bearing this in mind, let us look at what Gildas says about his time and the events immediately preceding it.

THE COMPLAINING BOOK

The story which Gildas tells of the 150 years leading up to his own time is this:

The destruction of Britain as a civilised and Christian community began when Roman usurper Maximus took the troops from the island to set up a

'Kingdom of Wickedness' on the continent. This left the country open to attacks by the barbarian Picts and Scots. Rescue missions by the Romans helped in the short term, but ultimately the Britons would have to rely on their own resources.

When a renewed attack by the old enemies coincided with a manpower shortage caused by a memorable plague, the government, a council and the Proud Tyrant (our Vortigern) decided to let the Saxons settle in the country in return for military service.

The Saxons fell out with their employer over supplies and broke into revolt. The fire burned from sea to sea, devastating cities and fields and almost the whole surface of the island to the shores of the western sea. All the *Coloniae* – York, Lincoln, Colchester and Gloucester – were laid low by battering-rams and their inhabitants slaughtered. Once their campaign of destruction had achieved its desired effect, 'the cruel plunderers subsequently returned home, that is to their settlements in the Eastern part of the Island'.

Those Britons who survived the general massacre and did not flee abroad or surrender themselves to slavery held out in high fortified hills, dense forests and sea cliffs. God gave them strength and people fled to them from all directions. Their leader was Ambrosius Aurelianus. Gildas describes him as 'vir modestus', an ordinary man, who 'perhaps alone of the Roman race' had survived the disaster. 'Surely,' says Gildas, 'his parents had worn the purple.' The 'citizens', as Ambrosius's followers are called (although they have abandoned their cities), sallied forth from their refuges and challenged the Saxons to battle. The war raged with victory going now to the Britons, now to the Saxons 'so that . . . the Lord could make trial of his latter-day Israel. This lasted right up to the siege of "Mons Badonicus", almost the most recent and certainly not the smallest defeat of the villains.'

This sets the scene for the denunciation of Gildas's contemporary kings and priests. Five of the tyrants are named: Constantine, Aurelius Caninus, Vortiporius, Cuneglassus and Maglocunus. Maglocunus is Mailcunus of the *Historia*. Gildas would therefore be living in the time of Outigirn and the famous poets. He says he was born in the year of the siege of Mount Badon, 43–4 years earlier. He would therefore have lived at least some of his life in 'the reign of Arthur'.

If Gildas really lived at the same time as Outigirn, and after Arthur and Vortimer, would we not expect him to refer to them by name? This argument is the one most frequently advanced by those sceptical about Arthur. It completely ignores the nature of *de Excidio Britanniae*. Proper names from Gildas's own era are kept to a minimum, irrelevant as they are to analysing and predicting trends. This allows the biblical parallels to stand out more clearly. Modern sceptical historians are happy to write Dark Age history without naming kings and warleaders of the period, and it seems quite unjustified to take Gildas to task for doing the same thing. When Gildas does single out individuals, his job is primarily to castigate the wicked, not to praise the good.

There is no special pleading here. Arthur is not the only unnamed person in a book otherwise teeming with Dark Age characters; Gildas names only one person in the hundred years or so between the appeal to Agitius and the denunciation of Maglocunus and the other tyrants. Only four Britons are named in the whole of history before Gildas's time, three of them saints martyred in the Great Persecution! In fact, only one person in Britain is named after Maximus left at the end of the fourth century, although Gildas was aware, from the work of the historian Orosius, of the names of the other Roman usurpers, for example. Although they are not named, many characters are referred to in the century preceding Gildas's own time. These include the Proud Tyrant and his councillors, Maglocunus's royal uncle and nephew, a good king who was the father of Vortiporius, the fathers (*sic*) and brothers of Aurelius Caninus, who died young as a result of their participation in civil wars, and two royal youths, who handled weapons more bravely than anyone else, treacherously murdered by Constantine. The list of these nameless but important characters could go on. Not being named by Gildas is hardly proof of non-existence.

We should not expect to find the name of Arthur in *de Excidio Britanniae*. We are looking for the reign of Arthur, its characteristics and events. For some of this, Gildas is a first-hand witness and on his testimony will the story we have deduced so far stand or fall.

THE END OF ROMAN BRITAIN

A flurry of tyrants and heretics had left the Island 'still Roman in name, but not by law or custom', Gildas wrote. For him, the watershed, when Britain lost its Roman name as well, came when the Roman usurper Maximus left to invade Gaul, despoiling Britain of 'her whole army, her military resources, her governors . . . and her sturdy youth'. From continental sources, we can date this to the period 383–8.

Here Gildas enters the most defective part of his analysis. He is hampered by a lack of sources, as he acknowledges, and some incorrect assumptions on the nature of Roman power and the origins of the barbarian threats. Gildas deduces that all the barbarian invasions of Britain, and the impressive military works built to defend against them, must be subsequent to Maximus's withdrawal of the troops. He cannot conceive of Picts and Scots successfully confronting the Romans, who have 'won the rule of the world and subjugated all the neighbouring regions'. He is further hampered in establishing an accurate chronology by imagining that the Picts are an overseas race like the Scots and the Saxons, who have only recently taken over the northern part of an island hitherto completely under Roman rule. Fortifications such as Hadrian's Wall therefore cannot date from the pre-388 undivided island.

The history of the generations that follow exactly parallels that of Gildas's immediate past: barbarian invasions, Britons timidly fleeing to remote locations, then trusting in God to secure a great victory. Then 'as it is now', the victorious Britons turned to debauchery, sin and civil war. They were, of course, heading for a worse disaster, the Saxon invasion. Now the cycle has been re-established and unless Gildas's contemporaries learn the lesson of the past and repent, surely an even worse calamity is in the offing.

The rhetorical purpose of this 'historical' account is obvious and its plausibility for us destroyed by its huge and demonstrable errors. Roman rule continued for a generation after Maximus, the northern walls and southern coast fortifications pre-date him, the Picts are probably natives under a new by-name. The description of the subsequent peace, begun by a British victory and dominated by sin and civil war, is almost identical to that of Gildas's own time, for obvious rhetorical reasons. Some writers have even considered that it *is* Gildas's present, that the Pictish and Saxon sections somehow overlap (Miller 1975a). However it is clearly set in the past and its similarity to the present pointed out specifically by the writer: '*sicut et nunc est*' – 'just as it is now'.

The point is that the events of the post-Maximus, pre-Saxon era have been forced into an incorrect framework to parallel modern, post-Saxon, history. Post-Saxon history has not been forced into an erroneous framework based on the past. Gildas has no reliable framework for past history, due to the loss of historical documents. All he can do is deduce what this period must have been like from his knowledge of recent history and a cyclical concept of time derived from the Bible. His understanding of the past is entirely shaped by his understanding of the present.

THE COMING OF THE SAXONS

During the period between the 380s and the mid-fifth century, Gildas tells us that 'Kings were anointed' according to a principle of survival of the fittest – 'in as much as they were crueller than the rest'. Gildas probably knows that two slightly different processes were at work. Until 408, these 'kings' are pretenders to the Roman Empire. The last of them, Constantine III, led the remnants of the Roman Army across to Gaul, following which the Emperor Honorius told the British *civitates*, local administrative units, to fend for themselves in 410. After this, the kings would be competing British rulers of whatever type (Snyder 1998). It is of this period that Zosimus writes: '[The Britons] revolted against the Roman Empire, no longer submitted to Roman law and reverted to their native customs.'

It is in the period of these 'sub-Roman' rulers that the next act unfolds. The dominating event was what has been known as 'The Coming of the Saxons'. The idea is traceable to the historiography of Bede, Nennius and the Anglo-Saxon Chronicle. All convey the idea that there was a particular date on one side of which there were no Anglo-Saxons in Britain, and on the other side there were. Gildas does not give such a date or even a rough estimate for the time when Saxon people first set foot in Britain. He never says that there were no Saxons, as invaders or settlers, in Britain before the arrival of the three shiploads of mercenaries. He knows that the Roman fortifications on the south coast (the Saxon Shore, as *Notitia Dignitatum*, the official record of imperial offices, calls it) had been built to defend against 'wild barbarian beasts'. He knows that the mercenary Saxon settlers are not the only people involved in the revolt which overthrew British rule – they 'heaped up and nurtured' the fire of revolt.

Once we accept that Gildas does not necessarily mean that there were no Saxons in Britain before the three keels, then we free the text from shaky chronological frameworks shoe-horning it into the evidence of the Gallic Chronicle of 452 and the *Life of St Germanus*, of Saxon activity in Britain in the early fifth century.

The focus of chronological attention is on the appeal to Agitius. This is the only incident with any chance of being dated by external sources between Maximus and Gildas's own time. Gildas is explicit that he does not have access to any historical documents. In spite of this, many historians continue to treat the appeal to Agitius as if it were an actual quotation from a 'file copy', somehow preserved without any other supporting material, in sixth-century Britain. Gildas makes it clear that he is not quoting the appeal to Agitius, but paraphrasing it when he writes '*hoc modo loquentes*' (speaking in this way) '*et post pauca querentes*' (and shortly after complaining). It is the obsequious and increasingly desperate style of the complaint, not its exact words, which he is trying to convey.

It is clear that, as with the rest of the section, Gildas is relying on traditions and analogy, not source documents. Here he may be drawing a parallel between Agitius and Ambrosius, contrasting a successful appeal to Roman Ambrosius with an earlier unsuccessful one to Agitius, a similar 'man of Roman power'.

All we can say for sure is that Gildas understood that the appeal, dated to 425 at the earliest and 462 at the latest (most plausibly 446–54), came from before the period of the Saxon revolt. Arguments resting on a mistaken placing of the document in the historical sequence, or a misunderstanding of which barbarians are involved, miss Gildas's purpose. He is no 'Nennius', sifting through various documents trying to make sense of them. He knows what sense they make already, based on the analogy with the present and with the Bible. Here, he intends his readers to understand that every remedy was tried before the Saxons were employed. With the appeal to Agitius, the last chance of any Roman leader coming back to help the Britons evaporated. He may have thought of this being the Roman warlord Aetius or the 'sub-Roman' King Aegidius, but either way, he is the last of his kind. The Britons now had two stark choices; to trust in God or to turn to the devil. The same two choices faced Gildas's contemporaries.

The appeal was made during 'many years' (DEB 20.3) of conflict between the Britons and the Picts and Scots. When it failed, the Britons, turning to God, were victorious. This British victory ushered in peace 'for a little while'.

This came to an abrupt end when Britain was struck by a 'deadly plague', 'a memorable plague' which sapped its manpower. At the same time, rumours of a new invasion by the Picts and Scots prompted 'everyone' to convene a council. For Gildas, the council, the embodiment of the culpable stupidity of the whole people, is the crucial feature. In his preface, he promises to write about 'a memorable plague, a council, an enemy more savage than the first'. Later historians saw the council as an incidental part of the drama. The 'Proud Tyrant' who, together with the councillors, invited the Saxons to settle in Britain, has been the focus of attention. It is now usually considered that he is a single major ruler, perhaps *the* Tyrant of Britain, and that the council is composed of 'his' councillors. This is not what Gildas says. The council is convened by everyone in response to a particular crisis. The councillors, like the foolish Princes of Zoan, give advice to the Tyrant to take a particular course of action (Gildas quotes Isaiah 19.11). The Tyrant is responsible for settling the Saxons in the eastern part of the island. He may, therefore, be one of several rulers, important because part of his territory borders the Saxon sea. The council may have persuaded him to do his part for the combined war effort. He may, alternatively, be a tyrant with wide-ranging authority, responsible for both beating back 'the peoples of the north' and for settlement in the eastern seaboard, as all subsequent writers assumed. Either of these concepts, at least, can be supported by what Gildas wrote.

Whether the Proud Tyrant was really called Vortigern is unimportant. The only name we have for him is Vortigern and there is no reason to think this is not his name. Too much may have been made of the possible pun on Vortigern's name Proud Tyrant = Foremost Prince. Later Gildas writes to '*superbis . . . principibus*' – the proud princes, without any suggestion that this is a pun (they all have different names after all). Nor is it an indication of supreme power; there are five of them named and some 'like them'.

It is worth noting that the Latin can be read as '[the council] devised that ferocious Saxons . . . should be let into the island', rather than implying that these are the first or only Saxons to set foot here. That this is not the first contact the Britons have with the Saxons is clear, as they already fear them worse than death.

The Saxons settle as a reward for fighting the northern barbarians. Their success inspires them to invite more of their compatriots over from Germany. These newcomers fall out with their employer over supplies, and revolt. Gildas never actually states that these are the first German troops to settle in Britain and we know from archaeology that some had been settled here from Roman times. The fire burned from sea to sea. All the *Coloniae* (the veterans' settlement towns) were laid low by battering-rams and their inhabitants slaughtered. Western Britain was neither conquered nor settled, but simply invaded and devastated. Gildas goes on to say that the 'cruel plunderers subsequently returned home, that is to their settlements in the eastern part of the island'.

AMBROSIUS AURELIANUS

We can now take a closer look at what Gildas says about the resistance, the crucial period which initiates the 'reign of Arthur'. The surviving Britons held out in high fortified hills, dense forests and sea cliffs. These are, of course, the types of sites found in the Arthurian battle-list. People fled to them from all directions. Their leader was Ambrosius Aurelianus, who 'perhaps alone of the Roman race' had survived the disaster. 'Surely his parents had worn the purple'. The 'citizens' sallied forth from their refuges and challenged the Saxons to battle. 'The battle went their way. From then on the victory went now to our countrymen, now to their enemies. . . . This lasted right up till the year of the siege of Badon Hill, pretty well the last defeat of the villains and certainly not the least' (DEB 26). 'The final victory of our country . . . granted in our times by the will of God' (DEB 2).

The only person Gildas names in the whole of this period is Ambrosius Aurelianus. He stands out as an important and unique figure. We must ask why he was so important to Gildas's view of the past. Although Gildas can be read, as Bede and many later historians have done, as meaning that Ambrosius fought the Saxons, even commanding the Britons at the siege of Mount Badon, this is not how the events were presented in the *Historia*. There, Ambrosius is an adversary of Vortigern and overthrew his government, establishing hegemony over the (western) British kings.

There is nothing in Gildas's account to contradict this. It seems likely that a necessary prelude to the war of the united Britons against the Saxon settlers would be the overthrow of Vortigern's government. This would be crucial if, as we have deduced and the *Historia* portrays it, this was now dominated by Hengist as the barbarian Masters of Soldiers were doing on the continent.

Subsequent retellings have clouded what Gildas actually wrote about Ambrosius Aurelianus. The phrase '*duce Ambrosio Aureliano*' means 'with Ambrosius Aurelianus as their leader (or king)' or 'led by Ambrosius Aurelianus'. His status is further complicated by Gildas's phrase '*parentibus purpura nimirum indutis*' – 'His parents had certainly worn the purple', interpreted as 'the imperial purple robes'. Bede paraphrased this as 'his parents were of royal rank and title', an interpretation which has been followed ever since. But is this the inference Gildas intended?

Some historians, worried about this throw-away reference to British 'emperors' in the generation before the Saxon wars, have suggested a less forceful interpretation along the lines of 'surely his parents must have worn the Purple' (read – 'one might have thought so, based on his leadership qualities.'). I do not think this passage gives any reason for ascribing real or imagined imperial qualities to Ambrosius. First, Gildas hardly considers royal descent to be a mark of virtue. The last ruler he has described is the 'Proud Tyrant' and his predecessors 'anointed as being crueller than all the rest'. The self-appointed Emperor of Britain, Maximus, has no legal claim to the title, forming a 'kingdom of wickedness'. Vortiporius and Maglocunus are none the better for coming from 'royal' families.

Second, Gildas does not use 'imperial purple' as a symbol for or synonym of imperial or royal status. He writes of Maximus's 'Imperial insignia' and 'the throne of his wicked empire'. His imperial adversaries are 'the crowned heads that ruled the world'. 'Kings were anointed' he writes, or figuratively of saints: 'They will receive the kingdom of beauty and a glorious diadem.' The tyrant Vortiporius sits on a 'throne full of guiles'. Thrones, crowns, anointing, these are Gildas's biblically inspired emblems of royal status, along with unspecified 'imperial insignia'. He never once refers to imperial purple robes as either real or symbolic attributes of rule anywhere else in the book, so why should we expect it here?

That is not to say that Gildas does not mention purple or purple robes. Quite the contrary, they are used as striking images, of *martyrdom*. When Gildas writes of 'the purple', he always means the blood shed by good victims of the ruin of Britain. A holy altar is 'touched by the purple cloak, as it were, of their drying blood'. The corpses of church leaders, priests and ordinary folk slain by the Saxons 'covered, as it were, with a purple crust of congealed blood'. This last description immediately precedes the fight back under Ambrosius, a mere 200 words before the use of *purpura* we are now discussing. Is it not, therefore, exceedingly likely that when Gildas writes that Ambrosius's parents had 'surely worn the purple', he means to imply not that they were emperors, but that they had been killed by the Saxons? Which is precisely what he does say: 'Ambrosius . . . had survived the shock of that notable storm which had killed his parents, who had undoubtedly worn the purple.' To make it abundantly clear that Ambrosius was not a tyrant, king or emperor, he is described precisely as '*vir modestus*', 'a man of ordinary status'.

What is actually most surprising about Gildas's description of Ambrosius is that he 'almost alone of the Roman race' – '*solus fortae romanae gentis*' – has survived the Saxon invasion. Even if we tone this down to read 'the last survivor from a proper Roman family', the implication is intriguing. Later writers have seen Ambrosius as a post-colonial civilised Romano-Briton, in contrast, perhaps, to Celtically named figures such as Maglocunus, the Gododdin heroes and, of course, Arthur. This, however, cannot have been Gildas's intended image. For him, the inhabitants of Britain were Britons or citizens. Throughout the book they are contrasted with the Romans, a continental people who once ruled Britain but have since departed. There was a time, granted, when harsh Roman rule transformed, as he says 'Britannia into Romania'. Those days are long gone. By the time of Maximus, 'The island was still Roman in name, but not by law or custom'. Romans returned twice to help the Britons against the Picts and Scots, but they 'bade farewell, never to return'. They returned home, and later Agitius, a 'man of Roman power' refused to help.

It is therefore a little unexpected to find that Ambrosius, perhaps alone of the Roman race, is still holding out in the island. The implication, from Gildas's usage of the word 'Roman', is that he considers that Ambrosius's family have continental origins, even though his parents have both been killed, presumably, in Britain. If Gildas does see Ambrosius as a continental Roman, then no native Britons are ever named in the book except three saints and five tyrants.

Why then, is he named at all? This is also fairly clear in context. The named characters are overwhelmingly the contemporary tyrants addressed by Gildas. The events of the past are used to make clear the patterns of the present and their likely future outcomes. The names in the past are most likely to be recalled for their importance in the present. What resonance does Ambrosius Aurelianus's name have in the present? 'His grandchildren have greatly degenerated from their ancestor's example.' It seems likely that these grandchildren are addressed directly by Gildas. Why would he not take them to task personally? Two of the named tyrants stand out as potential candidates, the only two who, like Ambrosius Aurelianus, have Roman names: Constantine and Aurelius Caninus, as if the similarity of Aurelius and Aurelianus were not enough to signal a connection.

The images of Gildas's Ambrosius ('last of the Roman race') and Nennius's Ambrosius ('king among the kings of the Britons') seem almost irreconcilable, but are not absolutely mutually exclusive. There is every reason to suppose that the former '*vir modestus*' used his position to establish a hereditary monarchy. The evidence for this is that Gildas saw fit to castigate his grandchildren. No ordinary people are criticised in *de Excidio*. Gildas's targets are the tyrants and the priests who should know better. The grandchildren fall short of Ambrosius's example. As Ambrosius's example was not a priestly one, it must be one of kingship. Logically, then, his grandchildren must be tyrants. Even the odd feature of Ambrosius as a fatherless boy has resonance in Gildas, where one of the few facts we are told about Ambrosius is that he is an orphan.

WHEN WAS THE SIEGE OF MONS BADONICUS?

It is nowhere explicitly stated that Ambrosius was the victor at *Mons Badonicus*. It is likely that the wars lasted for over a generation since Gildas, born in the year of the battle forty-four years before writing the book, is a contemporary of Ambrosius's grandchildren. There are at least four generations between the arrival of the Saxons and Gildas's own day. The first generation, that of Vortigern and the Council, included Ambrosius's parents, killed in the Saxon revolt. We know that the revolt itself lasted no more than a generation or two since some people have witnessed both the desperate blow and the recovery. The next generation was that of Ambrosius himself and the last that of his grandchildren. The generation between, that of Ambrosius's children, would be that of the battle of Mount Badon.

Gildas gives a precise dating for the siege of Mount Badon. In the work as we have it, he writes: 'That was the year of my birth; as I know, one month of the forty-fourth year since then has already passed.' The Latin is slightly obscure, but the implication is clear: Mount Badon was forty-three/forty-four years before the time of writing. Although Badon was not quite the last battle, there has been peace between the Britons and Saxons for most of the succeeding period. This long period of peace is not exactly what we would have expected from the later sources.

The *Historia* reads as if the Saxons began planning their counter-attack soon after their defeat at Badon, though if the wars are fought against Octha, and not resumed until Ida, a forty-four-year period of peace could be possible. In the *Annales*, Mailcun dies only thirty-one years after the battle of Badon. Gildas was a contemporary of this man, and does not seem to be denouncing someone thirteen years dead. The Anglo-Saxon Chronicle leaves a maximum gap of only twenty-five years between Saxon victories.

How is it possible to reconcile Gildas's versions of events – that Badon ushers in a relatively long period of peace, at least forty-four years – with the shorter period given in the later sources? Forty-four years might seem a long time to someone who has lived through it, but with the benefit of hindsight, may be nothing more than a hiatus, as it seems to Nennius. This, however, does not address the detailed discrepancies with the *Annales* and the Chronicle.

It may be that Gildas, based in the south, had not heard that fighting had already broken out in the north. How, though, could Gildas not have noticed the wars of Cerdic and Cynric in Hampshire and Wiltshire recorded in the Anglo-Saxon Chronicle? If we accept for the moment that the West Saxons were right about these wars, then there is an intriguing possible explanation.

The answer could lie in the concept of 'a long period of peace'. Though Gildas is often cited as living in an era of peace, he makes it perfectly clear that the years after the siege of Badon were not by any means peaceful. The British kings often wage wars, but only civil and unjust ones. It could be that Gildas regarded the wars of Cerdic and Cynric as being among them. The story of the establishment of Wessex in the Chronicle has some strange features if they are taken simply as wars between Britons and Saxons. Cerdic and Cynric are never called West Saxons. Their names are in fact British. Cerdic is the same name as Certic, the name of various British characters in the *Historia*, the Genealogies and the *Gododdin*. Cynric is a British name meaning 'Hound King', a popular type of name among Gildas's tyrants: Maglocunus (Hound Prince), Cuneglassus (Blue Hound) and Aurelius Caninus (Doglike – compare with Cinon in the *Gododdin*). The Chronicle does indeed say that they arrived in ships and proceeded to fight the British. This is a formula used for all the founders of Saxon dynasties in the Chronicle and derives from the established story of Hengist and Horsa.

Cerdic and Cynric are called aldormen, or *duces* in the Latin translation, right from their first mention, the only 'Saxon' leaders to be given titles before their arrival. The West Saxons, Stuf and Wihtgar, arrived nineteen years later. Five years after this, Cerdic and Cynric obtained the kingdom of the West Saxons. They went on to conquer the Isle of Wight and bestowed it on Stuf and Wihtgar.

The idea that Cerdic and Cynric led hordes of invading West Saxons into the country is at variance with the information in Bede. He says that the inhabitants of Wight and the adjacent mainland were Jutes and were still so called in his own time. He does not make the West Saxons important in the early colonisation of Britain, though he was well informed of their history by Daniel their bishop. He revealed that the area around Winchester, by his time the West Saxon heartland, had formerly been called *Gewissae*. This is a Saxon word meaning something like 'allies', an appropriate translation of the Latin word *foederati* used for the settled Germanic mercenaries. If the West Saxons are seen as participants in a British civil war, there is plenty of time in the Chronicle's version of events to accommodate a long period of peace.

An analogous situation occurred on the continent. Sixth-century Gallic writer Gregory of Tours recorded the career of the Roman *Magister Militum* Aegidius. He had started as a military officer of the empire. As this crumbled, he set himself up as 'King of the Romans' ruling the sub-Roman enclave around Soissons. When their own leader fled, the neighbouring Franks unanimously chose him as their king, in which position he reigned for eight years. His son Syagrius succeeded him as King of the Romans, until he was ousted by the new Frankish ruler, Clovis, in 486. Aegidius was probably known in Britain, his name influencing Gildas's 'Agitius'.

The problem with the explanation that Cerdic and Cynric are feuding Britons, perhaps allied to or employing Saxons, is that, had Gildas known, he would surely have castigated them. The simplest explanation is that the Chronicle is wrong, that the early history of the West Saxons did not consist of almost continuous warfare against the Britons. Even if it did, we have no reason to take the dates at face value. As noted earlier, it is unlikely that the various Saxon leaders had sequential careers. There were surely periods when all Saxons took advantage of British weakness and, as Gildas tells us, others when virtually all Saxon attacks ceased.

We should note that the Chronicle writers were working from a slightly different time-frame, derived from Bede's History. Bede had a much older text of Gildas than any which survive. It is conceivable that at some stage a copyist has inadvertently altered Gildas's meaning. As Bede reports it, the battle of Badon Hill was fought about forty-four years *after* the arrival of the Saxons (*c.* 493), not forty-four years before the time of Gildas. It has been argued that this a variant tradition, and that the battle could, coincidentally, have been forty-four years before the time of Gildas as well, but the odds are that the figure comes from a different reading of the manuscript source.

A forty-four-year period before Mount Badon implies the generational pattern already established, that the victor was of an age with Ambrosius's sons. Gildas's description of the siege of Mount Badon occurring 'in our time' might seem to place it nearer to him than forty-four years. Altogether, however, it is more reasonable to suppose that Bede has mistaken the rather obscure Latin than that all surviving versions of Gildas have followed one incorrect exemplar. Gildas mentions the time period to reinforce his certainty 'as I know . . .' because it was the year of his birth. His certainty is far more likely to derive from his current age than an (untestable) idea that the Saxons arrived forty-four years before he was born.

The *Annales* present a different picture to Gildas. Although Gildas's death is mentioned, fifty-four years after the battle of Badon, they show no knowledge of the contents of his work. There is no Vortigern, no Ambrosius and no Saxons. The only character in common is Mailcun/Maglocunus. Yet he is recorded as dying ten years before the date when *de Excidio* would have been written.

A crucial factor in creating a difference between the *Annales* and Gildas could be the starting date for the *Annales*. If this is actually 455, the start of the new Easter great cycle, then the events of the Saxon revolt could have taken place before this, or the Annalist might have imagined that they had. The contemporary Anglo-Saxon Chronicle gives 455 as the year of Horsa's death, with the revolt happening before this. Is the date a coincidence or is it indicative of tenth-century thinking? The last time the Christian Britons were known to be in contact with their continental co-religionists, when they accepted the Easter change of 455, could easily have been seen as a milestone by both sides.

I am wary of arguments based on tinkering with dates in Dark Age sources, especially the *Annales* and the Chronicle. This assumes that particular given dates are the 'true' ones. I do not believe the dates in the *Annales* and the Anglo-Saxon Chronicle have any objective reality. With Saxon events, the participants could not have known what 'the date' was. Rather the dates give an impression from the period of writing of when certain events occurred relative to others and to the present. As such, they are far more likely to have been calculated by estimating back from fixed points. It is hard to imagine, for instance, the preservation of a tradition that Arthur fought his great battle seventy-two years after the start of an Easter cycle, but easy to imagine it being remembered as occurring a hundred years before the reign of King Edwin.

If we allow ourselves to consider that the origin of the Arthur dates was not that his 'final' battle against the Saxons (Badon) was fought 100 years before Edwin, as the *Annales* report it, but that the remembered connection was actually with his final battle, in which he was slain (Camlann), the chronology takes on a much more consistent shape. The battle of Camlann would then take place twenty years earlier, at the date given for Badon, with Badon correspondingly earlier, between 486 and 499. This harmonises far better with the impression from the other sources that Badon was fought a generation (but no more) after the Saxon revolt, considered as happening in the middle of the sixth century. The Harleian Genealogies and the *Annales* have already allowed us to calculate a generation span of 32 or 33 years. Mailcun would then have died fifty years after Badon, in keeping with what we would expect from *de Excidio*. Gildas would have died at a venerable seventy-four, far more consistent with his reputation as a wise old saint. It would also leave enough time for a new and forgetful generation to have arisen between the time of Badon and Mailcun, as Gildas tells us it has. As I said, I am wary of manipulating Dark Age dates, but here the weight of all the other sources, especially Gildas's own testimony that he is forty-three/four years old, leads us to conclude that a minor mistake has been made establishing the *Annales* chronology of Arthur relative to Edwin of Northumbria.

WHO ARE THE VICTORS?

One recent suggestion is that Gildas has been read wrongly since the time of Bede. Higham argues that his true meaning is not that Badon is the last victory, followed by a British-dominated peace, but rather that it is the last victory, followed by defeats and Saxon domination. This conclusion is based on the biblical allusions chosen by Gildas and the assumption that his references to diabolical or bestial powers are consistently intended to mean the Saxons. Gildas only uses the word 'Saxons' ('name not to be spoken!') once, and thereafter refers to the invaders as wolves, devils and the like. As Higham understands the situation, a single powerful Saxon ruler, the Father Devil, exercises overlordship over Gildas's Britain (Higham 1994).

Although Higham does not himself allow evidence to be drawn from the later sources, it is possible to read them in this way. In the *Historia*, for instance, a literal reading is that the Saxon resurgence starts immediately after Mount Badon. This leads to Saxon victory and dominance, not a British-governed peace. Saxon kings are brought over from Germany to rule all Britain. They are distinct from the Saxons descended from the revolting mercenaries. One of these could easily be the 'Father Devil'.

The source of Higham's contention is the biblical material used by Gildas as a basis for his critique, especially his analogies with Jeremiah. The prophet begins his career and writings after the defeat of Israel by the Assyrians and ends after the Babylonian conquest. His images are all of defeat and despair, with no indication of triumphant Israelites.

This is an ingenious, but odd, reading of Gildas. He is convinced that the current peace has made his contemporaries forget the Saxon threat. If it had been brokered by the still-powerful Saxons after some more recent victories, then it is hard to see how the tyrants could have let this knowledge slip. It is difficult to see the Britons complacent and forgetful of the Saxon menace if they were living under Saxon overlordship, sustained by threats and extortion.

As noted, Gildas constructed his concept of what had preceded the Saxon wars on the framework of what came afterwards. What he imagined happening during that early period was based on the analogy of what had happened since. The Britons trusted in God, rallied and massacred the Picts and Scots who retreated from them. The Scots returned home, the Picts kept quiet, and a period of 'peace' ensued characterised by civil wars and cruel British kings. There were occasional returns by the Scots and plundering raids by the Picts; the massacre is thus not the last victory, but it is seen as far more important than the minor skirmishes which follow.

The whole point of Gildas's historical analysis is that, under similar circumstances, the British victory ushered in a period of complacency, sin and civil war. This in turn led to even greater destruction. The analogy with Gildas's own time is abundantly clear. It is no more likely that the tyrants of the present are subservient to the Saxons than that the Council and Proud Tyrant were pro-Pictish quislings.

Gildas's understanding of Jeremiah is also not as straightforward as Higham suggests. It is not clear from the Bible whether Jeremiah is always writing after the fact or whether his works are to be considered prophetically, describing the future. If Gildas casts himself in the role of Jeremiah, he may think of himself writing between the destruction of Israel by the Assyrians and the final defeat and exile of the Jews by the Babylonians. As he tells us, the eastern part of Britain has fallen to the Saxons and its previous inhabitants are slaves or exiles. In fact, the only explicit biblical parallel Gildas draws with the Saxons is that their assault on the Britons is 'comparable with that of the Assyrians of old' (DEB 24). And, like the remnant of Israel of old, the free Britons must mend their ways or face an even worse catastrophe. I should add that Gildas uses prophetic material from throughout the Old and New Testaments without necessarily drawing exact analogies with their historical context. Jeremiah's Lamentations are just one of the sources he cites in his introduction and draws on for inspiration.

To take every reference to the devil as figurative for Saxons seems highly unlikely. DEB 67 makes it clear that, in this case at least, the devil Gildas refers to is actually *the* Devil, not a Saxon lord. Those who go abroad for ecclesiastical promotion are in search of 'an illusion sent by the Devil' and return as 'instruments of the Devil', though obviously they must have gone to Christian lands for preferment. Exactly what use a pagan Saxon overlord would be making of such foreign-promoted clerics is a mystery!

On balance, the evidence seems to be that the traditional reading, that Britons dominate the post-Badon island, still seems the best.

WHERE WAS GILDAS WRITING?

Since the Dark Ages, almost every region in and around the British Isles has been suggested as the place where Gildas lived and wrote. Although certainty is not possible, there are some reasonable pointers to his location. This has an important influence on the analysis of what he wrote and its connections with later material:

1. Gildas is writing in Britain. He does not have access to the literary remains of the Britons which have been taken overseas by the exiles (DEB 4.4).
2. Gildas names very few locations in Britain, although his scheme covers the whole island. The locations named are: *Verulamium* (St Albans), *Legionum Urbs* (City of the Legions, Chester or possibly Caerleon), the Thames (twice), the Severn, Mons Badonicus (not certain), *Dumnonia* (Devon and Cornwall), *Demetae* (the Dyfed people). He knows about Hadrian's Wall and an associated turf wall (the Antonine Wall?), but not the names of any towns or forts associated with them. All the locations named of which we are sure are in the southern half of Britain. This is what persuades most writers that Dumnonia is not the other region of that name, in Strathclyde. It is likely that Mons Badonicus is somewhere in the region between Chester, St Albans and Devon.
3. Gildas is not in the east of England. The Saxons return 'home' to this area and leave Gildas and his contemporaries in unoccupied Britain.
4. Britons are unable to visit, because of the partition of the island, the shrines of the saints in Verulamium and the City of the Legions. We infer

Gildas's Britain.

that Gildas is in this position himself. Whatever location, Chester or Caerleon, we accept for the City of the Legions, it would be accessible to Christians in Strathclyde, Gododdin, Cumbria or Wales. Only Verulamium would be cut off by the Saxons. The only insular Christians who could not reach both of the shrines would be those in the West Country, menaced by Saxons in the Thames Valley.

5. Most commentators see a geographical scheme in the denunciation of the tyrants, albeit under the influence of a North Welsh location for Maglocunus not warranted by the text. Constantine of Dumnonia, first on the list, could be the nearest to Gildas. Gildas specifically claims to have recent knowledge of him 'This very year' he has killed the two royal youths, and Gildas knows for sure he is alive.

Medieval views that Gildas was from Strathclyde, a son of Caw of Pictland, have no support in DEB. No demonstrably northern location is referred to by name. Although Gildas does deal with Roman activities in the wall zone, his knowledge of the area is sketchy. Hadrian's Wall, he imagines, runs between towns which just happen to be there (DEB 13.2). He thinks that the northern border defences were built within the last hundred years or so, during which time the area north of them had seen the first settlements of the Picts, 'an exceedingly savage overseas nation' (DEB 13.2). Surely no local could make these claims, easily falsifiable by consulting any aged Pict. If Gildas's father were from Pictland, his descriptions of Picts as 'dark throngs of worms who wriggle out of narrow fissures in the rocks'; 'foul hordes . . . more ready to cover their villainous faces with hair than their private parts with clothes', would be very peculiar.

A voyage to Ireland by Gildas is recorded in *Annales Cambriae*, but his knowledge of that island, its Scottish inhabitants or the burgeoning work of Christian missionaries among them, is almost zero. South-western Britain therefore seems the most plausible location for Gildas.

5

TYRANTS AND KINGS

Gildas's historical analysis climaxes with his denunciation of the rulers of his own time:

Britain has kings, but they are tyrants; judges, but they are unjust
They often plunder and terrorise, but do so to the innocent;
they defend and protect people, but only the guilty and thieving;
they have many wives, but these are whores and adulteresses;
they swear constantly, but their oaths are false;
they make vows, but almost at once tell lies;
they wage wars, but only civil and unjust ones;
they chase thieves energetically all over the country, but love and even reward the thieves who sit with them at table.
They distribute alms profusely, but pile up an immense mountain of crime for all to see;
They take their seats as judges, but rarely seek out the rules of right judgement.
they despise the harmless and humble, but exalt to the stars . . . their military companions bloody, proud and murderous men, adulterers and enemies of God!

Through Gildas's condemnations, we can see a pattern of heroic 'Celtic' kingship, as celebrated in *Y Gododdin* and the poems of Dark Age Wales. Five rulers are singled out for special condemnation. Gildas then castigates the wicked priests, men who degrade even the harlots they lie with. They rejoice if they find even a single penny (indicating that some form of monetary economy is still in operation). Bishops, priests and monks are all mentioned. Most have bought their positions from the tyrants and even the best have not risked martyrdom by standing up to the wicked rulers.

It is worth noting that Gildas says nothing about a resurgence of paganism. The time when Britons misguidedly worshipped mountains, hills, rivers and idols is far in the past. Indeed the kings are specifically said not to be pagans: 'Just because they do not offer sacrifices to heathen gods, there is no reason for them to be proud, they are still idolaters because by their actions they trample on the commands of Christ.' There is also no mention of heresy, although Gildas left no stone unturned in searching out iniquity.

The five named tyrants are generally assumed to be kings, though this is not specifically stated. They are '*infausti duces*', unlucky leaders (DEB 50.1). They are not the only rulers of Britain. Gildas specifically tells us that some leaders have found the narrow path to salvation. In many ways, the wicked rulers are the focal point of *de Excidio Britanniae*. None of the exemplary rulers are mentioned by name, nor are any bishops or priests, good or bad, singled out from the general mass.

The first is Constantine, 'tyrant whelp of the filthy lioness of Dumnonia'. Whelps (*catuli*) and lionesses figure prominently in Gildas's vocabulary of condemnation. For example, he describes the Saxons as a pack of whelps issuing from the lair of the 'barbarian lioness', meaning their Germanic homeland. On the other hand, when Gildas earlier mentions a 'treacherous lioness' who rebels against Rome, it is not clear whether he is speaking figuratively of Britain or specifically of the leader of the rebellion – Boudicca.

Equally in Constantine's case, it is not possible to state categorically that it is his kingdom and not some notorious Dumnonian woman which is meant. The manuscripts of Gildas use the form 'Damnonia' or variations on it. Most commentators believe that Gildas is referring to Dumnonia, the *civitas* (Roman administrative area based on a British tribal area) which covered modern Cornwall and Devon. The latter county derives its name from the Welsh version of Dumnonia, Dyfneint. The error is most likely to be scribal, occurring as it does in other places too (Rivet and Smith 1979). The copyist is influenced by the word *damnatio* ('damnation') when faced with an unfamiliar name. Roman geographers recorded another *Dumnonia*, just south of the Clyde. It did not survive under that name into the Dark Ages, whereas Dumnonia/Dyfneint become one of the last surviving British kingdoms outside Wales. We note, however, that the early medieval *Life of Gildas* did connect Gildas to the Strathclyde area, perhaps influenced by this place-name.

Gildas shows that he has recent knowledge of Constantine. He says he knows for sure that he is alive, as if there is some doubt about this. His worst crime took place 'this very year' after he had sworn a terrible oath not to work his wiles on his fellow Britons. Dressed in the habit of a holy abbot, though armed with a sword and spear, he killed two noble youths in a church. Who these murdered youths were is not revealed, although almost no man could handle weapons as bravely as them. They were sheltering with their mother when Constantine killed them. Constantine is not himself a young man, as he put aside his lawful wife 'many years before'.

'What are you doing, Aurelius Caninus,' Gildas continues, 'are you not being engulfed by the same slime as the man I just talked about?' We are not told where Aurelius is from or whether he is actually a king. He is, however, described as a lion's whelp. This may be figurative. Gildas adds 'as the prophet says'. On the other hand, it may be that he really is a relation of Constantine. His name could also suggest that he is related in some way to Ambrosius Aurelianus whose living grandsons have already been mentioned. Aurelius's brothers and father died young, while he himself thirsts for civil war and plunder. There is no chance that he will live to a ripe old age, Gildas adds. He is very unlikely to outlive his descendants.

Fornications and adulteries, 'domestic wickedness' characterise the lives of Constantine and Aurelius Caninus, and they are equally present in the life of the next tyrant, Vortiporius. Figuratively he is like a leopard, spotted with his sins: murder, rape and adultery. Gildas gives us rather more circumstantial detail about Vortiporius than the previous two. We are told he is the Tyrant of the Demetae, the *civitas* of south-west Wales, the name of which survives in modern Welsh as Dyfed. Moreover, he inherited this position from his father, who was a good king. Vortiporius is not young, his hair is already whitening. His father, therefore, would have been one of those kings of the Badon generation.

We have corroboration of Gildas's words in the form of the sixth-century memorial stone from the borders of Pembrokeshire and Carmarthenshire, precisely in Dyfed. This commemorates 'Voteporix the Protector', inscribed in both Latin letters and Irish Ogham.

With the first tyrant in Devon and the third in Dyfed, it has seemed to most commentators that Gildas is following a geographical logic in his denunciations of the tyrants, working northward through the kingdoms of western Britain. It may be that he has some other pattern to guide him –

family relationships, similarity of crimes, prophetic inspiration or any
number of other factors. However, in the absence of any other evidence,
geography seems a reasonable starting point. That Gildas begins with
Constantine in Dumnonia suggests he may be the nearest tyrant, with the
others increasingly further away. The balance of probability is that Gildas
is writing from south-west England. The direct land route between
Dumnonia and Demetia would pass through three more *civitates*, the
Durotriges in Somerset and Dorset, the Dobunni in Gloucestershire and the
lower Severn and the Silures in Gwent, south-east Wales. These could be
possible locations for Aurelius Caninus and are also the areas we have
previously classed as 'South Welsh', areas of strong early Arthurian
tradition. Builth and Ercing, the locations of Arthurian wonders, might be
considered to lie between Devon and Dyfed. The area of south-eastern
Wales where the *Historia* placed Ambrosius would be defined in this way,
which would again suggest the possibility of a link between Aurelius
Caninus and Ambrosius Aurelianus.

Next comes Cuneglassus, another tyrant not specifically located nor given a
definite title. We are, however, given plenty of circumstantial detail about
him. He is no longer young, but has been wicked since his youth. He is a
rider, even a charioteer, with many horses or riders. (Some of the Gododdin
heroes are also called charioteers, probably an antiquated poetic image.) He
fights with weapons special or particular to himself, waging war constantly
against the Britons, and against God. Gildas says that his name, in Latin,
means 'tawny butcher'. In fact it means blue dog, though whether Gildas
really knows this or not is uncertain. Of Cuneglassus's domestic
arrangements, we know that he is rich and haughty, that he is surrounded by
holy men and that he has put aside his lawful wife to marry her sister.

Although all this material provides a fertile source for information about a
key character of Gildas's time, it is two odd and almost incidental parts of the
denunciation which have brought the most attention. Gildas calls him 'bear'
and 'charioteer of the bear's stronghold'. This is suggestive, as most scholars
derive the name 'Arthur' from *Arth*, the British word for a bear. One medieval
version of *Historia Brittonum* gives a possible translation of 'Arthur' as *ursus
horribilis* – 'horrible bear'. It goes on to translate Arthur's surname *mab Uter*
as 'terrible son' because he has been terrible even from his youth, exactly the
same information as Gildas gives us for Cuneglassus. This raises the question
of a connection between Arthur and Cuneglassus. If Cuneglassus is a

neighbour of Vortiporius of the Demetae, he could be the ruler of Ercing and/or Builth where the Arthur wonders are located.

Other features of the description of Cuneglassus coincide with features of the Arthur legend. Cuneglassus is a 'rider of many', and one of the characteristics of Guaurthur is his generosity with the horses of his own herd. Cuneglassus uses his own special weapons, and in medieval legend, Arthur's special weapons were famous. He has put aside his wife, a possible source of a breach with his son.

The stumbling-block to connecting Cuneglassus with Arthur is that he is a contemporary of Gildas. The whole rationale for these denunciations is that the Badon generation has passed away, leaving their sons to forget the lessons learnt. If such a crucial figure as the leader at the siege of Badon was still alive, it would be difficult to see how that knowledge would have slipped. Besides which, Cuneglassus is a villainous character, while Gildas views the kings of the Badon generation in rosy hues. We might imagine a heroic warleader who subsequently went bad and, for example, put aside his wife and killed his son. Gildas specifically tells us this is not the case with Cuneglassus, who has been wicked since his boyhood. If there is a connection between Cuneglassus *Ursus*, and Arthur, *Ursus Horribilis*, then it must be at some further remove.

One possibility is that *Ursus* was a dynastic name or title, and that Cuneglassus was a successor or descendant of Arthur, ruling over the same area. This is the suggestion followed in *King Arthur – the True Story* (Phillips and Keatman 1993). Here Arthur is identified with the Eugein Dantguin, Cinglas/Cuneglassus's father in the Harleian Genealogies. This is not particularly helpful, since we know far less about Eugein Dantguin than we do about Arthur. If Cuneglassus had indeed been related to the victor of Mount Badon, it is surprising that Gildas does not mention him as he does the forebears of Vortiporius and Aurelius and the uncle of Maglocunus.

Another possibility is that Cuneglassus is called a bear because he comes from a place connected with bears. *Receptaculum ursi* (bear's stronghold) could be a Latin translation of a British place-name. Other Dark Age writers translated the Welsh place-name element 'din' as *receptaculum*, suggesting that here Gildas is translating a possible 'Din Arth' or 'Din Eirth'. There are two places called this in modern Wales, one in north-east Wales, the other in Dyfed. The first is plausible for a Cuneglassus who is a relative of Maglocunus, while the latter makes better sense if Cuneglassus is a neighbour of Dyfed-man Vortiporius. Of course, there is always the possibility that other Din Eirths existed, now lost beneath English place-names. None of this precludes the possibility that Cuneglassus's stronghold might have been a previous base of Arthur, *Ursus horribilis*.

Although we may not be able to tell exactly why Gildas assigned the animal epithets he did to the particular tyrants (the last tyrant is called a dragon), his source for these images is the biblical Book of Daniel. In chapter seven, Daniel has a vision of various beasts who represent successive empires persecuting the people of Israel. They are all destined to have their power stripped from them by God. The bulk of Gildas's work consists of similar attempts to apply biblical prophecies to contemporary circumstances.

In the Latin version of the Bible, the first kingdom/beast is described as '*quasi leaena*' – like a lioness. Gildas gives us two tyrants called '*Leaenae Catulus*' (whelp of the lioness) and '*(ut propheta ait), catule leonine*' (as the prophet says, a lion's whelp). It is not clear why Gildas gives us two lions, perhaps because Constantine and Aurelius are related, or because the political situation had changed in the years before publication, replacing the rule of one lion with two. Gildas specifically says he has waited ten years before unleashing his polemic. The untimely death of, for instance, Aurelius's father may have changed the political landscape.

The next animal Daniel sees is '*quasi pardus*' (like a leopard). Gildas calls Vortiporius '*pardo similis*' (like a leopard). Then comes '*bestia alia similis urse*' (another beast, similar to a bear); '*urse*' (bear) says Gildas of Cuneglassus. The final beast in Daniel is '*Bestia atque terribilis atque mirabilis, et fortis nimis, dentes ferreos habebat magnos*' (a beast both terrible and wonderful, and incredibly strong, with great iron teeth), which Gildas renders concisely as '*draco*' (dragon). Why Gildas chose particular animals to represent particular rulers is not clear. Cuneglassus could be a bear just because he comes before the powerful Maglocunus. More likely, some points of similarity have prompted Gildas to make the particular connections.

Now Gildas's condemnations reach their climax: 'Last in my list but first in evil, mightier than many both in power and malice, more profuse in giving, more extravagant in Sin, strong in arms, but stronger still in that which destroys the soul' – Maglocunus *the Dragon of the Island*'.

It is clear that Maglocunus was one of the dominant figures of the age, not some petty regional tyrant. 'The King of Kings has made you higher than almost all the leaders of Britain, in your kingdom as much as your physique.'

Gildas spends as much time castigating him as all the previous tyrants put together. He hardly even bothers to exhort Maglocunus to repentance. The crimes of which he accuses him are too many and too serious.

Yet, practically every historian dealing with the period relegates him to the backwater of Anglesey and measures his importance solely as a founding father of medieval Gwynedd. Although logically Maglocunus seems to be based somewhere north of Dyfed, but one kingdom removed from it, this gives a range of possibilities of which Gwynedd is only one and Anglesey hardly likely at all. We have seen how the Gwynedd connection is found in exactly those sources which name Arthur as the leader at Mount Badon. Unlike Arthur, however, Maglocunus was used for partisan reasons, to bolster the claims of the burgeoning Gwynedd dynasty.

Gildas calls Maglocunus 'Insularis Draco', Dragon of the Island. With a north Welsh connection firmly in mind, historians pick the obvious island in North Wales, Anglesey, and locate the tyrant there. Later kings of Gwynedd did live at Aberffraw in Anglesey, although no sixth-century remains have been discovered there. In fact, archaeology suggests that the sixth-century centre of the kingdom was at the mainland site of Deganwy or possibly at Caernarfon. Even the normally sober historian Ken Dark has to construct a hypothesis of Maglocunus crossing the Menai straits to conquer the lands of the Ordovices. Nevertheless, most historians consider the epithet 'Insularis Draco' must mean no more than dragon of the Isle of Anglesey.

In context, there is no doubt what Gildas means by Insula (the island): throughout the text, it is used as a synonym for Britain as a whole. It is Gildas's preferred term when referring to his homeland. This is the sense in which he last used the word before the denunciation of Maglocunus: 'The remembrance of so desperate a blow to the island' – the Saxon revolt.

Examining Gildas's geography in greater detail, we find further proof that the epithet 'Insularis Draco' cannot have anything to do with Anglesey. None of the internal evidence gives us any reason to think that Gildas was living in a part of Britain where 'Insularis' would automatically evoke Anglesey. The complementary suggestions, by Higham and Dark, that Gildas is writing in the civitas of the Durotriges, would lead us to expect that a casual reference to the (offshore) island meant 'the Isle of Wight', as it would to a modern inhabitant of Dorset.

The linguistic evidence is that Gildas is more likely to have chosen the word 'promunturia' (translated by Winterbourne as 'promontory') to describe one of the off-shore islands, if that were intended. There is abundant evidence in the text that the whole of the island of Britain, not an obscure western corner, falls under the shadow of Maglocunus.

Insularis Draco should properly be translated as 'Dragon of Britain'. It is most likely to refer to Maglocunus's pre-eminent position among the British tyrants, not a geographical location. In the *Historia,* his title is *'magnus rex apud Brittones'* – Great King among the Britons. Gildas might use the Latin word *'Draco'* because of its similarity to *Dragon,* an actual title used of Welsh rulers. Rachel Bromwich was unable to find any early Welsh use of the word *'Dragon'* except as a title for a great warrior (Bromwich 1961). This would be similar to Snyder's suggestion that Gildas used the word *tyrannus* because of its similarity to the British *Tigern* (Snyder 1998).

We know from DEB 27 that some of the tyrants, presumably including Maglocunus, exercise jurisdiction beyond the confines of their own *civitates,* as they chase thieves everywhere *per patriam,* 'throughout the country'.

'The King of Kings has made you higher than almost all the leaders of Britain in your kingdom as in your stature.' This is a specific assertion of Maglocunus's power. If the British kingdoms are all derived from the Roman *civitates* (Dark 1994), then Maglocunus cannot be the king of the Ordovices. No one could describe this little kingdom, even if it has spread into the neighbouring territory of the Decangli, as 'almost the greatest kingdom in Britain'. The analogy Gildas makes with the King's physical height suggests the size of the kingdom, rather than its military or economic power.

Gildas proceeds to tell us how Maglocunus's kingdom has become so large: Maglocunus has 'deprived many of the aforementioned tyrants of their kingdoms and even of their lives'. Who are these aforementioned tyrants? They are kings from throughout the island, the tyrants of Britain, the 'kings of our homeland'. Gildas has never, to our knowledge, referred to the kings of the Ordovices, nor does he suggest that Maglocunus deposed a succession of kings of the same Ordovician area. Even if, like Dumnonia and the Demetae, most kingdoms do derive from the *civitates,* it is clear that Maglocunus must rule over more than one of them.

The phrase *'supra dictorum'* many of these 'aforementioned' tyrants, is problematic (DEB 33). Although it could be taken to refer to British tyrants in general ('Britain has kings, but they are tyrants' DEB 27), its most obvious meaning is that some of the tyrants who have just been named – Constantine, Aurelius Caninus, Vortiporius and Cuneglassus – are the ones who have fallen victim to the Dragon of the Island. Winterbottom glosses over this by translating it less precisely as 'these tyrants'. The difficulty is that Gildas has treated the other four as if they were alive. They are addressed as if they had the ability to repent and change their way of life. On the other hand, the vision of Daniel clearly refers to consecutive kingdoms. The terrible beast in Daniel was destined to overthrow some of the kingdoms, leaving others surviving and powerless. With the ten-year gap before publication, it is possible that some of the kings may have died since the first draft, but had been kept in, possibly as vindication of Daniel's prophecy.

Gildas's biblical models often leave some doubt as to whether the prophet is writing with hindsight or with prophetic foresight and it may be that we are encountering the same ambiguity here. Gildas frequently writes in a dramatic present tense about past events. It is worth re-reading the denunciations of the four tyrants to see if there is any hint that they have in fact been 'driven from their kingdoms or even their lives' by Maglocunus.

We have already wondered if the presence of two leonine tyrants rather than the expected one indicates that their predecessor has been removed, but what of Constantine and Aurelius themselves? Gildas specifically says in DEB 28 that he knows Constantine is alive, as if countering rumours that he is not. Though living, Constantine might have been cast out of his kingdom. His oath not to work his wiles on his fellow countrymen may have been part of a settlement following a defeat by Maglocunus. He may even have been forced to retire to the monastery where he 'masquerades' as a holy abbot. Bede and Gregory of Tours give examples of deposed Dark Age kings forced into virtual imprisonment in monasteries. Maglocunus's conquests included overthrowing his uncle and his forces 'Non catulorum leonis . . . magnopere dispares' (not greatly dissimilar to the whelps of a lion). This, as we suggest, must mean something more than pejorative epithet. If it merely meant that they were acting in an evil way, then Maglocunus's war against them would have been a good thing, which it clearly is not.

We are told in DEB 30 that some misfortune has befallen the rest of Aurelius Caninus's family: 'You are left like a solitary tree . . . Remember . . . the empty outward show of your fathers and brothers, their youthful and untimely deaths.' Maybe Gildas is trying to show that these tyrants are part of the same family. Aurelius may not even be alive as Gildas writes. Gildas's image of him being engulfed by the slime of his wickedness could be an indication that these prophesied events have already happened. His prophetic threat –

'The king will shortly brandish his sword at you' – could refer to God, as Winterbottom takes it, or equally to an earthly foe, perhaps Maglocunus.

LION'S WHELP, AS THE PROPHET SAYS

What exactly did Gildas actually mean by his biblical analogies? Higham argues that the heavy use of animal imagery by Gildas stems from his references to the Saxons. Having established that 'Saxons' is a name not to be spoken, he thereafter refers to them as wolves, dogs, villains, cut-throats and so on. Higham sees the application of similar terms to the Britons as marking their closeness to their putative 'overlords'. In reality, the situation is not so clear-cut. Generally, when the prophets, especially Gildas's favoured Jeremiah and Isaiah, refer to lions, lionesses or lion's whelps, they are symbols of God or his agents of judgement against the wicked. A lion's whelp had been established as a symbol of the tribe and kingdom of Judah and it is not surprising to find it used in this way. It is apparent, from the Maglocunus passage, that Gildas's use of leonine images cannot always be pejorative. If Maglocunus's victims are very similar to lion's whelps, this is not mentioned to exonerate him but to heighten his crime.

So there is no clear-cut way of understanding what Gildas means when he writes that Aurelius is a lion's whelp 'as the prophet says'. We have to make a reasoned guess as to which prophet and in what context. Gildas's prophet of choice is Jeremiah. For Jeremiah, lions, lion-whelps and leopards are agents of God's destruction on wicked Jerusalem, not necessarily evil in themselves. In one passage, however (DEB 51.38), he juxtaposes lion's whelps and dragons when castigating the Babylonians: 'The king of Babylonia cut Jerusalem up and ate it. He emptied the city like a jar; like a dragon, he swallowed it. He took what he wanted and threw the rest away . . . [Babylonia] will become a tomb and a habitation for dragons . . . the Babylonians will all roar like lions and growl like lion cubs.'

In spite of the suggestive language, it is difficult to see what this implies for Aurelius and the others, even in the vaguest terms. Gildas speaks with approval of Isaiah as the Chief of Prophets, but Isaiah too sees lions and lionesses as general instruments of God. The same use is made by the minor prophets to whom Gildas refers as his denunciations continue.

There is only one prophet who uses the words lioness and lion's whelp in a way which parallels Gildas: Ezekiel. In chapter 19 he writes:

The Lord told me to sing this song of sorrow for two princes of Israel: what a lioness your mother was! She reared her cubs among the fierce male lions. She reared a cub and taught him to hunt. He learned to eat people. The nations heard about him and trapped him in a pit. With hooks, they dragged him off to Egypt. She waited until she saw all hope was gone. Then she reared another of her cubs, and he grew into a fierce lion. When he was full grown, he prowled with the other lions. He too learned to hunt and eat people. He wrecked forts, he ruined towns, the people of the land were terrified every time he roared. The nations gathered to fight him, people came from everywhere. They spread their hunting nets and caught him in their trap. They put him in a cage and took him to the king of Babylonia, they kept him under guard so that his roar would never be heard again on the hills of Israel.

The lion's whelps are princes who should have protected Israel, something we would expect from the way the image is used by the other prophets. However, their vain and war-like shows have come to nothing when they confront more powerful foes. The lioness is figuratively the Israelite kingdom from which they come (Britain, to Gildas, is God's 'latter-day Israel') but could be their real mother, as they are both members of the same royal family, which is the obvious way the passage reads.

If this is how Gildas draws the analogy, that the lion's whelps are the princes who should be defending Israel, should be attacking the enemies of the kingdoms, and that there is a dynastic connection between them, he might see how the prophecy could be applied to the descendants of Ambrosius Aurelianus.

Intriguingly, Ezekiel later connects the images of lions and dragons (chapter 32): 'Take up a lamentation for Pharaoh, King of Egypt, and say to him: Thou art become like a lion of the nations and as a dragon that is in the sea.'

The historical background, as prophets like Jeremiah and Ezekiel make clear, is that the kingdoms of Israel and Judah were dependent on the military power of the Egyptian Pharaoh as his clients. They relied on Pharaoh for support against Assyria and Babylon, their adversaries to the north and east. The prophets maintain that this one-sided alliance is in vain, that either the Egyptians will not help or that, if they do, they will be defeated by the invaders. Instead, the Israelites must put their trust in God and turn away from wickedness. The prophets draw on their knowledge of the destruction of the earlier Pharaoh and his army during the Exodus and the recent defeat of the Egyptians by the Babylonians. It is this context, Pharaoh and the Egyptians being the uncertain military power, on which the Israelites place their reliance.

There is nothing at all in their descriptions to suggest that either Vortiporius or Cuneglassus had been killed or deposed by Maglocunus, so we are left with the possibility that it is the lion's whelps, the putative dynasty of Ambrosius, who have borne the brunt of his attacks.

THE DRAGON OF BRITAIN

Gildas gives us more biographical details about Maglocunus than about any of the other tyrants. Perhaps he knew him personally, or perhaps he simply saw the Dragon of the Island as such a significant figure in the destruction of Britain that it was worth covering the point in detail. Maglocunus began with the dream to rule by violence – that is, to take power violently. He was strong in arms and, in the first years of his youth, used the sword, spear and fire to despatch the king his uncle and nearly the bravest of his soldiers, whose 'faces were not very different from those of the lion's whelps' . As we last saw the phrase being used of Aurelius Caninus and (in modified form) of Constantine, I do not think it is unreasonable to draw a connection. The reference could be there to remind the first two tyrants that Maglocunus is a threat to them, or to emphasise the Dragon's crime.

If Maglocunus's uncle himself is such a close relative of Aurelius, then it suggests a dynastic motive for Gildas's writing. Close dynastic ties could exist between some of the tyrants, suggesting that they are united by more than the proximity of their kingdoms. If Aurelius is no longer alive, he might have been killed specifically in this coup.

Surprisingly, after this triumph, after pondering the godly life and rule of monks a great deal, Maglocunus repented of his sins, broke the chains of royal power and entered a monastery, 'bringing joy in Heaven'. Gildas stresses that Maglocunus's decision was voluntary, adding to the impression that Constantine's was not.

Gildas here speaks with warm approval of monks and their life. Later historians had no doubt that he himself was a monk. This is not clear from the text – he writes only of clerics of his order or rank, contrasted with bishops and priests. However, other works attributed to him concern the monastic life and there is nothing to suggest he is not a monk. In this case, it may be fellow-feeling for Maglocunus the monk, or even the possibility that they were in the same monastery, which prompts Gildas's vitriol.

Later, we hear that Maglocunus had as his teacher the most refined master of all Britain. This man was obviously an eminent cleric, as his teachings were religious admonishments similar to Gildas's own. Of course, the refined master might have taught Maglocunus when he was very young, before his coup. The most reasonable supposition, however, is that they met when Maglocunus was a monk. A further inference is that Gildas applauds the refined master and his teachings because he also was one of his pupils. That raises the possibility that Gildas and Maglocunus were contemporary disciples of the refined master. One point of note is that Gildas is clear what Maglocunus looks like – he is exceptionally tall. The one other tyrant whose physical features are described is Vortiporius, 'your head is already whitening', but this could be no more than a reference to his age.

Maglocunus did not remain a monk. Tempted by the devil he returned to his former life 'like some sick hound to your disgusting vomit'. Although Gildas expounds on this betrayal at length, it is not clear why Maglocunus left the monastery. Gildas says it was 'not much against your will' but this is suggestive that some political compulsion was behind it. Maglocunus did have a brother, who may have been ruling his former lands. All that Gildas tells us is that Maglocunus married as soon as he left the monastery. He soon tired of this woman, murdered her, then murdered his brother's son so that he could marry his wife. He was aided and encouraged by this latter woman, and married her publicly to the acclaim of his supporters.

This dramatic story is the last Gildas relays of Maglocunus. How he came to drive out and kill 'many tyrants' is not explained, and Gildas can hardly have meant just his uncle and nephew. Presumably, his civil wars occurred after he left the monastery, but we hear no more than that the Dragon of the Island has committed many sins.

One last interesting feature of Maglocunus's career is his chosen form of entertainment. 'Your excited ears hear not the praises of God from the sweet voices of the tuneful recruits of Christ, not the melodious music of the church but empty praises of yourself from the mouths of criminals who grate on the hearing like raving hucksters – mouths stuffed with lies and liable to bedew bystanders with their foaming phlegm.' These 'criminals' may also be the parasites whose lying tongues celebrate the king's new wedding. It is surely not fanciful to suggest that we have already met these characters. *Historia Brittonum* synchronised the reign to Maglocunus/Mailcunus specifically to the time when 'Talhearn Tataguen was famous for his poetry and Neirin and Taliessin and Bluchbard and Cian, who is called Gueinth Guaut, were at the same time famous in British poetry'. Perhaps some or all of these men were patronised by Maglocunus. At the very least, we have Gildas's surprisingly impassioned invective to inform us that such men were active at the Tyrant's court.

Gildas's chosen style, emphasising condemnation rather than praise, distorts our impression of his time. Although most rulers may be tyrants, a few, albeit a tiny number, do maintain 'controls of truth and justice'. Gildas tells us that this tiny minority of the just support him by their prayers and that all men admire them. At least one of the unnamed contemporary rulers must be very powerful indeed. We know this because mighty Maglocunus, Dragon of Britain, deposer of many tyrants, is only greater than 'almost all the leaders of Britain'. The likely explanation is that Gildas knows of a greater British ruler who is not a notorious tyrant. He tells us that he has reserved a special place for Maglocunus because he is first in evil, not because he is most powerful.

On the evidence of *Historia Brittonum*, we can probably name this man. He is Outigirn, who will fight against the Saxons when their attacks recommence, while his contemporary Mailcunus will not. Outigirn has a position distinct from that of the tyrants. The five named tyrants are likened to 'Five mad and debauched horses from the retinue of Pharaoh which actively lure his army to its ruin in the Red Sea'. This is not just a slightly forced metaphor meaning no more than that they, like the Egyptian army, will be destroyed by God. Gildas seems to be telling us that there really is a 'Pharaoh' whom they served. Earlier the councillors of Vortigern are called 'Stupid Princes of Zoan, giving foolish advice to Pharaoh'.

We have seen that Egypt represents for Gildas, as it does for Jeremiah and the prophets, the uncertain military power on which the Israelites rely instead of trusting in God. Vortigern, as Pharaoh, provides the military solution to the Council's problem, the settlement of Saxon mercenaries. The Pharaoh of Gildas's time could similarly be a military figure. This is an area we will turn to later.

So far, we have looked at Gildas's evidence on the generations of Vortigern and Ambrosius. We have also seen what he says about the generation in which he lives. This will help us now to define the generation between, the Badon generation, the reign of Arthur.

The Reign of Arthur

Because there is so little in *de Excidio Britanniae* about the generation which succeeded Ambrosius, it is worth reiterating exactly what Gildas does say about it. The fight-back began under Ambrosius, when the British challenged the Saxons to battle and were victorious. This ushered in a period of war between the 'Citizens' and their Saxon enemies. First one side, then the other, was victorious, up to the year of the siege of Badon Hill. There were then some more British victories, but the Saxons were completely cowed. One point to note is that Gildas remembers the 'year' of the siege of Badon as a glorious turning-point. The siege was the most dramatic, the most memorable victory, characterising the whole year, but it is the year which saw the pattern of consistent British victory established, presumably in more than one battle.

As far as *Historia Brittonum* was concerned, all of Arthur's battles were victories. This is unsurprising. The Anglo-Saxon Chronicle gives a picture of more or less victorious *Saxon* activity too. It may be that Arthur was exceptionally successful and that although the Saxons prevailed against other commanders and kings elsewhere, they could make no headway against him. This sounds slightly unrealistic, and the battle-list itself gives some grounds for thinking it may distort the real picture. Four battles were fought on the Dubglas. Even if the Britons were simply holding a defensive position against successive attacks, the scale of the victories did not permit a counter-attack or deterrence against the Saxons. The battle at the City of the Legion shows that the Saxons are still as far west as they were when they previously raged from sea to sea and destroyed Gloucester. They have thus regained militarily the position they yielded when they returned to the east before Ambrosius rallied the Britons.

Aside from Ambrosius, a leader of unknown rank, Gildas does not explain the military leadership required for the counter-attack, but military leaders there must have been. Battles and more importantly sieges could not just occur by the consensus of kings or citizens. The siege of Badon Hill implies the existence of a single military commander.

The key feature of the Badon generation, now forgotten by Gildas's contemporaries, is that 'kings, public and private persons, priests and churchmen kept their own stations' – '*reges, publici, privati . . . suum ordinem servarunt*'. It is hard to see how a king would avoid stepping out of line unless Gildas means they were subject to a higher, more legitimate authority. There was a 'Pharaoh' before the Saxon revolt and there is one in Gildas's own time, so it is reasonable to suppose a similar figure in the Badon generation coordinating the actions of the kings.

Although Gildas does not explicitly say that the kings were part of the military response to the Saxons, this is readily apparent. The kings clearly provide the military manpower of Gildas's time. Their ability to carry out civil war without hindrance demonstrates this. The men who feast at their tables are specifically called their 'fellow soldiers'. They are denounced primarily because their resources are not directed to the defence of Britain. It is inescapable that a similar situation existed in the Badon generation. The fight-back involved the military co-operation of the kings of the Britons, 'serving according to their rank', exactly as we are told in *Historia Brittonum.*

Gildas allows us to speculate who some of these kings were. One would have been the good King of the Demetae, the father of Vortiporius. If Vortiporius was sixty or more, then he might have fought in the war too. Maglocunus's uncle was another king in the same generation. So might have been the father of Aurelius Caninus, although he apparently died young in a more recent civil war and may not have been old enough to contribute.

This gives the lie to the argument that Arthur did not exist because Gildas did not name him. The victor of Mons Badonicus existed as much as Maglocunus's uncle or the fathers of Vortiporius and Aurelius Caninus. They, like every other member of their generation, are unnamed by Gildas. Yet the evidence for their existence is the effect they had on Gildas and his time. It was not part of Gildas's purpose to preserve those names in his work, but that is far from saying that their names were not preserved.

The picture Gildas presents agrees with the later sources. A generation of warfare separates the resisters of the Saxon revolt from the victors of Mount Badon. Those victors consisted of united British kings, public officials and private individuals, sticking to their allotted jobs. The wars saw British defeats, glossed over in British sources, it is true. Saxon sources also concealed their defeats, but there is no reason to discount a period which could see the Saxon conquest of Anderida, for example, alternating with the British defence of the City of the Legion.

Of all the possible scenarios, a supreme British warleader, coordinating the countrywide strategy of the kings, is the most likely. While that leader lived, remembrance of the unexpected victory at Badon kept the Britons united.

Could Arthur have been the son of Ambrosius? Ambrosius had at least one child, whom we might expect to have continued his legacy. There is nothing in *de Excidio* to contradict this. However, it seems strange that no British source makes this link, if it existed. We might add, however, that a man bearing the British name 'Arthur' was unlikely to be the offspring of the 'last of the Romans'.

As wars against the Saxons soon ceased after Badon, we can suppose that the Victor of Badon, if he died violently, was killed in one of the many civil wars. According to the *Annales*, Arthur was killed about twenty years after Badon. Gildas's formative years would therefore have been during the reign of Arthur. He tells us that he began to consider his denunciations thirty years or so after Badon, which would seem reasonable for a breakdown of the common cause among the Britons.

Medieval legends connected the death of Arthur to the incident where Constantine killed the two noble youths in church. The truth is, the battle of Camlann could have formed part of any of the civil wars Gildas mentions and Medraut, too, could be one of the unnamed participants in them.

Arthur, as he emerges from the sources we have examined, was the victor of the siege of Mount Badon. The *Gododdin* shows that the name and fame of Arthur were already known close to the time of Gildas and Maglocunus. He was so famous that just his name was expected to evoke comparisons with Guaurthur's fight against the English. Why is it so unreasonable to suppose that the names missing from Gildas are those provided by the *Historia* and *Annales*? Is it really so implausible that the name of the man who led the British forces at the siege of Badon Hill was indeed Arthur?

This is about as far as we can go following the narrative sources for the reign of Arthur. Clearly, we are not yet in a position to sum up a probable outline of the reign of Arthur. For that we must consider other sources. Since 1977, historians, deprived of the 'inadmissible' evidence we have spent the first half of the book considering, have turned to other sources to illuminate the fifth and sixth centuries. Archaeology is one source of data. Purely archaeological studies, however, have divorced the picture entirely from any written sources, eliminating wars, massacres and exiles according to the political whim or archaeological fashion of the writer. More recently, studies have linked the archaeological material firmly to linguistic evidence, comparative data from the continent and elsewhere in the British Isles, and the few 'admissible' contemporary written sources. These provide useful models which we can use to assess our picture of the reign of Arthur.

6

THE KINGS OF THE BRITONS

A good place to start our search is with Arthur's companions-in-arms, the British kings. When the Dark Age administrations emerge into the written records, Britain had become a patchwork of kingdoms. In the lowland (England), they are ruled by and named after Angles or Saxons. Their laws consider that most of their inhabitants are similarly Angles or Saxons. In the highland zones, the West Country, Wales, Cumbria and Scotland, the kingdoms are ruled by 'Celtic' kings, whether of British, Irish or Pictish origin, and are composed exclusively of such peoples. Where there is any higher form of government, it is imposed militarily by rulers of these kingdoms. These might be the Great Kings or *Bretwaldas* of the Anglo-Saxons, or the kings of Gwynedd. Where money, the Roman church, written bureaucracy or other features of Roman civilisation exist, they have been re-imported from overseas since the end of the sixth century.

On the other side of the historical divide, we have evidence of the administrative structures of the Roman Empire which dominated most of Britain. Most of this comes from *Notitia Dignitatum*, which seems to reflect late fourth-century reality. This shows Roman Britain with a hierarchy of civilian government operating alongside separate military structures. Coinage, public works, literacy and a city-based ecclesiastical structure were features of this system.

The transition between these systems must have occurred around the time we are studying. The nature of the reign of Arthur depends on how far we can see this transition as having progressed. The nature and timing of the transition form the basis of Dark's work, most notably in *Civitas to Kingdom*. Many of his conclusions are taken for granted here, and I refer readers to his work for further clarification. Needless to say, Dark is very much of the view that Arthur and his reign rest on inadmissible evidence and I stress that the interpretation of his work offered here is my own.

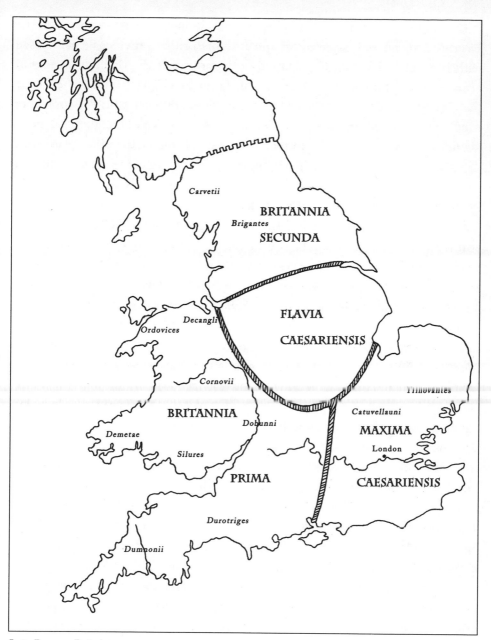

Late Roman Britain.

Roman Britain formed a diocese of the late Roman empire. Its governor, the *Vicarius Britanniarum* (viceroy of the Britains/British provinces), was based with his staff in London. He reported to the prefect of the Gallic provinces in France. Under him were five provincial governors. The technical term for these governors was '*rectores*' (singular *rector*) although the British governors used several different titles. One of the provinces, Valentia, has not been identified. However, as it was formed from part of one of the other provinces, its fate will be covered with whichever province it came from. Maxima Caesariensis and Flavia Caesariensis covered the lowland zone, and Britannia Prima and Britannia Secunda the highlands.

Beneath the provinces were the *civitates* (singular *civitas*). They were county-like areas centred on Roman cities, with their own municipal governments. Some un-Romanised areas do not seem to have been organised as *civitates* in the technical sense of the word. *Coloniae*, the major towns founded by Roman veterans, also had their own governments.

Although the *Vicarius* had some troops at his disposal, the main military units were independent of civil structures. The commanders reported to the *Magister Militum* in Gaul. The most senior was the *Comes Britanniarum*, the companion or (as the title became in the Middle Ages) Count of the Britains. He held the mobile reserve which helped the static commands or defended against civil unrest or invading Irish. Next came the *Comes Litoris Saxonicii* – the Count of the Saxon Shore – who ran the *limitanei* or frontier troops and their settlements on the south coast, defending against Saxon invasions. Finally, the *Dux Britanniarum* (leader or duke of the British provinces) commanded the *limitanei* and forts of Hadrian's Wall and their supply lines. This was the front line of defence against the Picts. The official titles vary between *Britanniae* (of Britain) and *Britanniarum* (of the Britains) and the latter clumsy designation would soon fall out of use.

There were also unofficial sources of power. The powerful landowners fell into two groups. One were the Romanised villa-dwellers, involved in the political and economic lives of their towns. They were sponsors, and presumably adherents, of Roman pagan cults. As the empire became less stable, with barbarians and local peasants a source of threat, they supported private armies of *bucellarii*, heavies who protected their social position and capital.

On the western fringes, particularly in the province of Britannia Prima, urban and villa life did not really take hold. Here, as Roman rule collapsed, the local magnates who took power dwelt in refortified hillforts, patronised missionary and monastic Christians and favoured a culture more similar to that of their pre-Roman ancestors or their un-Romanised Irish neighbours. Their troops were far more likely to be semi-noble warbands than the mercenaries or tenants who formed the *bucellarii*.

The Romans based their *civitates* on the pre-existing tribes of Britain. In the west, it is conceivable that the Celtic warlords who re-established control after the end of Roman rule were actually the descendants of the former tribal kings four centuries earlier. Tribal kingship and identity proved very resilient in Ireland, by way of analogy. These Celtic kings look familiar to us. They are the archaeological manifestations of the rulers denounced by Gildas and the ancestors, real or imagined, of the kings of Dark Age Wales.

According to Gildas, the Roman civil and military structures disappeared when Magnus Maximus used them to usurp the Roman Empire. In this, he was wrong in detail – Roman military commands survived at least until soldiers from them backed Constantine III's invasion of Gaul. At this point, according to Zosimus, the Britons drove out Constantine's placemen in the civilian government and ruled themselves. It may or may not be significant that when the Emperor Honorius wrote to the Britons in 410 formalising this arrangement, he wrote specifically to the *civitates*, the lowest tier of government, as if the higher levels no longer existed.

It used to be the fashion to see characters such as Ambrosius as hanging on to old Roman posts. This does not seem to be borne out by the evidence. Gildas, for instance, is convinced that Roman rule is a thing of the distant past. On the other hand, it is possible that the new British rulers resurrected Roman structures for their own benefit.

KINGDOMS OF THE WEST

The kingdoms of the Dark Age Britons derived, Dark argues, from the *civitates*. There is an indication of this in Gildas, explicitly in the case of Vortiporius, Tyrant of the Demetae – the *civitas* which would become the kingdom of Dyfed. It is also probably implicit in his description of Constantine. The *civitas* of the Dumnonii will become the Kingdom of Dyfneint.

Dark argues that in the east the *civitates* evolved into 'kingdoms' ruled by the Romanised magnates. In the west, the successors were the hillfort-dwelling 'Celtic' chieftains, whom he sees as the 'kings' proper. The *civitas* model allows us to refine the tentative geography we have used so far for the reign of Arthur. The locations and extents of the Roman *civitates* are much easier to determine than the early Dark Age kingdoms. We can therefore be much more precise about the 'north-eastern', 'Kentish' and 'South Welsh' Arthurian locations we have demonstrated earlier, as well as having a clearer idea of Gildas's geography.

First, the most reasonable location for Gildas is the *civitas* of the Durotriges, extending from immediately south of Bath (the Wansdyke seems to be its frontier defence), down to the south coast. The 'kingdom' is bounded by Dumnonia to the west and Penselwood and the Saxons in Hampshire to the east. This fits the evidence from Gildas's text exactly. It is also the conclusion reached by Higham from studying the geographic references in *de Excidio Britanniae*.

As Gildas starts his denunciations with the tyrant of the neighbouring Dumnonia, rather than his own land, we can suppose that he considered the ruler of the Durotriges as one of the handful of admirable rulers. It might be in deference to this local leader that Gildas calls Maglocunus greater than '*almost* all the leaders of Britain'.

The major centre of the kingdom would be South Cadbury Hillfort, replacing the Roman town of Ilchester. As the largest of the refortified hillforts, and because of later legends, South Cadbury has frequently been identified as the 'Camelot' of King Arthur. The *Linnuis* region where Arthur fought four of his battles could even be a mistake for *Lindinis* – Ilchester. Hitherto, we have given the consensus view that *Linnuis* is Lindsey. However, Lindsey does not feature as an area of conflict between Britons and Saxons in Dark's analysis. It had been intensively settled since the early fifth century and has no obvious sub-Roman neighbours. Ilchester, on the other hand, was clearly in a war zone.

The Durotriges and the next polity north, the Dobunni (incorporating the lower Severn Valley, Bath, Gloucester and Cirencester) are where we would expect to find the battle of Mount Badon. Overall, the *civitas* of the Durotriges looks a promising candidate for Arthurian activity.

Dark acknowledges the existence and role of sub-kings within each kingdom, answerable to over-kings of the *civitas*. It is therefore possible that Aurelius Caninus and Cuneglassus, not linked explicitly to any *civitates*, are sub-kings noted for their wickedness rather than their power. However, like practically all other writers, Dark assumes that, since Constantine and Vortiporius are specifically linked to *civitates*/kingdoms, they are the over-kings of them, and the other tyrants hold similar positions. This means that, in the absence of any contradictory data, the three unlocated tyrants can be assigned to *civitates*/kingdoms around those fixed points of Dumnonia and Demetae.

On this assumption, Aurelius Caninus would be king of one of the three *civitates* between Dumnonia and Dyfed: Durotriges, Dobunnii or Silures/ Gwent. If Gildas is in Durotriges, this is an unlikely base for Aurelius, about whom he gives no up-to-date information.

Dobunni looks a rather better candidate for Aurelius's kingdom. The Wansdyke, protecting Durotriges from the Dubonni, is indicative of civil wars between them, with the Dobunni as the aggressors. If the civil wars for which Aurelius is denounced focused on Gildas's home *civitas*, this may have contributed to his animosity. It is the first of the *civitates* in what I have loosely referred to as 'South Wales' when discussing Arthurian sources. As a frontline area between the Saxons and the Britons, it would be an ideal setting for the careers of Ambrosius and Arthur. The broad geographical area where Mount Badon is likely to be located encompasses this *civitas*. We know it has previously been a target for the Saxons, as Gloucester is one of the Coloniae laid low by their battering rams.

The next *civitas* is that of the Silures. Dark suggests this would split into two polities in the sixth century. In the east would be Gwent, derived from the urban elite of Caerwent (*Venta Silurum*, from which it took its name), and Glywysing in the west, ruled by the hillfort-dwelling chieftains. A third kingdom, Brecheiniog, was formed within the *civitas* at this time.

The *civitas* of the Silures is a prime location for preserving traditions of Arthur. Some writers (e.g. Gilbert, Blackett and Wilson) have argued that Arthur was a native of Gwent, usually identified with Atrwys ap Meurig, from the Genealogies. *Historia Brittonum* specifically made Ambrosius a native of Glywysing. If that is true, then Aurelius Caninus, as his descendant, could plausibly be based here.

The region of Ercing, where the grave of Arthur's son Anir was a wonder in the ninth century, is in this *civitas*. Davies speculates that Ercing was a distinct sub-kingdom of Gwent, derived from the Roman town of Ariconium. Although most of Davies's sources, such as the twelfth-century *Book of Llandaff*, are not ones I would consider for evidence, it is interesting to note that the area is defined by a cluster of churches dedicated to St Dyfrig (Dubricius). Similar clusters for different saints mark out the extents of

Elmetsaete

ELMET

Pecsaete

GWYNEDD

Wreocensaete

POWYS

Tomsaete

ERCING

Magonsaete   Arosaete

BRECHEINIOG

DYFED   **GWENT**

GLYWYSING

Cilternsaete

SILCHESTER

Sumorsaete

DYFNEINT   Dorsaete

KEY	
///	Evidence of Anglo Saxon occupation c. 500 AD
🟫🟫	The Wansdyke

Britons vs Saxons.

Glywysing and Brecheiniog. The later existence of a tribal area of the Magonsaete in the area may also be significant. The Durotriges were to be divided between the Dorsaete and the Sumorsaete (whence the modern counties of Dorset and Somerset derive) and the other sixth-century British frontier areas were also to be characterised by tribal areas with the -saete suffix (Snyder 1998, Davies 1978).

If Arthur was the *sub-king* of Ercing, it would go some way to explaining the evidence which gives him either royal or less than royal status. Arthur would be positioned between the over-kings of Gwent, Powys and Dobunni. Self-preservation if nothing else would give him a reason for investing in alliances with them. It is easy to imagine him leading these 'kings of the Britons' against the invading Saxons.

That the kingdoms of the South Welsh did co-operate in such a way is an inference we can draw from the Anglo-Saxon Chronicle entry on the Battle of Dyrham. This saw the destruction of the *civitas* of the Dubonni and the conquest of its major cities, Bath, Gloucester and Cirencester. Three British kings died at the battle. Most historians have made the equation three cities = three kings, meaning that each city has its own king. This is not what the Chronicle says. Not only is it unlikely *per se* – what kind of tiny kingdom would include just one of these neighbouring cities? – it is not borne out by Dark's analysis of the evolution of political control in the area. The kingdom of the Dobunni derives from the Roman *civitas*, centred on Cirencester, rather than the individual cities with their individual characteristics. Bath was a cultic spa centre and Gloucester a veterans' settlement. If the three kings are not minuscule princelings, the only remaining hypothesis is that they are allies, quite possibly the rulers of Gwent, Powys and Dubonni.

If Arthur's battle at the City of the Legion is really at Caerleon this would be within the Gwent kingdom. If Gloucester was attacked by Saxons in the previous generation, a battle at Caerleon is a possibility. Vortiporius is clearly located in Dyfed, leaving Powys and Gwynedd as possible locations for the other two tyrants, as well as areas for consideration as bases for King Arthur.

Paradoxically, the Kingdom of Gwynedd is the most difficult to trace back to a Roman *civitas*. It seems to bear a Celtic tribal name, but not that of the tribe who lived in the area during the Roman period, the Ordovices. We do not know whether the Ordovices were even organised as a *civitas*. As Gwynedd evolved in the Dark Ages, the non-Ordovican areas of Clwyd (the Decangli) and Ceredigion, became disputed border areas.

If we set aside the traditional attribution of Maglocunus to Gwynedd, we can see that on the evidence of both Gildas and Dark he might equally well be the King of Powys. Dark sees Powys evolving from the urban elite of the Cornovii. His choice of tyrant, chariot-riding Cuneglassus of the bear's stronghold, seems an unlikely candidate for king of such a political unit. Dark is forced into some strained speculation to fit him into this pattern. It is rather more likely that Cuneglassus is a sub-king either of Ercing or of a North Welsh location. Dark sees the area of the Decangli as a debated zone between Gwynedd and Powys. It also boasts one of the likely Din Eirth locations. The Harleian Genealogies, used to support the identification of Maglocunus with the ruler of Gwynedd, link Cuneglassus to the same North Welsh Dynasty. If this is reliable in any sense, then Maglocunus and Cuneglassus could both be North Welsh, leaving Powys as one of the few kingdoms whose ruler is not a tyrant.

Powys is an area likely to have contributed to Nennius's Arthur material. Carn Cabal, now Carn Gafallt, is in Powys, as was Chester, the more plausible of the two Cities of the Legion. Chester shows signs of sub-Roman use or occupation. The Book of the Blessed Germanus clearly has a Powysian slant to it, as does Nennius's local knowledge of Fernmail, whose lands, Builth and Gwerthrynion, are sub-kingdoms of Powys. According to the *Historia*, Fernmail's named ancestors were rulers of Builth after Ambrosius. If these are real characters, then we have proof that Gildas's tyrants are not the only rulers between Dumnonia and Gwynedd.

Powys would constitute an obvious area for conflict between the Britons and the English. We could either see Arthur as a King of Powys, or the King of Powys as one of his major partners among the 'Kings of the Britons'. If Arthur was actually King of Powys, it would be odd that Nennius does not mention the fact. He could have linked him to Catel, the dynastic founder in the Germanus material, or placed him in the genealogy of the contemporary rulers. The Powys dynasty of the later Dark Ages left genealogical material extending back to the sixth century and beyond, but did not choose Arthur as one of its members. The odds are that, although the King of Powys must have been a participant in the wars before Gildas's birth, he too 'was not Arthur'.

All these *civitates* fell within the province of Britannia Prima. Later we will look at the possibility of any higher authority binding them together. For the moment, we can say that the 'South Welsh' Arthurian material is not only fully in accord but also makes much better sense when understood in the context of the *civitates* of Britannia Prima. To examine the 'Kentish' material, we will have to look elsewhere.

Dark identifies the *civitates* of the Trinovantes and the Catuvellauni north of the lower Thames as a surviving sub-Roman unit. Later, the area would be ascribed to the Cilternsaete. Within this area, the cities of Verulamium, Colchester and London continued to be inhabited. The Anglo-Saxon Chronicle saw London as a place of refuge for Britons fleeing the men of Kent. Additionally, there was an isolated sub-Roman pocket around Silchester.

Wars between the Saxons and these eastern enclaves could easily have been the source of the Kentish Arthur material. Their disappearance before the end of the sixth century could provide a convincing reason for the lack of details of Arthur or his family. Place-names associated with his rule or his victories would have been replaced soon afterwards by English ones. Later legends did show Arthur ruling in lowland England, but unfortunately these are just as likely to be anachronisms based on the medieval political geography of Britain as preserved tradition.

If Arthur came from the *civitas* of the Trinovantes, then self-preservation might have prompted him to give help to the western kings simply to ensure their support for the enclave. Alternatively, the Britons of the west may have felt loyalty to their beleaguered compatriots. Perhaps even a residual diocesan government in London might have encouraged joint action.

On a map, the Chilterns kingdom seems completely isolated, and it is difficult to imagine how Arthur could actually have fought campaigns here and in the west. In fact, the Saxon settlements could hardly have constituted an impervious ring of steel around the Chilterns. For instance, it would still have been accessible by sea via the Thames estuary. As Snyder points out, there is the distinct possibility that some of Arthur's battles are intended to be naval. The battle by the mouth of the River Glein and some of the others on rivers could have been fought by boat. This should hardly be surprising since the Saxons had at first been exclusively sea raiders. Alfred's campaigns against the Vikings required both land and sea forces and this could have been the case in the earlier period. Gildas bears witness to Britons travelling overseas, where some went into exile. Archaeologically, Mediterranean luxury goods show that the Britons had contacts with seafarers who presumably could have transported men and military materials as required.

Alternatively, it would have been possible to move from the South Welsh kingdoms to the Chilterns by the Ridgeway. Blocking or opening such a vital communication route would have been an obvious source of continuous conflict. John Morris, among many others, saw the Ridgeway as a location for the Arthurian wars. One of the strategic points along it, such as Liddington Castle (Badbury), would be an ideal setting for the siege of Mount Badon. Either side could be conceived of as besieging the other if their opponents occupied a defensive position astride the way. A siege from which the Britons emerged victorious could sound a devastating blow to the Saxons by ensuring the continuance of a British kingdom deep in their heartland.

Once again, the *civitas* model provides a convincing explanation for the later Arthurian evidence. It provides a framework whereby Arthur can lead united British kings with South Welsh connections against the kings of the men of Kent, exactly as *Historia Brittonum* would have it. Can the same analysis be applied to the northern material?

The Carvetii, the *civitas* around Carlisle, which was still functioning in the fifth/sixth centuries, became a sub-Roman kingdom. The north-west, however, is not an area where any of our sources would have placed Arthur. It is the north-east which gave rise to the earliest reference to him.

Although not a *civitas*, the tribal Votadini and their Dark Age descendants, the Gododdin, formed a Dark Age kingdom. An obvious possibility is that, like Guaurthur, Arthur was from the kingdom of the Gododdin. Aside from some North Welsh heroes, added later in the poem's development, there is no reason to suppose that anyone else mentioned in the poem has a different homeland. The Votadini/Gododdin were only occasionally part of the Roman Empire. However, there are signs in the poem of some Roman influence on them. The poem itself bears witness to the warriors' fellow-feeling to other Britons and their antipathy to the Saxons. It is therefore conceivable that the attack on Catraeth is part of an ongoing history of campaigning in sub-Roman Britain.

Having said this, it would be difficult to account for Arthur of the Gododdin fighting in South Wales, other than for sheer love of adventure. Nennius, who describes the exploits of Cuneda of the Gododdin in Wales, does not record any tradition that Arthur, too, was from that area.

South of the Wall, North Britain had been dominated by the large *civitas* of the Brigantes, identified as one of the Dark Age kingdoms. Some scholars have argued that the Welsh word *Brenhin* (king) derived from the name of this powerful realm. The Brigantes would have been the largest *civitas/* kingdom, allowing us to deduce that Manglocunus, 'greater than *almost* all the leaders of Britain', was not its king. At some time before the Gododdin expedition, Angles had overrun the southern part, known by the British name 'Deira'. Subsequently the northern part, Bernicia, was also conquered. By the end of the sixth century, only the sub-kingdom later attributed to the Pecsaete, known as 'Elmet' or 'Loidis Regio' (Leeds area) retained a British identity.

The absence of an English settlement here in the late fifth/early sixth century would suggest a strong military showing which could have resulted in the fame of Arthur among the Gododdin. They would have been going to fight in his old stamping grounds. Of the battle sites, Binchester (Castellum Guinnion) is in the Brigantian area. So is the River Glen known to Bede. The Caledonian Forest and the City of the Legion (if Chester) are within reach of a Brigantian king. The lack of surviving Brigantian material could account for the lack of background on Arthur.

To counter this plausible suggestion, it is not quite clear what he would be doing in the South Welsh or Kentish zones. Unlike the kings of Britannia Prima, clearly benefiting from unity against a common foe, it is hard to see why, apart from sheer patriotism, the King of Brigantia would have made common cause with the southern *civitates*. His enemies, sea-borne or Humberside Angles, were not the Mercians or Saxons fighting in the south.

The evidence collated by Snyder, and Dark's own analysis, points to a different source of British resistance in the area – the command of the *Dux Britanniarum* spanning the *civitates* of Carvetii and Brigantes. Before looking at the implications of this, we must first consider if the focus on *civitas* kings has excluded different types of ruling authority in the fifth and sixth centuries.

BRITAIN HAS GOVERNORS

Dark identifies two different types of rule at the *civitas* level. He argues forcibly (Dark 2000) that the western tribal rulers are specifically the *kings*, and that the bureaucratic Roman rulers of the eastern *civitates* are not, although one, Gwent, actually survived to become a British 'kingdom'.

I do not believe that Gildas and other contemporary evidence support such specific use of terminology. If any distinction is made by Gildas between western kings and eastern bureaucrats, then a good place to start is with the word *rector*. Gildas states that Britain has *rectores*, if not too many of them, at least no fewer than it needs. On first impression, he means there are simply many rulers. Dark, on the other hand, suggests that he is making a distinction between (Roman bureaucratic) *rectores* and (Celtic British) *reges*.

This is not correct. Gildas does not contrast *rectores* and *reges*. He writes *Habet Britannia rectores, habet speculatores* '– Britain has governors, it has intelligence officers' – that is, people whose job it is to find out sin and to correct it, the two tasks he now takes on himself. The actual rank of the *rectores* is not clear. They may include bishops as well as secular rulers, for instance.

Technically, rectors were the civilian governors of the provinces into which Roman Britain was divided. However, there is good reason to suppose that, by the end of the Roman rule, this term was no longer confined to this official usage. Even during the Roman period, the title could be used loosely. One rector in Cirencester called himself both 'Praeses of Britannia Prima' and 'Primae Provinciae Rector' on his memorial column, although formally these terms were not synonyms (Snyder 1998).

The writer Aminanus used *rector* for emperors, provincial governors, military officers and barbarian client kings (Snyder 1998). When Gildas says that Britain has, if not too many *rectores* at least no fewer than it needs, it seems unlikely that he means it has almost too many official Roman provincial governors; he seems to mean a superfluity of feuding petty kings, as he shows later. One of the Gododdin heroes, Tutvwlch, is specifically given the title *rector* (YG B36) along with the epithets helmsman, rampart and citadel. He is unlikely to be the official holder of a Roman civilian governorship! Nevertheless, there does remain the possibility that *rector* means something specific to Gildas.

If a *rex/rector* dichotomy is not supportable, it is still possible that Gildas's language permits that interpretation that different types of government, royal and bureaucratic, coexisted in Britain.

When Gildas does write of different secular rulers, he contrasts *Reges habet Britannia, sed tyrannos; iudices habet, sed impios*: 'Britain has kings, but they are tyrants; judges, but they are impious.' This presents a better case for two different types of rule. It is a contrast Gildas knew from the Bible, where the judges of Israel are non-royal rulers, distinct from the kings.

It is generally assumed that *reges* and *iudices* are synonyms used for rhetorical effect. When Gildas denounces the priests, in similar formulae, he calls them *sacerdotes*, *ministri*, *clerici* and *pastores*, all synonyms for 'priest'. This is the simplest reading of the *reges/iudices* passage. However, for those arguing for different types of rule, there may be some support in this seeming contrast.

First and most simply we should consider whether they are actually judges, in the literal sense. Gildas tells us that the rulers in general go into the seat of judgement but rarely seek out the rules of right justice (DEB 27), that is, that both *reges* and *iudices* have judicial functions.

On Dark's analysis, it could be that the *reges* are the actual 'kings' of the west and the *iudices* are the Roman bureaucrats of the east. This argument is based on an academic prejudice against the idea of sub-Roman kings. In *Civitas to Kingdom*, Dark simply used 'kingdom' as a blanket term for the sub-Roman polities, but by his later works he has become polemical in asserting that the only *reges* were the westerners. All we can add is that Vortiporius, called 'tyrant' by Gildas, calls himself *Protector* (strictly, imperial bodyguard) on his tombstone. This demonstrates that contemporaries of Gildas could be called kings or any convenient euphemism, without altering the nature of their power. It is even possible that Gildas uses *Rex* and *Iudex* in exactly the opposite way. He calls the legitimate Roman emperors 'kings', as he does the Roman usurpers who rule after Magnus Maximus ('kings were anointed'). Ammianus and the Bible both use *Iudex* as a title for a non-Roman ruler of kingly status (Dumville 1990), which might imply that they, not the kings, are the tribal rulers. This suggestion is further supported by the use of the title Ut Eidyn (*Iudex* of Edinburgh) among the tribal Gododdin.

Another possibility is that the *iudices* rank below the kings, the normal relationship between kings and judges. They could be sub-kings or officials within the same kingdom. On the other hand, it is even possible that they are of higher status! The Roman law code, *Codex Iustinianus*, is more or less contemporary with Gildas. Justinian, the Roman emperor responsible for its compilation, was in contact with the western states, including Britain. He specifies precisely '*iudices . . . hoc est provinciarum rectores*' – '*Iudices*, that is provincial governors.'

The named 'tyrants' are not all said to be kings. Gildas does not say that Maglocunus is just the greatest *king*. His kingdom and height set him apart from *cunctis paene Brittanniae ducibus* – 'nearly all the *leaders* of Britain'. These could include both royal and non-royal rulers. Only Vortiporius is said to be a hereditary monarch of a *civitas*/kingdom. Constantine comes from Dumnonia and we might guess he is the ruler of the *civitas*/kingdom. Aurelius Caninus, however, is not said to be a king. There is no need to slide him westwards into

Glywysing as Dark does. He might equally be the military commander or leader of the bureaucratic rulers of the Dobunni (for argument's sake) as a tribal 'king'. Gildas calls all the tyrants kings when he goes on to deliver his prophetic analogies, yet another indication that, if a distinction exists, it is not one Gildas acknowledges terminologically. All this confirms my view that Gildas and other sixth-century Britons used a variety of titles and descriptions for their rulers, without any systematic logic we can detect.

Dark is reluctant to speculate that any forms of authority operate in sub-Roman Britain above the *civitas* level. Gildas, however, provides evidence that higher levels of rule must exist. The roles of Vortigern and Ambrosius are not explicable if they are simply *civitas* kings.

First we must reconsider Gildas's categorical statement '*habet Britannia rectores*' – that Britain has *rectores* (provincial governors) – in his own time. Hitherto, we have dismissed this as yet another synonym for the *Duces*, *Reges*, *Iudices* and *Tyranni* who rule Britain. Although we may balk at taking him so literally, is it possible that he means us to understand them as different or higher than the kings? The evidence is that 'Roman provincial governor' is the only sense in which Gildas uses *Rector*. He writes of *Rectores* twice more: rebellious Britons during the Boudiccan revolt butcher the Roman *Rectores* and Magnus Maximus despoils Britain of her *Rectores* during his usurpation. So there is a good case for seeing this as meaning something particular. In both cases, low-level rulers, of a British tribal nature, are obviously excluded. They have been taking part in the rebellion in the first case. In the second, usurping and cruel kings will be ruling Britain immediately after. If we only had these two passages, there would be no question but that Gildas was using the word in its technical Roman sense. Only the prejudice that he 'cannot' be using it in this sense in his introduction prevents it being understood in this way.

One of the features of the good generation before Gildas's time is that 'kings, officials and ordinary citizens served in their allotted roles' or 'kept to their appointed station'. Does Gildas mean they were subject to the legitimate governor of the province? The *publici* could be the officials of non-royal bureaucratic government, again contrasted with the kings.

One indication that, in some sense, provinces continued beyond the end of Roman rule is that the four met different fates in the fifth and sixth centuries. This is demonstrable by the patterns of Saxon settlement. Maxima Caesarienses was settled along the lines of the former *civitates*, with concentrations in strategic areas. The *civitas* name of Kent survived. This indicates settlement while the Roman-style administration was still functioning. Flavia Caesariensis had settlements of Saxons with little regard to the Roman patterns, as though carried out in a disorganised free-for-all. The two Britannias were hardly settled at all. Britannia Prima would come to be dominated by warlike kings while Britannia Secunda saw Roman static defences re-employed. It is likely these differences arose from different provincial responses to the crises of the mid-fifth century.

There are basically two models for how provincial authority could still exist. If it is independent from the *civitates*, then some degree of consent must exist. The *civitates* would have to provide food, supplies and manpower to the administration, which had no hinterland for itself. Perhaps more plausible is that the provincial ruler is also one of the *civitas* rulers, using his local power-base to achieve hegemony. This is the way the Saxon Bretwaldas derived their power. In this case, the King of the Dobunni (for instance) might exercise authority over the other *civitates* in his province.

Another indication that the concept of the Province of Britannia Prima still existed in Gildas's day is that, as far as we can tell, all the tyrants he denounces come from that area, as Higham points out. We might even suggest that the survival of the name Britannia for the whole island was influenced by the two provinces where sub-Roman/British rule survived being those called Britannia.

Could Arthur be one of these provincial governors, of Britannia Prima perhaps, in the previous generation? Is that the reason he is distinguished as fighting with 'the Kings of the Britons'? If they are the rulers of *civitas* kingdoms and he is not, this would make sense of the apparent distinction made by Nennius.

Alternatively, the governor of Britannia Prima might be the coordinating authority, employing Arthur as his *Magister Militum* to lead the British rulers against the Saxons. This does not preclude any of the other suggestions. Arthur could be a sub-king, king, non-king or non-Briton to occupy this role. He could be chosen by the provincial governor or, as happened elsewhere in the west, he could have dominated the provincial government by virtue of his military power. Commitment to the province as a whole could explain why even Gildas's tyrants chase thieves energetically all over the country. If Arthur acted in a similar way, it could explain his presence in Ercing and Builth. They would be in different kingdoms but parts of a single province.

Another possibility is that the kingdoms of Britannia Prima are linked by dynastic alliances in the previous generation, explaining why three of the kingdoms seem to have been ruled by lion's whelps. In Gildas's time, hegemony over the province might have been imposed by coercive power. Maglocunus, Dragon of the Island, is able to depose or kill other tyrants. In the Badon generation, however, the import of Gildas's approval of the kings, officials and private persons who kept to their stations is that they consented to a legitimate overlord.

An indication that some kind of provincial responsibility lingered in the minds of the northern successors is the fact that the northern forts were maintained. These included locations already discussed: Cataractonum (Catraeth of the *Gododdin*), Vinovium (Castellum Guinnion?) and Camboglanna (Castlesteads). These were occupied and fortified by some kind of successor authority.

The forts ran across the territories of the Kings of the Carvetii and Brigantes. The kings must have cooperated with a revived Roman office for mutual defence, possibly a governor of Britannia Secunda, or a new *Dux Britanniarum*. If Arthur held one of these positions, then we might imagine him fighting at a civil war centred on forts like Camboglanna.

The official responsible for the forts, according to the *Notitia Dignitatum*, was the *Dux Britanniarum*. This role, as we have noted, has often been attributed to Arthur by modern historians. There is no sign of the forts having a single administrative centre or a hinterland as distinct from the *civitates* in which they were found. The *Dux* must therefore have acted in cooperation with the kings of the Britons. A hypothetical Arthur as *Dux Britanniarum* would have defended the Wall and adjacent areas against attacks from the north and maybe the south as well.

The *Dux Britanniarum* controlled the frontier troops stationed in the region of Hadrian's Wall. By the fifth century, these border troops were often hereditary, making it far more likely that they had been left behind by usurpers like Maximus when they used British forces in their struggles for power. However, all sources' view of the end of Roman Britain hinge on the idea that, without Roman garrisons, the Walls cannot repel the invading Picts and Scots. It is the clear import of the Honorian rescript, and Zosimus's account of the Britons' own response to the barbarians, that there is no major surviving Roman military presence in the island. The whole rationale for the Saxon settlement, to fight the Picts and the Scots, is that there were no continuing garrisons in the Wall area. Dark provides an answer to this conundrum: his analysis of the *Dux Britanniarum* forts shows that, while they are not continually occupied from the period of Roman rule, they are reoccupied and fortified during the Badon generation, perhaps when a new *Dux* was set up (Dark 2000).

An invigorated British resistance, combined with a sense of responsibility for the Province of Britannia Secunda or the Diocese, might have seen the British appoint their own *Dux Britanniarum*. *Publici* (state officials) served in their correct ranks, as Gildas says. If Nennius is actually making a point about the different nature of Arthur's power as *Dux*, against the kings (Roman-derived and military in nature – as opposed to the civil, taxing and quasi-judicial role of a king) then his description does make a lot of sense. Arthur would be appointed by British kings acting responsibly for the good of the wider region. He is fighting with the authority of the kings of the Britons, but he was himself the *Dux Bellorum*.

It is hard, unfortunately, to see how Arthur's role can be limited in this way. There is no obvious reason for the frontier-defending *Dux Britanniarum* to be associated with wars in South Wales or the Chilterns. The only model which explains this is that the whole military structure, with both *Dux* and *Comes Britanniarum*, had been re-established. Arthur could even, in this theory, have been the *Comes Britanniarum*, his northern victories attributable to his support for the *Dux*. This has brought us back to that old theory of Arthur the cavalry leader, by other means! The existence of the *Comes* would imply other levels of authority. Even more than the *Dux*, the *Comes* required extensive civil support. He had no territorial hinterland to supply his troops, no fortified bases and no widespread supply depots. For a military command of this nature, there would have to be a supportive civil authority at provincial level.

Furthermore, if the *Dux Britanniarum* were supported by a mobile reserve, there would have to be a coordinating *Magister Militum*. It is almost impossible to imagine any organised relief for static garrisons which would not rely on a single strategic commander. Arthur as *Magister Militum* across the British provinces fits the evidence very well. If we look at the northern archaeological evidence from another perspective, we might suggest that, rather than being the *Dux Britanniarum*, Arthur was the man who drove out the Saxons and re-established the frontier command to consolidate his victories. We know Saxons must have been in the Wall zone precisely because they were Vortigern's defence against the Picts, as Gildas tells us. Arthur as *Magister Militum*, fighting with the kings of the Britons (presumably the Brigantes, Carventii and perhaps the Gododdin), who provided troops and supplies, could have driven out the Saxon frontier troops, re-established control of bases such as Castellum Guinnion and hunted the fugitives into the Caledonian Forest. British garrisons could then have been re-established under a subordinate official, with guarantees from the kings to maintain them. Peace treaties guaranteed by religious sanctions are a feature of the next generation and we can imagine such an agreement to uphold the system. Small wonder that the Gododdin, coming to support the southern Britons by driving Saxons from one of the region's forts, could draw an analogy with Arthur and his battles.

The idea that Arthur was a *Magister Militum*, perhaps supporting the command of the *Dux Britanniarum* in the north and the *Comes Britanniarum* in the south, for successor provincial authorities makes a lot of sense of the evidence. It explains that his military power was different in nature from 'the kings of the Britons' and why he could be found fighting across the Diocese. It may be that Arthur switched voluntarily from one province to another, was wooed by greater rewards or was deployed in different provinces by a residual diocese-wide authority.

This raises the vexed question of whether there was a 'ruler of Britain' in the late fifth/early sixth centuries. The Saxons had a vague concept of overlordship, embodied by the great kings, the Bretwaldas. Later kings were apparently acknowledged as Bretwaldas, and the tradition was passed on that late fifth-century Aelle and mid-sixth-century Caelin had been as well. Was this a relic of the concept of 'diocesan' rule? If there could be only one Great King/Bretwalda in the island at any one time, is it not possible that the long gap between Aelle and Caelin might have been filled by a British overlord?

There is ample evidence that Britons before and after the Arthurian period could conceive of a great king of Britain. Gildas hints, and all subsequent writers infer, that Vortigern was 'the ruler of all Britain'. The epithet *Insularis Draco*, as we have seen, could mean rule across the whole island. Nennius, too, conceived of Ambrosius and Mailcunus as being great kings of Britain.

We cannot detect such a figure from direct evidence, but diocese-wide authority, based on the *Vicarius* (Roman governor) or an imposed high kingship on the Bretwalda analogy would make the British resistance more understandable. Having a single strategic direction would have been a great boon to the British. This seems a pretty clear reading of Gildas's kings, public and private persons keeping to their station, which implies subordination to a legitimate authority.

We have to say that, if any sort of diocesan ruler did exist, capable of moving Arthur's forces around the island to cooperate with the kings of the Britons, then he has left no independent trace in tradition, legend or history. Some, doubtless prominent, members of the Badon generation did sink without trace. The children of Ambrosius were real, their own children were contemporaries of Gildas. Yet no trace of them survives in any later source, however legendary. However, the disappearance of the man who coordinated the second generation of the British resistance from history really defies belief. In other words, if such a man existed, it would be inconceivable that he was not Arthur.

We do have one other pre-eminent ruler of the period with whom a comparison can be made – Vortigern. Was Vortigern *the* tyrant of Britain? It is not clear if Gildas imagined Britain still having a central authority by this time. The kings of the civil wars replace one another, for example, rather than ruling in hostility over smaller kingdoms. By the time of the fight-back, Britain does have multiple kings who '*suum quique ordinem servarunt*' – 'serve according to their rank'. At what point in the transition between diocesan rule and multiple kingdoms did Vortigern come?

The settlement patterns show provinces acting separately. The implication is that Vortigern is more than a *civitas* king. If he is not the ruler of the whole diocese, then he must rule Maxima Caesariensis, the province of the fifth-century settlements. This would give him some interest in stemming the seaborne raids of Picts and Scots on his coast. The two provinces called Britannia, however, would be those most vulnerable to these attacks, but do not have Saxon settlements.

Historia Brittonum associates Vortigern with the western province. If this is true, the only explanation of their long range of authority is that either Vortigern or the council have authority over the whole of Britain. The Province of Maxima Caesariensis had to be coerced or persuaded into accepting Saxon settlement by rulers concerned with or coming from Britannia Prima or Secunda. The diocesan framework is the only one which makes sense of all the information. Even if the *Historia* evidence of a western Vortigern is not accepted, Gildas supports the concept too. The Saxons, in his account, are settled in the eastern part of the Island. That their employers are in the west is made explicit when the mercenaries do not receive their due supplies. They do not just turn on cities such as London, around which their settlements can be detected by archaeology. They raged from sea to sea, that is into the western provinces, to seek redress.

An alternative is that the tyrant and council have nothing to do with existing structures, a high-kingship, a rule by force of some kind. This is unlikely, as the idea of settling the Saxons seems a purely Roman concept, clearly not understood by later writers, who can only see it as mindless folly, perhaps prompted by lust. Gildas used the technical vocabulary of the Roman Foederati/Laeti system to describe the deals and disputes with the Germanic settlers.

The clear implication is that Vortigern and the council represent, at the very least, provincial or more likely diocesan-level authority. We can speculate therefore that it is at this level that both the Saxon takeover and the British resistance take place.

We posited that Gildas and Nennius mean that the distinguishing feature of the Saxon revolt against Vortigern was that Saxons, perhaps with Hengist as *Magister Militum*, took over the diocesan government. This is supported by the Gallic Chronicles of 452 and 511. Their reports of Saxon rule in Britain are usually considered as derived from the intensive Saxon settlement in the areas nearest to Gaul. This ignores the fact that travel between Gaul and Britain was not limited to the 'ferry crossings' of the Pas de Calais. If Britons could turn up in Armorica and Mediterranean goods in Tintagel, there is ample reason to suppose a Gallic chronicler would hear news from outside the occupied zone.

What the chroniclers actually wrote is that in *c.* 441 'The Britains [the British Provinces] . . . yielded to the power of the Saxons'; 'The Britains . . . were reduced into the power of the Saxons' (Snyder 1998). It seems clear that the rule of the provinces has been taken over, not that thousands of Saxons have flooded into the Kent and Sussex coast.

If some form of higher authority, above that of the *civitates* kings, existed in the Badon generation, it is quite possible it continued to Gildas's time. We are told that, just as when the Saxons first arrived, this generation has a Pharaoh. Gildas says his generation's Pharaoh is heading for disaster, driven on by his reckless horsemen, the tyrants of Britannia Prima. *Historia Brittonum* shares the view that Arthur's torch has been passed on. It is Outigirn who leads the fight against the Saxons in Mailcunus's day.

Historia Brittonum supports the view that the Saxon fighters' power or authority is different in nature from that of the kings. Vortimer leads the first fight, although his father is the main king. Arthur is, as we have seen, given a title implying military power against that of the *reges* he commands. Outigirn exists alongside Mailcunus, the great king of the Britons. Gildas's version, in which Maglocunus is *Insularis Draco* while at the same time being in the retinue of Pharaoh, harmonises with this.

Thus, Dark's analysis of the *civitates* origins of the sub-Roman kingdoms fits perfectly with the model of the Arthurian period we have deduced from Gildas and from Nennius and its supporting material. Furthermore, the *civitates/* kingdoms model necessarily implies, even in Gildas's geographically limited picture, that some sort of legitimate higher authority must have existed in the Badon generation. This would be established by the Roman Ambrosius Aurelianus, and utilised by Arthur in the Badon generation, characterised by the united kings and lesser Britons keeping to their stations. We know that Gildas must view this higher authority as legitimate as he is not tarred with the name of tyrant or Pharaoh – which in turn implies that it is a return to the official Roman structures, rather than the imposed hegemony which characterised the earlier tyrants.

Historia Brittonum has exactly the same picture, both explicitly with the *Dux Bellorum*, Arthur, existing at the same time as the kings of the Britons, and implicitly in the battle-list and its origins, which spread his activities across the *civitates* and even the provinces.

KING ARTHUR?

The combination of sources so far has yielded several plausible roles for Arthur, the victor of Badon Hill. He could be a sub-king of Ercing, of lesser rank to the main kings, but giving him access to his own warband and lands. This would make sense of his South Welsh connections. He equally could be the over-king of one of the *civitates*, Trinovantes, Dubonni, Durotriges or Brigantes, which did not yield lasting British dynasties. All these are in the war-zone and could provide us with a 'King Arthur'. He could even be a great king, with power over several British kings, as medieval legends imagined him.

Other analysis has suggested that Arthur was a military figure, perhaps even of non-British origin, employed as *Magister Militum* by a dominant *civitas* king or, much more likely, by a coordinating authority such as a successor provincial or diocesan ruler. His power would therefore be different in origin to that of the *civitas* kings. That may, however, create a false impression of the extent of his power. Dark Age experience shows that the controller of the soldiers could soon become the power behind the throne, or even the one sitting on it. There was usually only a thin line between what constituted a *Magister Militum* and the 'ruler of a kingdom'.

I have specifically avoided phrasing these as contradictory alternatives. Alcock used the analogy of Wellington and Arthur, arguing that Wellington and Waterloo are so strongly linked that the commander's name would be assumed in any reference to his victory. We might say that, if detailed knowledge were lost, it would be difficult to judge Wellington's status. We could find sources to show he was an Irish soldier, an Indian general, an English duke, a Spanish grandee, a British field marshal and the prime minister of the United Kingdom. The reality is that these are not conflicting possibilities but changing roles during a successful military and political career.

There is no reason why Arthur should not have been a non-royal, perhaps non-British, military figure who came to rule a British kingdom or sub-kingdom while also being the *Magister Militum* for civil authorities. One would expect that, even if a successful Dark Age general started in subordinate or non-royal role, victory would pretty soon be translated into civil power. The *Historia*'s battle-list might read as a progression showing how Dux Arthur, fighting with the kings of the Britons, comes to a final victory when he alone now has the power to turn back the Saxons.

Arthur the Warrior

If Arthur was primarily a warrior and warleader, what sort of wars did he fight? Discussion has been clouded by a fixation on Arthur as a leader of heavy cavalry, often no more than an attempt to preserve the image of medieval 'knights'. Battle sites in forests, river mouths, hills, castles and cities all look unlikely ones for such a force. Gildas and Nennius give sparse information, but the warlike *Gododdin* provides, unsurprisingly, ample material. Supporting explanation is supplied by the early Welsh poems in the *Black Book of Carmarthen*. These may date back at least to the era of *Annales Cambriae*, and they work in much the same poetic idiom as *Y Gododdin*.

Gildas's vocabulary is drawn extensively from the Latin Bible and from Vergil, and may not always be appropriate to his own time. He says the

Romans left Britain, stripping the island of all its armed soldiers and military supplies. The remaining Britons were ignorant of all ways of warfare. After twice coming to their aid, the Romans advised them to arm themselves with the *ensis* (a general word for sword), the *hasta* (a spear that could also be thrown) and the *pelta* (a light skirmisher's shield). These contrast with the *gladii* (short stabbing swords) and *scuta* (large rectangular shields) used in earlier times (DEB 6). They also left '*exemplaria instituendorum armorum*', which could be training manuals or less specific instructions on how to use them. The *ensis* and the *hasta* evidently took on. The tyrant Constantine is twice described as using them and they were the weapons Maglocunus employed against his uncle's forces.

Horsemen are referred to again briefly, when Cuneglassus is called a rider, or horsemen, of many. He is also described as a 'charioteer'. Gildas may have meant that he rode a chariot into battle, as he goes on to say that Cuneglassus fought with weapons peculiar to himself. On the other hand, there is no reason to suppose a military context, as we learn from Gildas that some Britons travel on horseback or in vehicles and so consider themselves superior to other men. Gildas writes evocatively of cavalry warfare as practised by the Roman rescue force, yet does not say they passed on the technique when they left (DEB 17).

The military organisation of the Britons is only touched on. Revealingly, the companions of the kings are called 'soldiers in the same company', suggesting a military atmosphere at court. The only formation mentioned is the generic 'battle-line'. Fighting men are called soldiers, and they fight for booty or reward.

Historia Brittonum has little to offer on warfare. The Roman army includes soldiers and horses, and is controlled by *duces*. *Miles* (soldier) is a word used for warriors in all armies, including the Saxons and Arthur himself. However, *exercitus* (army) is only used for anti-Saxon forces. There is no suggestion that armour is worn. The Severn Bore, for instance, is said to be able to over-whelm armies, with their 'clothes' and horses.

In contrast, *Y Gododdin* is fertile with military details. The weapons used are again the sword and the spear. Spears are the more common, as supported by archaeology. They are long and yellow, usually of ash wood. Spearheads are 'square-pointed', presumably in section. Their sockets are dark blue metal, though their tips are only ever red – with blood. They can be used for cutting and tearing or thrusting and pushing. They are also thrown. Swords are bright blue, shining, sharpened and used for swift, slashing blows.

Shields are as common as spears and are used in conjunction with them. The most frequent word for them, *sgwyd/ysgwyd*, is derived from the Latin *scutum*, but these are not rectangular. Other words used are *cylchwy* and *rhodawg/rhodawr* (circular and round shield). They are light and broad and generally white, though some are decorated with gold. Although they make a noise like thunder when struck, they are not very strong. If described, they are always 'shattered', 'splintered' or 'not solid'. Even spears can shatter rather than pierce them. A reasonable explanation is that they lacked a strengthening metal rim. In this, they correspond to the *pelta* mentioned by Gildas, which in the late Roman army were edged with leather.

The warriors of the *Gododdin* are armoured. Their armour is dark blue or iron. It takes the form of the *llurig*, derived from the Latin *lorica*, in this period a shirt of bronze or iron scales or mail. Probably the latter is intended as one warrior is specifically 'mail clad'. Limb armour and helmets are not mentioned.

The warriors fight on foot and on horseback. Their horses are fleet, slender and long-legged. The horsemen fight 'in dark blue armour, with shields, spear shafts held aloft with sharp points, shining *loricae* and swords'. Spears are held or thrown from moving horses. One warrior uses strokes, then spears, from his slender bay horse. A saddle is mentioned, which must have helped keep them steady. They are heavy cavalry, making close-order charges against formed bodies. They charge swiftly against enemy spears, trampling on arms and weapons. They tear through the armies with surging fury. Blood flows up to the thighs of the riders. The infantry fight in close ranks, with 'the best men in the forefront', 'the chosen warriors in the front rank'. The mass of men is called a 'stronghold of shields', a 'wall of battle', a 'stockade' or 'battle-pen'. It stands steadfast. Spears point out from it as, when two forces meet, there is a pressure of spears and a clash of spears. Spears are shattered at the start of battle. The poet refers frequently to the noise of battle. Aside from the thunder of struck shields, there is uproar and fury. Warriors laugh and sing a song of war. They shout a battle cry and 'after the cry of jubilation there was silence'. After the battle, they give no quarter in pursuit of the Saxons, whom they cut down like rushes. They collect booty.

The engagement in which the Gododdin fell is conventionally described as 300 men against 100,000. These extreme figures are found only in the later verses, not in those likely to derive from the sixth century. Usually in the poem where sizes of groups and armies are given, they are smaller than a thousand men. The command structure of the Gododdin is not made clear. They seem to be divided into three sections, but we cannot tell who was in overall command.

The *Black Book of Carmarthen* poems, *Gereint, Pa gur, Stanzas on Graves*, provide a correlation with the previous sources. Spears are made of ash wood, with sharpened blue points. They may be thrown. Swords are used and in *Gereint son of Erbin* edges of blades are in contact. Shields are employed. In *Pa gur*, as in *Y Gododdin*, they are shattered and fragmentary. However, the only mentions of armour are in the *Stanzas on Graves*, where some of the dead were formerly armoured horsemen. One of Gereint's warriors has blood on his head and is presumably not wearing a helmet.

In the poems, horsemen wield spears in battle. Even when they lack armour, they are used in a heavy cavalry role. Horses gory in battle charge against resisting forces. A poet sees the spurs of men who would not flinch from dread of the spears. The horses are magnificent swift racers, usually white in colour, though sometimes this is caused by sweat. In the *Stanzas on Graves* there is a reference to warhorses being specially bred. Guaurthur of the Gododdin bred horses as well, possibly for military use.

Gereint's battle begins with a shout after which there is a terrible resistance, a terrible impulsion and a fearful return. Many armies begin their battles with a distinctive shout, and this may be what is implied by the poets. The fifth-century *Life of St Germanus* tells how the saint organised a British army to oppose the Picts and the Scots. Following Germanus's lead, the army gives a shout of 'Alleluia' which frightens the attackers away before battle is joined. This may be the first example of the British 'battle-shout'.

Forces are led by a 'regulator of hosts', 'one who marshalled the armies', 'the conductor of the toil'. In *Gereint* this figure is Arthur, which exactly parallels Nennius' description of him as '*Dux Bellorum*' (warleader, or leader of the campaigns). *Pa gur* gives the figures of 600 and 900 men for the size of the forces.

The poems give a consistent picture of Arthurian warfare, supporting the terser accounts of the Latin historians. They may not tell the whole story, of course. Close order charges make for much better poems than less dramatic tactics. They do, however, give a first glimpse of those battlefields where 'Arthur fought in those days'.

FROM HISTORY

The early sources are coherent and plausible. Not only does Arthur, military leader of the kings of the Britons between Ambrosius and Maglocunus, fit the facts, it is the only explanation which makes sense of them: the victory of Badon Hill, the reactivation of the northern command, the defeat of the Saxons across the island, the good order shown by contemporary kings and their subjects. All of this can scarcely have come about by chance. They are the evidence which both demonstrates and requires the existence of a British leader of battles. Of course, we have no way of being certain what his name was, but a name he undoubtedly had. No other name has ever been applied to him by any British writer, no matter how eager to aggrandise their ancestors or dynastic founders. Under such circumstances it seems churlish to deny him that last piece of recognition and argue that he was not Arthur.

 PART TWO

INTO LEGEND

7

ARTHUR'S BRAVE MEN

It seems there was an Arthur and that he was a very significant figure in Britain at the time suggested by the romances. At that level, we have answered the question whether he existed. A large number of basic Arthurian features, however, remain to be established or dismissed. Moreover, there is much in the picture which does not feature in any standard image of Arthur.

Those who dismiss all Arthurian material as legendary should consider how few of the episodes we have studied entered into legend at all. No legend, oral, poetic, romantic or pseudo-historical has survived to shed light on the incident where Arthur killed his son Anir. The battle at Castellum Guinnion, on which Nennius dwelt at length, vanished completely. We shall never know why Arthur carried the image of the Virgin Mary on his shoulders for three days and nights. Most of the other battles in the list will never reappear. Outigirn features in no tales, only a misplaced reference in the Harleian genealogies. Even the great battle of Badon all but disappeared from the traditions of the Britons. Of all the details the written sources have so far furnished us about Arthur, only the boar hunt with his dog Cabal and his death alongside Medraut at Camlann can truly be said to be the stuff of later legends.

The loss is greater when we consider the historical material in Gildas. Most of the characters we have identified are never heard of again. The twelfth-century writer Geoffrey of Monmouth incorporated Constantine, Aurelius, Vortiporius and Maglocunus in his history, but based purely on what he found in Gildas. There is nothing about Vortiporius's good father, Maglocunus's uncle or any of Aurelius's family. Perhaps the strangest loss to legend was the family of Ambrosius Aurelianus. He had children, and they had children in their turn, but they were never to feature in any tale, genealogy or history. The legends which spread throughout the Middle Ages had little in common with the historical material studied so far.

In contrast, it is worth considering what aspects of the legends have yet to be encountered. Many modern Arthurian theories take the concept of Camelot as a starting point. Place-names, strategic locations and impressive archaeological remains are pressed into service to identify Arthur's supposed capital. Yet nothing in what we have studied has given us any reason to think that Arthur had any capital or single base at all. His campaigns seem energetic, ranging across the country, through rivers, forts, mountains, forests and cities. Gildas specifically denigrates the idea of fleeing to fortified locations, making it unlikely that his victorious Britons followed such a tactic. If any capitals or bases are implied, then they are those of Arthur's allies, the kings of the Britons. Even they, like all Dark Age rulers, would have led itinerant lives, moving their courts constantly to oversee their lands and collect supplies. In the re-fortified defences of the north we see no single Camelot – rather, a complete military network. The nearest name to Camelot we have encountered is Camlann, site of the last battle.

Avalon has not featured in the evidence. Neither has the Grail, the Round Table, the sword Excalibur (stuck in a stone or rising from a lake), or foreign wars. This suggests that theories which rely on identifying such features in the historical or archaeological record are likely to be wide of the mark. There is no need to suppose that any of them figured in Arthur's historical career.

Perhaps most surprising, we have not encountered any of Arthur's men. He is not connected with a fellowship of famous knights, or a warband of any sort. There is nothing to suggest he led heavily armoured cavalry, carried a dragon banner or even rode a horse into battle. These are all features of later legends, not Dark Age history.

How can we draw a line between material we can legitimately consider historical, and that which is probably legendary? We have a reasonable chronological criterion in that material written after *Annales Cambriae* and the tenth-century recensions of *Historia Brittonum* is unlikely to be completely independent of the sources we have studied. In their written form, they were being collected, copied and studied from this time. Material which post-dates this must be judged, where possible, on its provenance. We can also compare each source with what we have already deduced about fifth/sixth-century reality.

Between *Annales Cambriae* and the explosion of Arthurian romances at the end of the twelfth century, three types of source have been proposed as offering additional evidence for the reign of Arthur. These include Welsh legends, thought of as the final expression of an oral transmission stretching back over the centuries. Next are the lives of the saints, and related ecclesiastical material, where churches may have preserved details of Gildas and his contemporaries. Finally, there is the most important Arthurian work of all, the one which established Arthur's 'historical' career and has influenced subsequent interpretations of his time, Geoffrey of Monmouth's *History of the Kings of Britain*. The romances themselves fall outside the scope of this book, as they are clearly works of fiction, drawing loosely on an established historical background, but by no means bound by it.

WELSH POEMS

By the late thirteenth century, the Britons faced defeat. Llywellyn ap Gruffydd, Prince of Wales and 'descendant' of Maglocunus, was killed. His adversary, Edward I of England, descendant of the West Saxons, sent the former's head to the Tower of London and his regalia, including 'The crown of King Arthur' to join the royal treasures in Westminster. For Edward, an Arthurian enthusiast himself, the stories of Arthur would live on in French romances and in Latin histories, not in the recitals of Welsh bards.

It is against this background that the first surviving Welsh Arthurian materials came to be written down. Works which had doubtless circulated orally for many years, even centuries, are first found in manuscripts of the late thirteenth and early fourteenth centuries. Without the patronage of Welsh-speaking princes, there was no other way for these legends to survive.

The oldest of the major manuscripts, the *Black Book of Carmarthen*, was written in the late thirteenth century specifically, it seems, to preserve the ancient traditions. The poems it contains vary in age, but there is little doubt that some of them are very ancient indeed; exactly how ancient is a matter of much debate. For our purposes, it is enough that some of those referring to Arthur were written between the tenth-century composition of *Annales Cambriae* and the establishment of an 'authorised' version of Arthurian history in the twelfth century. The three we will consider could be at least as old as the *Annales* and the Vatican Recension.

One of the poems is entitled *Gereint fil. Erbin* (Gereint son of Erbin). The poet describes how he 'sees' Gereint and his men, fighting at the battle of Llongborth: 'At Llongborth were slain Geraint's brave men from the lowlands of Diuvneint (Devon)'. Medieval genealogies made Gereint a ruler of Devon and Cornwall, a reasonable inference from the poem. In these genealogies,

Erbin was the son of Constantine of Cornwall, the tyrant denounced by Gildas. A King Gerent of the Britons is mentioned in the Anglo-Saxon Chronicle as fighting against the West Saxons in 710. This cannot have been the same person, but indicates that the name was in use by a southern British dynasty, presumably Diuvneint. There is nothing in the poem to confirm that Gereint son of Erbin is either a grandson of Constantine or an early eighth-century king. He may have been neither.

Gereint's adversaries are not named. *Llongborth* appears to mean 'warship port'. It is popularly identified with Langport on the Parrett in Somerset. The name is similar, and it would have been on the borders of Diuvneint. This, as we have seen, would have been a viable location for sixth-century warfare, but could equally represent an eastward thrust by a later ruler of Devon.

The verse before that identifying Gereint's men as coming from Diuvneint reads:

> *In Llongborth I saw Arthur's*
> *brave men, they hewed with steel*
> *Emperor, leader in toil.*

The poem is often misread as 'In Llongborth I saw Arthur'. This is a product of the obscurity of the language and the fact that Arthur ends the line and, as in *Y Gododdin*, is the rhyme for the other lines. There is, however, now no doubt that the poet sees Arthur's men at the battle. Arthur is clearly present himself, just as Gereint is, confirmed by the description of him as conductor of the toil.

Ashe argues that the verse preserves a tradition that Arthur's men carried on the fight after his death (Ashe 1982). If so, this is the sole piece of evidence. For Gildas, the fighters of the Badon generation are forgotten. Arthur's men have never previously been mentioned.

Does this verse mean the men of Diuvneint are like those of Arthur, the heroes of an earlier age? This would make a similar comparison to that of the *Gododdin*. If the poet implies, literally, that both Gereint and Arthur are at the same battle, then either he has wrongly dated one of them or Gereint cannot be either of the later characters above.

If we disregard later material contextualising him two generations after Gildas, perhaps Gereint son of Erbin actually did fight with Arthur at the battle of Llongborth. If he is ruler of Dumnonia, then his fighting alongside

Arthur is wholly consistent with what we have deduced so far. It is interesting that Arthur is given both a Roman title, indicative of the different nature of his rule, and a Welsh title which is a virtual synonym of *Dux Bellorum*.

Llongborth is not listed as one of Arthur's twelve battles, but it might be another name for one of them. A 'warship port' might be located on any of the riverine locations. If it is Langport, then this might have been one of the battles in the Linnuis (Ilchester?) region with Dubglas as an alternative name for the Parrett. Losing Gereint and his men might have made such a victory pyrrhic and led to further campaigns in the area. Alternatively, it could be part of a civil war, after the battle of Badon. Llongborth would border on the *civitas* of the Durotriges, after all. It is exceedingly unlikely the poem means that Gereint and Arthur were adversaries.

The poem has one other important aspect to it: the first introduction of the concept of 'Arthur's brave men'. Before exploring this further, let us look at another of the Black Book poems, the *Stanzas on Graves*.

The *Stanzas* describe or locate the graves of various heroes, some of whom feature in later legends, others of whom are unknown. Two tell of the grave of Owain, son of Urien Rheged; three describe the grave of Cynon, son of Clydno Eiddyn of the Gododdin. Bradwen, given as a comparison in *Y Gododdin*, also has his grave mentioned. Other verses refer to various Welsh locations like Llanbadarn.

Two of the verses are of particular interest. One reads

> *The grave of the son of Osvran is in Camlan,*
> *After many a slaughter the grave of Bedwyr.*

The other

> *The grave of March, the grave of Gwythur,*
> *The grave of Gwgawn Gleddyvrudd (Red Sword);*
> *A mystery to the world, the grave of Arthur.*
> (Coe and Young 1995)

The last line, '*Anoeth bin u bedd Arthur*', is translated in various ways from the apocalyptic 'concealed to Doomsday, the grave of Arthur', to the prosaic 'unknown is the grave of Arthur'. It could be understood as meaning that Arthur's grave is at a place called Anoeth. Earlier in the poem we hear of the

Tribes of Oeth and Anoeth. In the prose tale *Culhwch and Olwen*, Arthur's porter says that he (and possibly Arthur as well) has been in Caer Oeth and Anoeth. The context indicates some fantastic, faraway place.

The stanza is commonly taken to mean that no one knows the location of the grave of Arthur, this in turn indicating the tradition that Arthur has no grave because he is still alive. This story was around in the early twelfth century, with Arthur awaited as a messianic Celtic deliverer. It was common when the *Stanzas* were written down. However, the only evidence we have from the tenth century, the earliest date for the *Stanzas*, is quite the opposite. He was known to be dead. This is stated as specifically as possible in *Annales Cambriae*. At the battle of Camlann, Arthur and Medraut fell down dead. No one else so described in the *Annales* is considered to be alive, so we have to conclude that Arthur's survival is a later development, perhaps partially derived from the *Stanzas*.

We might wonder why, if the grave of Arthur was simply unknown, it was included in the *Stanzas on Graves* at all. There must have been plenty of other figures the location of whose graves was unknown. It seems odd to put one of them in a poem whose sole intention is to record details of the graves.

The final possibility is that the grave is not unknown at all. *Anoeth* means a wonder or a marvel. It is the word used in the story of *Culhwch and Olwen* for the marvellous and seemingly impossible tasks set the hero by a giant. We already know from *Historia Brittonum* that in the ninth century Arthur was credited with a grave that was a marvel, one of the *Mirabilia* of Britain. It was a marvel because it could not be measured twice and yield the same result. In the *Historia* this grave is said to be built by Arthur for his son Anir, but as we can see, Anir and his death at Arthur's hands dropped rapidly out of tradition. There is no trace of it in any tenth-century or later source. It is surely conceivable that the grave of Arthur which is *Anoeth*, in the *Stanzas on Graves*, is the same one which the author of the *Mirabilia* claimed to have tried to measure. 'A marvel to the world is the tomb of Arthur.' What appears to be the same monument, outside Hay-on-Wye in ancient Ercing, is now called 'Arthur's Stone', not Anir's Grave.

The longest poem dealing with Arthur in the Black Book is called *Pa gur*. These are its opening words ('What man . . . ?') addressed to the porter, Gleuluid Gavaelvaur (Strong-Grip) by Arthur. There are many translations of this obscure poem. I will use the version recently published by Sims-Williams (Bromwich *et al.* 1991). Although the details differ from one translation to another, the basic premise is clear. Arthur and Cei Guin (fair Kei) are seeking admittance to the place which Gleuluid guards. The porter refuses to let them in until Arthur reveals who he is travelling with: '*Guir goreu im bid*', says Arthur, 'the best men in the world'. There seem to be about ten or eleven of them although counts vary both on which words are names, and which men are actually with Arthur and which have only taken part in others' exploits.

Kei is pre-eminent. He was named with Arthur at first, and his exploits are told at length. Kei slaughtered adversaries three at a time when Kelli was lost. He killed a witch in the hall of Awarnach, he pierced Pen Palach in the Dwellings of Disethach. He killed *Cinbin* (dog heads – a term of abuse or mythical monsters?) at Minit Eidin (the mountain of Edinburgh). He is a sword in battle, a strong leader, possibly a tall man, a man who could drink like four but kill like a hundred. If God had not brought it about, it would be impossible to kill Kei. He killed nine witches on the peak of Ystawingun; he went to Anglesey to kill lions and his shield was a polished mirror, or a broken fragment against the fearful *Cath Palug* (Palug's Cat), which used to eat nine-score champions.

To all intents and purposes, the poem is one in praise of Kei the monster-slayer. Arthur appears in the fourth line: '*Arthur a Chei guin*', providing the full rhyme for the previous line '*Tu gui ueyouln*' (what man asks it?). Arthur is not explained. We infer that he is the leader of the best men in the world, but he is nowhere linked to their exploits. Nothing which Kei did features any locations or actions previously connected with Arthur. Arthur is enigmatically said to be doing something while Kei is fighting in the hall of Awarnach, 'laughing', says Sims-Williams (Bromwich *et al.* 1991), 'playing', say Coe and Young, both presumably more accurately than Williams's earlier 'distributing gifts', but no more clear. Other than that, he plays no role in the poem (Coe and Young 1995, Williams 1972).

The Mountain of Eidin would be part of the Gododdin territory. Two more of the men, Anguas Edeinauc ('the winged' or 'the swift') and Lluch Llauynnauc (windy-hand) were defenders of Eidin, so presumably Kei was a defender too. This would put them in an area and (for what it is worth, given the opponents are dog-heads) a possible historical context. Speculation in the twelfth century would place Arthur's battle of Mount Agned at Edinburgh, but nothing we have seen so far would lead us to this supposition.

Kei fought with Llacheu, perhaps as an ally, though the line is ambiguous. By the time the Black Book was written, Llacheu was known as a son of

Arthur, equivalent to the romance figure Loholt. The romance *Perlesvaus* has Loholt killed by Keu (Kei), but we are going far beyond the evidence of *Pa gur* to surmise that this was the poet's implication (Bryant 1978).

Kei's only rival among the 'best men in the world' is Beduir Bedrydant (perfect sinew). Like Kei, Beduir killed by the hundred. 'His nature was ferocious as regards sword and shield.' He fought against Garuluid on the shores of Trywruid. Another warrior, Manawidan ab Llyr, was at Trywruid, too, where he bore shattered shields (or spears). This is of great interest, since Trywruid is the same name as Tribuit, site of Arthur's tenth battle. The Vatican recension glossed this as 'Which we call Traht Treuroit', exactly the Traetheu (plural of Traeth) Trywruid where Beduir fought.

There are three warriors mentioned in the poem, possibly described as wizards: Mabon, son of Modron, servant of Uther Pendragon; Kyscaint, son of Banon, and Guin Godybrion. Another warrior, Mabon, son of Mellt, would stain the grass with blood. Given that Modron derives from matrona (matron/mother) it could be that this is the same person as Mabon, son of Modron, with first a matronymic then a patronymic given, or they may be intended as separate warriors.

One familiar name is mentioned. Kei hurries before 'Rieu Emreis' (the kings or local lords of Ambrosius). What this means is unclear. Does the writer think that Emreis is a place, Dinas Emrys, for example, or are these the 'kings of the Britons' among whom Ambrosius is a (great) king, as the *Historia* tells us? Are the Rieu Emreis the warriors of the poem, and if not are they adversaries, allies or rivals of Kei? One thing seems fairly clear: if the Black Book spelling is original, the poem must post-date Nennius, who gives Ambrosius's name in the older form of *Embreis*.

The poem breaks off in the middle of the description of Kei's adversary, Palug's Cat. We cannot tell how many more men were to be enumerated (perhaps Medraut, Anir and Gereint, the other names so far associated with Arthur would have featured). We never find out to whom Arthur was seeking admittance.

For anti-Arthurians, this poem is the smoking gun. Up until this point, none of the references to Arthur seem inherently mythological. *Pa gur* makes no claims about Arthur, but here he seems clearly guilty by association. His companions are slayers of witches, lions and dog-heads. Arthur's overthrow of 940 men in a single charge is seen as of like nature to the hyperbole of Kei and Beduir killing by the hundred.

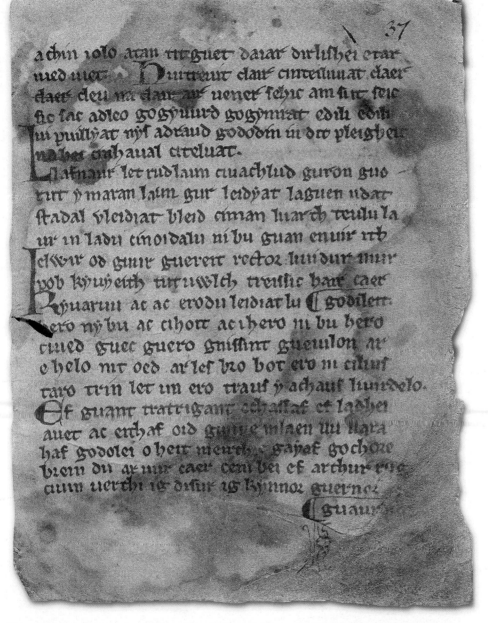

The earliest reference to Arthur. His name can be seen in the lower right corner. From *Y Gododdin*, in the fourteenth-century Book of Aneirin (*Cardiff Public Library Ms 1 (2.81) f37. Reproduced courtesy of Cardiff Council and the National Library of Wales*)

Catterick. There are no surface remains of the Roman fort, which stood in the foreground of the picture. (*Julie Hudson*)

Carn Cabal (Carn Gafallt). The cairn itself sits beyond the ridge to the right of the summit. (*Julie Hudson*)

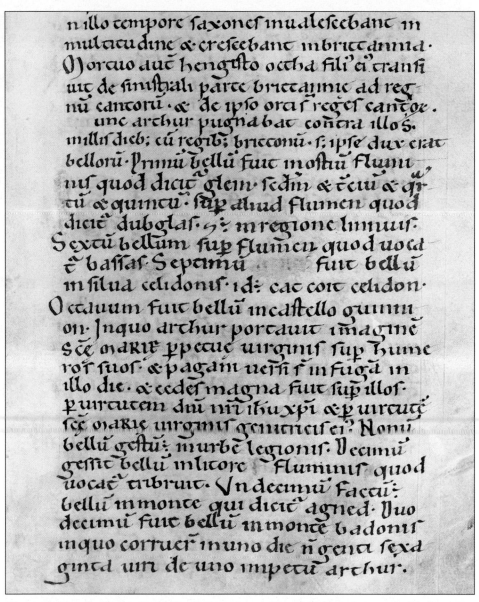

n illo tempore saxones inualescebant in
multitudine & crescebant inbrittannia.
Mortuo aut hengisto octha fili' eí transi
uit de sinistrali parte brittannie ad reg
nú cantorú. & de ipso orti s reges cantoꝛ.
    unc arthur pugnabat contra illos.
millis dieb; cú regib; brittonú. s; ipse dux erat
bellorú. Primú bellú fuit inostiú flumi
nis quod dicitꝛ glein. secdm & tciú & qr
tú & quintú. sup aliud flumen quod
dicitꝛ dubglas. q; in regione linnuis.
Sextú bellum sup flumen quod uocat
e bassas. Septimú   fuit bellú
in silua celidonis. i d; cat coit celidon.
Octauum fuit bellú incastello guinni
on. Inquo arthur portauit imagine
sce marie ppetue uirginis sup humeros
ros suos. & pagani uersi s in fuga in
illo die. & cedes magna fuit sup illos.
p uirtutem dni nri ihu xpi & p uirtute
sce marie uirginis genitricis ei? Nonú
bellú gestú; inurbe legionis. Decimú
gessit bellú in litore Fluminis quod
uocat' tribruit. Vndecimú factú;
bellú in monte qui dicitꝛ agned. Duo
decimú fuit bellú in monte badonis
inquo corruer' inuno die n̄ genta sexa
ginta uiri de uno impetu arthur.

The Arthurian battle-list. From the earliest manuscript of *Historia Brittonum*. (*Harleian Ms. 3859 f187. By permission of the British Library*)

The Arthur Stone, Dorstone, near Hay-on-Wye. Apparently the tomb of Anir from *Historia Brittonum*. (*Julie Hudson*)

Liddington Castle. A frequently suggested site for Mount Badon. (*Julie Hudson*)

Little Solsbury Hill, overlooking Bath. Suggested as a site for Mount Badon. (*Julie Hudson*)

Chisbury Camp at Great Bedwyn. Possible site of Bedanheafod/Mount Badon. (*Julie Hudson*)

Binchester. Possible site of Castellum Guinnion. The unexcavated defences lie some way beyond the wooden fence. (*Julie Hudson*)

Mouth of the River Glen, in Northumberland. The sub-Roman and Anglian centre of Yeavering dominates the site. (*Julie Hudson*)

Ivory carving of a fifth-century Roman general, said to be the *Magister Militum* Stilicho. Monza Cathedral. (© *The Bridgeman Art Library*)

The facing leaf of the 'Stilicho' diptych, showing the general's wife and son. (© *The Bridgeman Art Gallery*)

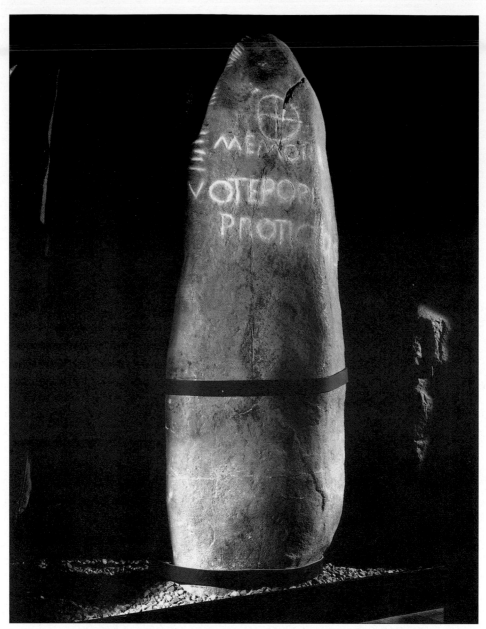

The Vortiporius Stone. The sixth-century inscribed stone from Dyfed bears the name of Voteporix Protector, identified with Gildas's Vortiporius. (*Crown copyright: Royal Commission on the Ancient and Historical Monuments of Wales*)

The *Annales Cambriae*. The Arthurian entries on Badon and Camlann can be seen in the third column. (*From the earliest manuscript, Harleian Ms. 3859 f190. By Permission of the British Library*)

Camboglanna (Castlesteads). View towards the valley which gives the site its name. Seen from the site of the Roman fort, levelled in the eighteenth century. (*Julie Hudson*)

Camlan on the Dyfi in North Wales. A possible site for the battle of Camlann. (*Julie Hudson*)

Slaughter Bridge, Camelford. Traditional site for the battle of Camlann. The sixth-century inscribed memorial stone lies on the bank of the Camel River. (*Julie Hudson*)

The Wansdyke. Part of the sub-Roman earthwork defending the land of the Durotriges, to the left, from attacks from the North. (*Julie Hudson*)

Caerleon. Identified, since the tenth century, with the City of the Legions. View across the Roman amphitheatre. (*Julie Hudson*)

The 'Arthur stone'. Inscribed slate bearing the name Artognou, excavated at Tintagel. (© *English Heritage Photo Library*)

There is no denying that Arthur is in very odd company here. Manawidan ab Llyr is none other than Mannanan Mac Lir, a euhemerised Celtic sea god in the Irish *Lebor Gabala*. He is the title character of one of the four medieval Welsh tales called the 'Mabinogi'. In both sources he is seen as a prehistoric figure, not a sixth-century Saxon-fighter. Mabon, son of Modron, is the most clearly mythological figure. He is the Celtic god Apollo Maponus, worshipped in pre-Christian times in the Hadrian's Wall area. Their presence does not give us much cause to hope that Fair Kei, Lluch Windy-hand and Anguas the Winged were real inhabitants of Dark Age Britain. And the same might also be said of the man who introduces them, Arthur himself.

The anti-Arthurian position is that *Pa gur* presents the mythical 'reality' from which a seemingly Dark Age historical figure has been spun. In this view, Arthur and his superhuman warriors are inhabitants of the timeless never-never land of the Mabinogion. These mythical fighters of lions, man-eating cats, hags and dog-headed creatures have been transposed to a historical milieu against the more realistic Saxons. Support for this comes from Arthur's inflated total of kills at the battle of Badon, his hunt for the boar Troynt and his association with a marvellous tomb.

Some of this could be cleared up by a more accurate dating of *Pa gur*. It should post-date Nennius, if the form Emreis is anything to go by, making it, possibly, contemporary with *Annales Cambriae*. If it is later than Nennius, then it cannot have influenced him.

There is no connection between Arthur, the sixth-century leader of the Britons at the siege of Mount Badon and the figure in *Pa gur*. No one else in the *Gododdin* is a mythical superman. For the poet to say that Guaurthur was no Arthur, if Arthur was a superhuman monster-killer would surely diminish his achievement and the pathos of his passing. Arthur in the *Gododdin* was, from any rationale, a real person. None of the other 'best men in the world' feature in the poem, even though some are supposedly defenders of the Gododdin stronghold, Eidin.

The siege of Mount Badon was not a mythical occurrence. It was a real event of the year when the equally real Gildas was born. The British commander was a real man. We would have to accept the far-fetched conjecture that the man who led the British at the battle has been forgotten, in favour of a figure of mythology. How could that have happened? Cassivelaunus features in mythical company in the Mabinogion, but no-one forgot his role as the adversary of Julius Caesar. *Historia Brittonum* wishes to set the record straight that Britons had a heroic past, with victories against the Saxons, and it seems odd that, among all the real characters, the writer had to pick a mythical monster-slayer to lead these campaigns. Such an inclusion would greatly diminish the effect of the history, throwing the whole concept of a British resistance into doubt.

If Nennius did make use of *Pa gur*-like sources, his use of them would defy explanation. The chronological placing would be arbitrary. With no Saxons or other historical opponents, the poem gives no clues as to the date it is supposed to be set. *Historia Brittonum* covers the whole of British history from the Trojan War to the seventh century. If the writer simply wanted to include a local hero, surely we would have expected to find his monster-slaying exploits in the distant past, not in an era covered by other historians.

The ambience of the *Historia* and the poem is completely different. In the *Historia*, Arthur is a Christian warlord, fighting against pagans. His companions are the kings of the Britons. Nennius shows no knowledge of his wonder-working companions. If Arthur could be given a spurious historical career, why not Kei, Beduir and the others? The *Historia*'s battle locations are generally obscure, while *Pa gur* has chosen familiar ones like Edinburgh and Anglesey. All indications are that the background of *Pa gur* is not that drawn on by the *Historia*, if such legendary material even existed at that time.

It is far more plausible that Arthur the warleader acted like a magnet, attracting to his banner legendary characters from different mileux. We know this process continued through the Middle Ages. *Culhwch and Olwen*, for example, places legendary Irish characters among his men. If Arthur is equally a mythical character, why must he play a secondary role to the other legendary warriors? It was a poet of limited imagination who could only think of Arthur 'playing' or distributing gifts. The legendary material, clearly, featured Kei and the other 'best men in the world' attached here to Arthur.

Before the tenth century, Arthur appeared as a more or less lone character. His manpower is provided by the kings of the Britons. Any idea that he has a famous warband of his own is absent. However, in *Gereint*, we see, with the poet, the 'brave men of Arthur'. Did he mean the 'best men in the world', the legendary warriors accompanying Arthur? Was he numbering Gereint among them, figuratively perhaps, rather than placing him historically in the late fifth or early sixth centuries? Witnessing the heroic accomplishments of Gereint, the poet might feel he is seeing again feats such as those attributed to Kei and the other 'brave men of Arthur'.

Everything indicates that it is the superhuman warriors who are an accretion to the Arthur story. There is no description of them in any source composed before the Black Book poems. Even the most 'mythological' construction it is possible to put on the *Historia Brittonum* battle-list, that Arthur killed 940 men single-handedly, leaves no space for the supermen of *Pa gur*.

Pa gur shows the direction the Arthurian legends are to take. Arthur is relegated to the background, while heroic champions dominate the picture. The brave men will emerge decisively into Welsh legend in the first Arthurian prose tale which survives, *Culhwch and Olwen*.

SPOILS OF THE OTHERWORLD

Another poem cited in favour of the 'mythological Arthur' is found in the *Book of Taliesin*. Some of the Taliesin poems concern Urien Rheged and his son Owain, figures from late sixth-century northern Britain. They may be the work of the historical Taliesin, given as a contemporary of Neirin in *Historia Brittonum*. Other works in the book have a mythological bent. They date from the early Middle Ages, and are generally considered more recent than the Black Book. One of the poems is Arthurian. It is called *Preideu Annwfyn* – the booty of the otherworld. Dates for this range from the late ninth century to the early twelfth century. As with all the Welsh materials, dates for composition are continually being revised. Here, an early date would suit the idea that Arthur was primarily mythological and that famous French romances like the Holy Grail derived from partially discernible Welsh originals. A later date would prove the reverse. For argument's sake, we will assume it pre-dates *Culhwch and Olwen*.

Preideu Annwfyn is told in the first person. The poet takes on the persona of Gwair, singing before the spoils of Annwfyn. He is held prisoner in Caer Sidi, bound by a heavy gold chain 'according to the tale of Pwyll and Pryderi'. As Caer Sidi means 'Fairy Fort', we assume some otherworldly location.

Gwair sings: 'Three loads of Prytwen we went there. But for seven, none returned from Caer Sidi.' Later he sings: 'Three loads of Prytwen, we went on the sea.' From this it is generally inferred that Prytwen is a ship in which Gwair and his companions sailed. If that is the case, the writer implies a shuttle service, ferrying the companions to the otherworld in three batches, which seems unlikely. The companions went together to Caer Sidi, in which case 'the fullness of Pytwen' is used as a measure of how many men went on the expedition, presumably far more than seven. Perhaps the capacity of

Prytwen was a known bardic image, three times which would be a large number, of which seven would be a significant small fraction. For example, if the capacity of Prytwen were taken as 70, three times this would be 210, meaning that one man in 30 had survived. It does not, however, necessarily imply that all the men actually travelled in Prytwen.

In *Culhwch and Olwen*, Prytwen is said to be Arthur's ship, probably a direct inference from *Preideu Annwfyn*. Geoffrey of Monmouth, apparently from an older source, gives Pridwen as the name of Arthur's *shield*. In as far as it means 'white face', and that the shields of the *Gododdin* and the other early poems are white, this seems rather more likely than 'ship'. I think it possible that Arthur is understood in the poem to be a giant. *The Dream of Rhonabwy* is explicit that Arthur is gigantic, and in *Preideu Annwfyn*, he takes the part of Bran in the Mabinogi, who is so large that no ship can hold him. The capacity of his *shield* could be described by a poet as being able to hold many men.

Through the poem runs the refrain 'save seven, none returned from . . .'. Unless Gwair had the misfortune always to take part in disastrous expeditions with the same result, the verses all refer to the same adventure, with synonyms given for the otherworldly fortress. Gwair says that his song is heard in Caer Pedryvan (four-cornered) which must be the same as Caer Sidi, where he is imprisoned. It is later called the staunch door of the island, implying, as does the sea voyage, that the castle is on an island. The poem makes it clear that Arthur leads the expedition. 'And when we went with Arthur, a famous toil, save seven none returned from Caer Vedwit [drunkenness]', 'but for seven, none returned from Caer Rigor [numbness]', 'Three loads of Prytwen went with Arthur, save seven none returned from Caer Golud [obstruction]' and so on, with the name given as 'Caer Vandwy', and Caer Ochren' (meanings unknown).

What happened on the expedition is not clear. The poet sings of various objects and phenomena (the speckled ox, the lost grave of a saint) but whether to demonstrate an episode on the quest, his wide knowledge, or the inscrutability of the universe is impossible to tell. Two episodes stand out. In one we learn: 'Beyond Caer Wydyr [glass] they could not see Arthur's valour, the three-score hundred men who stood on the wall. It was difficult to speak to their watchman.'

More comprehensibly, the first incident concerns the Chief of Annwfyn's cauldron. This is warmed by the breath of nine maidens and will not boil the food of a coward. This seems to be the booty of the otherworld, as no other objects apart from the ox's collar are referred to. 'Lluch Lleawc's sword was raised for it and in a keen hand it was left.' He might be defending or seizing the cauldron. Either way, only he, Arthur and Gwair are named in connection with the expedition.

Lluch is a familiar name from the early poems (there is another one in the *Stanzas on Graves*). Whether we are to understand that there was one character with various surnames or that there are several Lluchs distinguished by their surnames is uncertain. No more than one Lluch is named in each poem, making the latter less likely. Although Arthur is said to be the leader, he takes no part in the action. Instead, a great warrior performs amazing feats, here connected with the cauldron of Annwfyn.

We can easily demonstrate that the story has no necessary connection with Arthur. The story of Pwyll and Pryderi exists. It is found in the four branches of the Mabinogi preserved in the early fourteenth-century *White Book of Rhydderch*, alongside explicitly Arthurian tales. Fragments of it are known earlier still, in a manuscript, Peniarth 6, written *c*. 1225.

The story of Pryderi is spread unevenly through the Mabinogi. He is born in the first 'branch', the son of Pwyll, Lord of Dyfed, known as the Chief of Annwfyn because he once swapped places with the King of Annwfyn for a year. The magic cauldron features in the second branch, here connected not with Annwfyn but with Ireland. The British sail across the Irish sea, led by their gigantic King Bran, who has to wade. Although the Britons are victorious, only seven survive to return with their wounded king. Bran is so badly wounded that his body has to be amputated, his head staying alive for the next eighty years. Of the seven who return, one is Pryderi, another Manawydan, son of Llyr (the heroes of the next branch) and a third, Taliesin himself, presumably to tell the tale. Pryderi is killed in the fourth branch and buried in North Wales (his tomb is mentioned in the *Stanzas on Graves*). The tales are set in pre-Roman times.

Although some details of *Preideu Annwfyn* are not repeated, the Mabinogi cover the same story of Pwyll and Pryderi which the poem gives as its source. In prose the story has no Arthurian elements at all. It is inconceivable that Arthur was removed from a tale which originally featured him, in the early thirteenth-century heyday of the Arthurian legends. It is far more likely that the poet has grafted Arthur on to pre-existing material relating to Pryderi. It is another example of the 'best men in the world' being attached to the figure of the pre-eminent warleader.

Proof that the legendary material in *Preideu Annwfyn* existed independent of any connection with Arthur is found in *Historia Brittonum*. Early in the book, the writer presents an account of the settlement of Ireland: 'Three sons of Miles of Spain [or 'a soldier of Spain'] came with thirty keels between them and thirty wives in each keel . . . they saw a glass tower [*turris vitrea*] in the midst of the sea, and saw men upon the tower, and sought to speak with them, but they never replied . . . [one ship was wrecked] the other ships sailed to attack the tower . . . the sea overwhelmed them and they were drowned, and not one escaped [save] the crew of that one ship that was left behind because of the ship-wreck' (HB 13).

This is, effectively, the story found in *Preideu Annwfyn*: the glass fort beyond the sea, the guards on the wall, the difficulty in talking to them, the tiny number of survivors. If the capacity of Prytwen were seventy, then the ratio of survivors-to-slain would be identical. The Taliesin poet has added the Arthurian context to a story which in the early ninth century existed without it. In this case, we have the evidence to show that Arthur is not the mythological hero of an assault on the otherworld, inserted into real history. The process here is unarguably the reverse; a poet has plucked Arthur from a historical context and added him to a legendary tale. The Taliesin poet would have had an easy job doing this if he knew *Historia Brittonum*. All that was needed to make the Glass Tower episode Arthurian was to change the hero from 'Militis Hispaniae' to 'Arthuri Militis', as he is described in the *Mirabilia*.

The process is the same as in *Pa gur*: legendary warriors, the 'best men in the world', Gwair, Llwch, Pryderi, have become 'brave men of Arthur', bringing their exploits with them. The process of accretion to Arthur becomes abundantly clear in the first surviving prose legend – *Culhwch and Olwen*.

'HOW CULHWCH WON OLWEN'

Culhwch and Olwen appears in the *White Book of Rhydderch* and, slightly updated, in the later *Red Book of Hergest*. Its language and content date it to the tenth or eleventh century, and for argument's sake we will accept the earlier date favoured by its most recent editors, Bromwich and Evans. It cannot go back much further than this because of its dependence on the Black Book poems.

The story is a display of virtuosity and wide knowledge. On a frame similar to the classic tale of Jason and the Argonauts are hung several encyclopaedic compilations of legendary knowledge. Culhwch, son of Kilyd, son of Kyledon Wledic (the ruler of Caledon), is cursed by his wicked stepmother never to wed except to Olwen, daughter of Chief Giant Yspadaden. The giant is a homicidal maniac armed with poisoned stone spears who needs mechanical aid to raise his enormous eyelids. He sets Culhwch a series of impossible tasks to complete before he can marry Olwen. Culhwch succeeds, Yspadaden is killed and the couple wed and live happily ever after.

Culhwch taunts the giant after each task is set: 'That will be easy for me to get, though you think it will not be easy', and reveals why at the end of the episode: 'my lord and cousin Arthur will get everything for me'. This must have come as a shock to the giant as many of his 'impossible' tasks involved securing the cooperation of Arthur's men. For instance 'Arthur and his companions must come and hunt [the boar] Twrch Trwyth, for he is a powerful man, yet he will not come for he is under my thumb'.

The reference to Twrch Trwyth, the boar Troynt from the *Mirabilia*, is an indication of the writer's erudition. He can be assumed to know most of the material we have already covered. He is not necessarily an independent witness to the traditions he relays.

After setting out Culhwch's birth and curse, the author turns to *Pa gur*. In his version, the hero Culhwch comes to *Arthur*'s court. He asks the question: 'Is there a porter?', and is answered by Glewlwyt Gavaelvawr. Glewlwyt recites a catalogue of strange faraway places, including Caer Oeth and Anoeth. Arthur lists his own inviolate possessions but it is left to Culhwch to enumerate the warriors of Arthur.

Glewlwyt's catalogue is interesting because it credits Arthur with overseas victories. He mentions Greater and Lesser India, 'Lychlyn' (Norway), Europe and Africa, Greece and other locations such as Sach and Salach – unknown to us and probably to the author, too. They give us no confidence that they are anything other than legendary encounters spread throughout the world. Actual locations where Dark Age Britons were active, such as Brittany or the Loire Valley, are not mentioned. The one slight Breton connection is that Arthur is said to have killed Mil Du, son of Ducum, a giant in an early life of St Malo.

The next catalogue is of Arthur's possessions. He lists his ship, his mantle, his sword Caletvwlch, spear Rongomynyat, his shield Wyneb Gwrthucher, knife Carnwenhan and wife Gwenhwyvar. The ship is later named as Prytwen. This catalogue seems to be of some antiquity. We know this because

Geoffrey of Monmouth preserves it in an earlier form. Bromwich and Evans point out that Geoffrey's version, *Caliburnus* (from whence our form 'Excalibur' derives) comes from a much older form than *Caletvwlch*.

Geoffrey knows Arthur's spear simply as *ron*, an old word meaning spear. It is not used in *Culhwch and Olwen*. *Gomyniad* means striker/slayer and is used in the *Gododdin*. It seems that the writer has mistaken this description as part of the name.

For the reasons covered above, it seems likely that Geoffrey's naming the shield Prydwen is an earlier tradition. The name *Wyneb Gwrthucher* means 'face – evening', suggesting a dark colour rather than the universal white in the early poems.

This list sees the first appearance of Arthur's wife – 'The first lady of the island' – Gwenhwyvar. Geoffrey gave her name, too, and her appearance in *Culhwch and Olwen* is evidence of a common tradition older than the tenth century. She plays no part in the action. We cannot say what stories were told about her, whether, for instance, she is the mother of Gwydre, son of Arthur, killed later in the story.

Gwenhwyvar is listed as one of the 'gentle gold-torqued women of the island' alongside her sister Gwenhwyach. The Triads connect the two with the battle of Camlan, but *Culhwch and Olwen* does not. Instead, it gives Arthur's man, Gwynn Hyvar, 'Mayor' of Devon and Cornwall, as one of the nine men who 'threaded out' the battle of Camlan. This shows that the name Gwenhwyvar/Gwynn Hyvar was given to the causer of the battle of Camlan, but that different stories have been spun from that meagre tradition. For the author, Camlan is a battle featuring three larger-than-life characters, presumably derived from a triad on the survivors of Camlan. The three men who were not struck by weapons at the battle were Morvran, descendant of Tegit – 'because of his ugliness everyone thought he was a devil helping', Sande Angel-Face – 'because of his beauty everyone thought he was an angel helping', and St Cynwyl, 'the last to leave Arthur', possibly implying that this was the battle where Arthur died. Medraut is not mentioned in the story, nor Badon, nor any of the other battles in *Historia Brittonum*, another indication that the *Historia* and *Annales* have different sources from *Culhwch and Olwen*.

The men who escaped Camlan, and the gold-torqued ladies, are part of the catalogue of Arthur's companions. Some have feats attached to them, others short descriptions, the majority are just names. From *Pa gur* come Kei,

Bedwyr, Anwas Edeinawc, Glewlwyt Gavaelvawr, Llwch Windy-hand, Manawydan son of Llyr, and Gwynn Gotyvron. Mabon, son of Modron and Mabon, son of Mellt turn up later, although they are not in the catalogue. Only Llacheu and Bridlau are unaccounted for.

Gwair, the prisoner of *Preideu Annwfyn*, could be one of four warriors of that name, 'all uncles of Arthur, his mother's brothers, all sons of Llwch Windy-hand from beyond the fierce/Tyrrhene sea'. Presumably the author intends that Llwch is Arthur's grandfather. Taliessin the chief bard is also among Arthur's men, as is Gildas!

One warrior mentioned is Gwawrdur, the man compared to Arthur in the *Gododdin*. His three sons Duach, Brathach and Nerthach 'sprung from the highlands of Hell' and his daughter Gwenwledyr are named in the catalogue. Gwawrdur himself is called 'the hunchback'. If the author knows the *Gododdin*, which is quite likely, he may construe the verse differently from the way we have interpreted it. If Gwawrdur is a hunchback, it could be read that his feats were comparable to Arthur's although physically 'he was no Arthur'. The poet may intend to invoke surprise that, in extremity at Catraeth, the physically unfit Gwawrdur fought as well as even the famous Arthur, a more flattering and dramatic comparison.

Culhwch and Olwen is the first source to present a comprehensive picture of who 'King Arthur' is. The six sons of Iaen, 'all men from Caer Tathal', are related to Arthur on his (unnamed) father's side. Llwch Windy-hand has already been mentioned. Culhwch himself is Arthur's first cousin and therefore shares one of his grandfathers, Kyledon Wledig or Anlawd Wledig. Gormant, son of Ricca, chief elder of Cornwall, is described as Arthur's half-brother, sharing the same mother.

Gereint, son of Erbin, and his son Cadwy are in the catalogue. A Custenhin and his son Goreu (often interpreted as Gorneu – of Cornwall) figure in the story. There may be some connection between this Custenhin, a gigantic shepherd, and Custenhin Gorneu (Constantine of Dumnonia) given in genealogies as Erbin's father.

Although Arthur has jurisdiction over all Britain and beyond, his home base is at Celli Wic in Cornwall. Both these concepts are novelties.

The catalogue has scoured many sources of legend and history. Saints rub shoulders with heroes from Irish legend. Some warriors, like Kei and Bedwyr, were already associated with Arthur while others, such as Gwenhwyvar and Gwalchmei, son of Gwyar, become so intermeshed with the Arthurian legends that it is impossible to believe their association with Arthur began here. Between the extremes of association and independence lie most of the named characters. Stories are embedded in the catalogue, such as that Gwydawc, son of Menester, killed Kei and was killed by Arthur in revenge. If the author wanted to show what his predecessors had meant by 'the brave men of Arthur', he rests his case here.

The next section is the *Anoethiau*, strange, impossible to achieve and often interconnected wonders. Culhwch, accompanied by Arthur's men Kei, Bedwyr, Cyndelic the guide, Gwrhyr interpreter of languages, Gwalchmei, son of Gwyar and the enchanter Menw, son of Teirgwaed, asks the Chief Giant Yspadaden for the hand of Olwen, and is set these seemingly impossible tasks. The tale expands the descriptions of the Arthurian heroes. Kei could hold his breath for nine days and nights under water. He could also be as tall as the tallest tree in the forest if he wanted to be. Bedwyr, though he has only one hand, is one of the three handsomest men of the island of Britain (clearly a triad) along with Arthur and Drych, descendant of Kibdar.

Arthur's companions in *Historia Brittonum*, the kings of the Britons, are more or less absent. The king does not lead Britons in wars against the Saxons, nor does he feature in most of the adventures. Soon his men advise him 'Lord, go back, for you ought not to accompany the host on this sort of petty errand' and he returns home.

The fulfilment stories contain the major set piece, the hunt for the boar Twrch Trwyth and a doublet adventure, the hunt for chief boar Yskithrwyn. The author prefaces this with the search for Mabon, son of Modron. This Mabon assists the hunt for Twrch Trwyth while the other (?) Mabon, son of Mellt, hunts Yskithrwyn.

Another short but apparently independent episode about Arthur and Gwynn mab Nud precedes the hunts. Two stories feature Kei and Bedwyr tricking powerful warriors, Wrnach the giant and Dillus the Bearded. A similar story forms the denouement of the tale: tricking the unbeatable giant is a common folk-tale motif. Arthur plays a small but vital part in the adventure of killing the black hag. He also goes with his men to capture the pups of the bitch Rymhi. This is a rather short and inconsequential episode, as the pups were neither requested by the giant nor used to fulfil the tasks, and had previously been listed among Arthur's men!

The seizure of the cauldron of Diwrnach is a story with which we are already familiar, from *Preideu Annwfyn* and the Mabinogi. Diwrnach is the steward of Odgar, son of Aed, king of Ireland. The cauldron is intended to boil the meat for the wedding feast, perhaps an echo of the poem's 'it will not boil the meat of a coward'. The cauldron has to be taken by force from Ireland (Mabinogi). Arthur sets off with a small force in his ship Prydwen (*Preideu Annwfyn*). The cauldron is seized by Bedwyr and Arthur's servant Hygwydd, while Llenlleawc the Irishman uses Caletvwlch to kill Diwrnach and his retinue. Finally, the heroes load up the cauldron with the booty of Ireland and return to Britain. This episode of the booty of Ireland only features Arthur as the owner of Prytwen, an inference drawn from *Preideu Annwfyn*. The use of his inviolate sword Caletvwlch is not remarked on. Llenlleawc appears twice in the catalogue, the second time after the sons of Llwch Windy-hand. It could be that there is a confusion here – in *Preideu Annwfyn*, Llwch plays a similar role.

Diwrnach has a name similar to Wrnach the Giant, whose sword is another of the *Anoethiau*, fulfilled by Kei and Bedwyr. The episode opens in a paraphrase of *Pa gur*, but this time the heroes conceal their identity, claiming to be furbishers of swords and scabbards. This trick allows Kei to get hold of Wrnach's sword, the only weapon which can kill the giant, and chop off his head. Goreu, son of Custenhin, plays a minor role. After an argument over precedence, he crosses over the walls of the fortress and is acknowledged the best ('*Goreu*'). He and the men with whom he is arguing have been given separate lodgings. This is so that they can kill the giant's lodge-keepers without him knowing. What actually happens is that Goreu defeats and beheads Chief Giant Yspadaden before, at the end of the story, seizing his land. Goreu's prominence in the story, coupled with the low profile of Culhwch, suggests that the author is using two 'Giant's Daughter'-type stories to create a larger whole. The giant's name recalls the Hall of Awarnach in *Pa gur*.

The *Historia* names Cair Urnach as one of the twenty-eight cities of Britain, with no indication of an Arthurian connection. The story in *Culhwch and Olwen* does not feature Arthur, it does not have even the loosest chronological placing, there are no Saxons, kings of the Britons, Christian imagery or anti-pagan content. In short there is nothing in it to warrant the idea that Nennius drew his Arthur from such tales. At the very least, he could have made Cair Urnach the site of one of Arthur's battles. All indications are that Nennius did not extrapolate his historical Arthur from sources such as this.

Kei and Bedwyr later take on Dillus the Bearded, 'the greatest warrior who ever avoided Arthur'. After Kei has returned to Celli Wic, Arthur composes an *englyn* (a type of three-line poem):

> *A leash from a beard made Kei,*
> *Ripped from Dillus son of Eurei.*
> *If Dillus were well, Kei'd die.*

This enrages Kei, who thereafter would have nothing to do with Arthur, even when Arthur was weak or his men were being killed.

In the mass of such material, there is only one element reminiscent of the Arthur of *Historia Brittonum*: the hunt for the boar Troynt. There are actually two boar hunts in *Culhwch and Olwen*. The first, and much shorter, is the most similar to the *Historia*. Arthur hunts the chief boar Yskithrwyn with his dog Cavall. The context is that Yspadaden will be shaved with the boar's tusk, taken from it while still alive. Though there is much confusion over this episode, it appears in origin to be the same as the story of Twrch Trwyth and could easily form the background to the *Historia*'s wonder of Carn Cabal.

There is little conformity between the tasks relating to the boar in the *Anoethiau* and the episode of its hunting. In the hunt, Arthur retrieves some dogs from Brittany and a huntsman from western Ireland, neither specified by Yspadaden. Odgar, son of Aed, King of Ireland, helps hunt the superfluous huntsman, rather than pluck the tusk from the living boar as he was supposed to. Caw of Pictland kills the boar while mounted on Arthur's mare Llamrei, rather than look after the living boar's tusk. Finally, the boar is hunted using Drutwyn, the pup of Greid, son of Eri, specified as necessary for hunting Twrch Trwyth, and with the assistance of Mabon, son of Mellt, who may or may not be the same as the Mabon, son of Modron that Arthur's men have just spent several pages searching for, again to hunt the other boar. No location is given for the boar-hunt.

The second hunt is for Twrch Trwyth, the boar Troynt of the *Historia*. How much of the later story was known by the author of the *Historia* is a difficult question. In *Culhwch and Olwen*, the hunt never specifically runs through the country of Builth. Neither do Arthur and Cabal play a particularly important part. The author was, doubtless, responsible for the many embellishments of the tradition. One example of this is the incorporation of William of France and the men of Normandy, who clearly demonstrate their post-1066 origin. If we can acknowledge that they are later additions, not present in whatever story Nennius knew in the early ninth century, why not the other fantastic 'best men in the world'?

While the hunt for Yskithrwyn is little more than a huntsman's tall tale, the hunt for Twrch Trwyth is positively baroque, with absurd hyperbole and shifts in scale. This time, Yspadaden requires the comb and the shears which lie between the ears of Twrch Trwyth in order to straighten his hair. The boar can only be hunted by the pup Drutwyn, held by special leash, collar and chain, managed by Mabon, son of Modron (who disappeared aged three days and can only be found with the help of his cousin) mounted on the horse Gwynn Dun-Mane. The giant also specifies the arrangements for another pair of unnamed hounds, who may be the two from Brittany used to hunt Yskithrwyn. These pups must be held by the leash made from Dillys's beard, managed by Kynedyr the Wild, son of Hettwn the Leper, who is 'nine times wilder than the wildest beast on the mountain'. In an extra twist, the boar must be hunted by Gwynn, son of Nud 'in whom God has set the energy of the demons of Annwfyn, in order to prevent the destruction of this world, and Gwynn cannot be turned loose'. Gwynn, we learn, has sent a character called Kyledyr the Wild mad by feeding him his own father's heart. Although this Kyledyr is the son of Nwython, and is used to hunt Yskithrwyn, he is obviously supposed to be the victim of Gwynn, and getting them to cooperate on the hunt an impossibility. Yspadaden stipulates that Gwynn must be mounted on a particular horse, and that Gwilenhin, king of France (William the Conqueror or William Rufus) and Alun Dyvet, two unspecified animals Anet and Aethlem, Arthur and his companions, and the three sons of Kilyd Kyvwlch, whose fantastical array of attributes and property includes the dog Cavall, must also join the hunt.

If the *Anoethiau* were complex, this is nothing to the hunt. A fifth of the section covering the fulfilment of all the tasks is devoted to the search for Mabon, son of Modron alone, another fifth to other pre-tasks and fully a third to hunting the boar. Twrch Trwyth is the son of the ruler Tared, a king turned by God into a pig for his sins. He exudes poison and is accompanied by seven young pigs, equally monstrous and enchanted.

The enchanter Menw, son of Teirgwaed and Gwrhyr the Interpreter fail to get the comb, shears and razor by stealth or persuasion. They each try in the form of birds, and have previously been encountered talking to the most ancient animals in the search for Mabon, son of Modron. Arthur tries to defeat the boars by the combined might of the warriors of Britain with its three offshore islands, France, Brittany, Normandy and the Summer Country. The beasts are first encountered ravaging Ireland, where Arthur's protection is sought by all the saints. Arthur fights the boars for nine days and nights, but only succeeds in killing one piglet.

Twrch and his boars then cross the Irish sea, pursued by Arthur in Prytwen, and devastates south-west Wales and the Prescelly mountains. 'Arthur went after him with all the forces in the world . . . Bedwyr with Arthur's dog Cavall at his side.' They fight at the Nevern valley, where Arthur's son Gwydre is killed. Twrch is tracked across Wales, losing two breakaway pigs before he arrives between Tawy and Ewyas, heading for the Severn and a chance to break out of Wales.

Arthur summons the men of Devon and Cornwall to meet him on the Severn. At the river, the main champions try to stop Twrch Trwyth, including Mabon, son of Modron, Goreu, son of Custenhin, Keledyr the Wild and Manawydan, son of Llyr. Although they seize the shears and the razor, the boar escapes into Cornwall, bearing the comb. Two characters who are killed by the boars at around this time are sometimes suggested as possibly remembered Saxons. Osla Big-Knife could be Octha of the *Historia*. Echel Pierced-Thigh could be Icel of the *Historia* genealogies. If so, nothing remains of their Saxon heritage or, at least in Osla's case, of his role as adversary to Arthur.

Arthur eventually drives Twrch Trwyth out of Cornwall and into the sea, without fulfilling the quest, and retires to Celli Wic in Cornwall to bathe and rest, as he did after the hunt for Yskithrwyn. Celli Wic, which seems to be the enclosure Kelly Rounds in North Cornwall, is the only headquarters assigned to Arthur. If this is the same Kelli referred to in *Pa gur*, then its fall was presumably when it was taken by Arthur.

Is this the 'truth' about Arthur? Was he merely a mythical figure, surrounded by bizarre superhumans? Were his adversaries always enchanted pigs, hags and giants, scattered all over the British Isles for no more than dramatic effect? This is the argument central to Arthur's detractors. They charge *Historia Brittonum* with taking this mythical image and giving it spurious legitimacy by setting it in an arbitrary historical period, replacing supermen with 'kings of the Britons' and boars with Saxons. It is time to gather these allegations to show how unlikely it is that the legends developed in this way.

First, there is the simple matter of chronology. The historical versions of Arthur in *Y Gododdin* and *Historia Brittonum* pre-date the legendary ones. This is true even if we take the most extreme dates possible, that the *Gododdin* reference is only as old as the ninth-century North Welsh phase, and that the Arthurian battle-list originates with Nennius in the 830s, with *Culhwch and Olwen* a survival of the tenth century.

Second, there is no evidence at all that Nennius was given to rationalising mythical sources. He could produce them without noticeable alteration from Irish works; he set the Arthurian battle-list in a context of prophetic worms and city-destroying saints. It is only a modern view that he would have wanted to make his history more 'plausible' by editing out gigantic boars and supermen. Bede and the *Mirabilia* both show a contemporary world characterised by expanding tombs, miraculous relics and supernatural apparitions. It seemed as reasonable to a Dark Age audience that a hunting dog should leave an indelible footprint on a stone as that a king's hand which had once given alms to the poor should never decay. Both wonders were visible to contemporaries to verify the stories attached to them.

Third, somebody did fight the Saxons and lead the Britons at the battle of Mount Badon. If Arthur is mythological, then he must replace absolutely and without trace the real victor. But how could this happen? Nennius was not the final arbiter of all history. While he might have decided for his own reasons to replace a real Dark Age hero with some legendary chimera, how is it that he was followed by *Annales Cambriae* and preceded by *Y Gododdin*, and destroyed all conflicting versions of the story? It is beyond belief that Arthur of an indeterminate mythological period was chosen by all concerned, independently, to stand in the place of a real fifth/sixth-century warlord. This absurdity is compounded by the context. No poet would compare Guaurthur unfavourably with a godlike superhuman. Nennius puts Arthur in the context of other anti-Saxon fighters. Are they too mythological beings given spurious historical life?

The most sensible explanation is that which has been accepted since the Middle Ages. Arthur was a real historical figure, the leader of the Britons at the fifth/sixth-century battle of Badon. His fame as a warrior, and his convenient role as leader of various kings of the Britons, made him a perfect magnet for unrelated stories of heroes, 'the best men in the world'. He himself takes little part in these stories, the warriors come complete with their exploits, families and contexts. We can see this process in the Middle Ages with the addition to the Arthurian milieu of such fictitious knights as Lancelot and Galahad and knights from other legendary cycles, like Tristan. One example of such an out-of-context warrior is Owain, son of Urien. His father is mentioned in *Historia Brittonum,* and both are celebrated in the early Taliesin poems. Urien lives in the generation after Mailcunus, so two generations after Arthur. His son cannot have been one of Arthur's men. He has become attached to a King Arthur who did not originally feature in combined stories. It is the legends which have accreted to the king, not the king who is extracted from the legends.

CAER VADDON

Arthurian material in Wales after *Culhwch and Olwen* falls broadly into two groups. The first owe their structure and tone to Geoffrey of Monmouth and the French romances. Others present a different, supposedly more primitive picture, and it is to these that we now turn our attention.

The Dream of Rhonabwy is found in the *White Book of Rhydderch.* This is a consciously literary work, with a specific claim that it is too complex to be reproduced orally. Its interest to us is that, alone of the Welsh poems and stories, it connects Arthur with both Camlan and Badon. The story is set in the middle of the twelfth century and must therefore have been composed later than that. The author knew the Welsh translations of Geoffrey of Monmouth, the Bruts, which cover both battles.

The author, in as much as he thinks in such terms, imagines the reign of 'the Emperor Arthur' as being in the mid- or even late sixth century. This makes Arthur a contemporary of Owain, son of Urien, Rhun, son of Maelgwn, Gildas and Avaon, son of Taliesin. Some of Arthur's men come from Geoffrey (Cadwr of Cornwall, rather than the Welsh Cadwy, son of Gereint). Others are from *Culhwch and Olwen* (Gwalchmei, son of Gwyar, Goreu, son of Custenhim, Gwrhyr, interpreter of languages, Menw, son of Teirwaedd and Mabon, son of Modron). Many other warriors from the catalogue are given in this writer's version of the list.

As we do not know exactly when the story was written, other features which would be innovations in a twelfth-century context could be derivative by the early fourteenth century. One of these is Llacheu, son of Arthur, who was mentioned briefly above. The others are Drystan, son of Tallwch (Tristan) and March, son of Meirchiawn (his uncle, King Mark). These characters featured in an independent legendary cycle, not fully integrated with the Arthurian legends until the mid-thirteenth century. In the same way, the writer makes Owain, son of Urien, a contemporary of Arthur. Chretien de Troyes, in the late twelfth century, was the first writer to make Owain one of Arthur's knights. It seems unlikely that the Welsh writer came up with a connection between Arthur, Tristan and Owain independently. He could be aware of and draw on the continental sources, while a continental writer could not have used the *Dream* as inspiration for his own work. Logically the *Dream* must derive its information from continental works, rather than vice versa.

The most significant aspect of the *Dream* is that the writer refers to both the battle of Badon and the battle of Camlann. The context is that Rhonabwy dreams about going back in time to the eve of the battle of Badon. The first person he meets is Iddawg, son of Mynyo, embroiler of Britain, who explains his role in the battle of Camlann. He leads Rhonabwy to Arthur's camp, where the men are preparing for the battle of Badon. This has been interpreted as either the author's confusion or his playful inversion of the true order of the battles. I cannot believe that this is the intention of the writer. Since the story is a dream, it is perfectly understandable that Iddawg should be able to explain his future role, including how he procured his name, although chronologically this cannot yet have happened. Arthur, too, is aware that Rhonabwy comes from the future.

Iddawg explains that he is called the embroiler of Britain because he was 'one of the messengers at the battle of Camlann between Arthur and his nephew Medraut'. Because he was such a high-spirited young man and eager for battle, he deliberately stirred up ill-feeling between them. 'When the Emperor Arthur sent me to remind Medrawd that Arthur was his uncle and foster-father, and to ask for peace lest the sons and nobles of the island of Britain be killed', Iddawg repeated his kindly words as rudely as possible. Nevertheless, he repented 'three nights before the end of the battle' and went off to Scotland.

That Arthur and Medraut are adversaries at Camlann seems to be the intention of *Annales Cambriae*. Geoffrey made this clear and is the first writer to state that Medraut was Arthur's nephew. He does not see any opportunity for the two to parlay and make deals. This motif first appears in continental sources in the early thirteenth century. Here again, the inconclusive dating prevents us from ascertaining whether *Rhonabwy* has come at this idea earlier and independently or later and derivatively. The only source to suggest that the battle was brought about by human guile is *Culhwch and Olwen*, where Gwynn Hyvar and others plan the battle. Iddawg says that his intervention wove the battle, but a similar story might have seen repeated transfers of envoys between the reluctant opponents. That Arthur is Medraut's foster-father and that the battle dragged on for more than three days are features unique to the *Dream*.

On the battle of Badon, the writer has the troops, the leaders and the warriors of the Britons mustering at the ford called Rhyd y Groes on the Severn. They set off in the direction of Kevyn Digoll, away from the Severn Valley. The force descends until they are below Caer Vaddon, the City or Fortress of Badon, possibly the City of Bath, as in Geoffrey, but whether the author sees it as a real location in Somerset is not clear. Arthur and his men are giant supermen and rush off to Cornwall by nightfall, so whether Baddon is supposed to be near Rhyd y Groes, Cornwall or amazingly distant from one or the other is impossible to tell. The story makes it seem that Arthur is besieging Caer Vaddon, but it may be that he is attacking another army in the field close by. His enemy is Osla Big-Knife. If the writer knows this is the Saxon Octha or decides to make that connection for himself, or even if he just plucks the name out, he is acting completely independently of Geoffrey, for whom Cheldric is the Saxon leader. The writer does not even say whether Osla's men are Saxons or Britons. In the event, there is no battle of Badon between Arthur and Osla. Instead, Arthur's men fight Owain's ravens while their masters play the board game Gwyddbwyll.

This strange tale hints at other possible interpretations of the Arthurian legends, although we cannot dismiss the possibility that these are derived from the author's imagination, presented as 'eye-witness' corrections of current views.

RED RAVAGER OF THE ISLAND OF BRITAIN

The vast majority of Welsh Arthurian tales was undoubtedly oral. Traces of this body of tradition are preserved in the 'Triads of the Island of Britain'. These group three related names or events, such as 'the three exalted prisoners of the Island of Britain'. Grammatical or stylistic triads were used by Welsh bards as mnemonic devices and it is theorised that the legendary triads were used in the same way. Recalling one story would naturally remind the bard of the other two. The tales in the White and Red Books show how these Triads would be unpacked. They could be delivered at length (as with the Triad of the three fortunate concealments, which takes a whole tale of the Mabinogi to develop) or simply dropped into a larger text (the three unfortunate blows, or, presumably, the three men who survived Camlan) to add depth by resonance and comparison.

The earliest list of triads is in the manuscript Peniarth 16. This is either early or late thirteenth century (the usual Welsh source caveats apply). The scribe responsible wrote a version of the Brut (the *Brut Dingestow*) so knew the standard Geoffrey of Monmouth material. The same triads are specifically described as relating to Arthur and his men in another manuscript, Peniarth 45. Triads on famous horses are included in the *Black Book of Carmarthen*. The White Book adds more, updated by the Red Book. More Arthurian triads turn up in fifteenth- and even sixteenth-century manuscripts. In no sense are these later triads independent. They know the Mabinogion, Geoffrey of Monmouth and French thirteenth-century romances. What is interesting is the different picture of Arthur and his men that the triads present to the standard sources, even when they obviously have knowledge of them.

Fifteenth-century triads stress Gwenhwyvar's adultery as leading to Arthur's downfall, a thirteenth-century concept. They single out Gwenhwyvar as more faithless than all the Three Faithless Wives and Camlan as one of the most futile battles because of her part in causing it. These add little to our understanding of early Welsh tradition. If we look at the thirteenth-century triads, we can see some very different interpretations of the Arthurian legends.

Peniarth 16 begins with the threefold division of Britain, exemplified by Arthur's chief tribal thrones as ruler of Wales, Cornwall and the north. In Wales he is connected with St David as Chief Bishop and Maelgwn as Chief Elder, with his seat at St David's. In Cornwall his throne is at Kelli Wic, as it is in *Culhwch and Olwen*, while his seat in the north is at Pen Ryonyd.

The second triad links three characters known by the epithet *Hael* ('The Generous'), with the additional information that Arthur was more generous than the three of them. His generosity is stressed in Geoffrey of Monmouth and hence in the Bruts. This prevents us from stating that Arthur was known independently to be generous. However, one of the characteristics of Guaurthur in the *Gododdin* was that he too was extremely generous.

In the ancient triads of the horses, we encounter again Gwgawn Red-sword, Morfran descendant of Tegid and Kei, but no context. Bromwich draws attention to a horse poem in the *Book of Taliesin* which seems to draw on the triads, but with additional material. This includes the lines: 'A horse of Guythur, a horse of Guardur, a horse of Arthur, fearless in giving battle.' Guardur is none other than Guaurthur of the *Gododdin*. Guaurthur's horses, along with his generosity and warlike prowess, are among his attributes. We can see here, again, that the poetic comparison 'he was not Arthur' could imply more than simply 'they were both warriors'.

Many triads feature Arthur's famous men. Llacheu mab Arthur appears with Gwalchmei mab Gwyar as men well-endowed (by their ancestry) to rule. It may be that Llacheu was always known to be Arthur's son, and that the audience of *Pa gur* would be expected to realise this when he was mentioned fighting with fair Kei, but that early poem does not give him a patronymic. Three characters appear grouped as three 'Unben' (head ones) of Arthur's court, two from *Culhwch and Olwen*, but their legends and why they were singled out for this treatment are lost. Gereint is named one of the seafarers of the Island of Britain, which might give us a clue as to why he is fighting at a place called Llongborth (warship port).

Four 'Arthurian' warriors feature together as the battle-diademed men. Drystan, Hueil, son of Caw (from *Culhwch* and the *Life of Gildas*), Kei, son of Kenyr elegant-beard (from *Culhwch*) and finally Bedwyr, son of Bedrauc, 'diademed above the three of them'. Morfran descendant of Tegid, one of the three who escaped Camlann, turns up as one of the slaughter-blocks of Britain, in the company of Gwgawn Red-sword, from the *Stanza on Graves* which includes Arthur.

Triad 30 shows how unconnected warriors could be added to the Arthurian story. One of the three faithless warbands is that of Alan Fyrgan, the late eleventh-century Count of Brittany. We are surprised to see that his men are faithless because they deserted him before the battle of Camlann, where he was killed. I have no doubt that, were this the first reference to the battle of Camlann, we would have sceptics declaring it was clearly an early twelfth-century action which Geoffrey of Monmouth had spun out to include the legendary Arthur. What we have, in fact, is more proof that the embellishment worked the other way round. Arthur's death at Camlann has attracted other famous stories of death and betrayal. We know this, since even at the most pessimistic estimate the actual manuscript of *Annales Cambriae* giving Camlann as the battle where Arthur and Medraut fell was written down before Alan Fyrgan was born.

Arthur is named one of the three red ravagers of the island of Britain. He also appears, surprisingly, as one of the three frivolous bards. There need be no more behind this than the story in *Culhwch and Olwen* of Arthur offending Kei by his ill-judged verse. On the other hand, the *Triad of the Three Battle Horsemen* is said in the *White Book of Rhydderch* to be an englyn composed by Arthur himself on the three of his favourites who would not endure having a court official placed over them.

Triad 26 gives the most detail of its three stories, showing the kind of material which could lie behind the terse entries on the other triads. It also links clearly with the next two triads, showing how one group could be used as a mnemonic for further elaboration. It deals with the three powerful swineherds of the island of Britain. These were not actually swineherds, but much more powerful men who at one point in their careers had to guard swine. The first was Drystan, son of Tallwch, guarding the swine of March, son of Meirchiawn, while the actual swineherd was off delivering a message to Essyllt. 'And Arthur was seeking to obtain one pig from among them, either by deceit or by force, but he did not get it.' Two significant features of this triad are Arthur's rapacity, similar to that he shows in the *Life of St Padarn*, and the assimilation to Arthur of the unrelated Tristan-cycle characters. The White Book extends the episode to include Kei, Bedwyr and March himself, presumably trying to catch Drystan out.

The second swineherd was Pryderi, son of Pwyll. The third was Coll, son of Collfrewy, guarding the sow Henwen, who he hangs on to while she tours Cornwall and Wales giving birth to various prodigies. One is a kitten which Coll throws into the Menai Straits off Anglesey. It grows up to become 'Palug's Cat', the monster of *Pa gur*.

This triad presumably served as a reminder to the next one, 'Three enchanters', which starts with Coll, son of Collfrewy, whom we might otherwise have thought just a swineherd. He is in the company of Menw, son of Teirgwaedd, from *Culhwch and Olwen*. This triad leads to a third: *Three Great Enchantments of the Island of Britain* which shows how Menw and Coll obtained their powers (the first from Uthyr Pendragon, the second from Gwythelyn the dwarf). The first enchantment, of Math, son of Mathonwy, taught to Gwydion, son of Don, features in one of the branches of the Mabinogi.

We can see here the pattern of different layers of story which doubtless underlie the other triads too. Peniarth 16 is earlier than the manuscripts preserving the Mabinogi or the early poems and shows those stories in circulation before they reach their final written form.

The triad of the three concealments, while easy to decipher, implies knowledge of its counterpart, the three unfortunate disclosures, although this is not found with it in the earliest version. We know that the triad cannot be of any antiquity, however, as it makes use of the story of Lludd and Llevelys which post-dates Geoffrey.

In the Red Book we learn that the unfortunate disclosure of Bran's protecting head was performed by Arthur, 'because it did not seem right to him that this island should be defended by the strength of anyone, but by his own'.

Although, having Peniarth 16, we can tell that the extended version of the Triads in the White Book and the Red Book are later and not likely to preserve pristine ancient traditions, it is worth looking at the new material they present. They may illuminate the ideas of the scribes who collected *Culhwch and Olwen* and the other Arthurian materials. The two texts, as with the prose stories, cover the same materials.

Arthur appears first as one of the nine worthies of the world, a late thirteenth-century concept. From this we know that the writer is aware of the standard genres of medieval romance. When he expands at length on the 'three dishonoured men who were left in the island of Britain', we can see at once he has simply taken the story of Medraut's betrayal of Arthur direct from the Bruts.

It is therefore a great surprise to find completely unprecedented Arthurian material in this collection. The 'Three Exalted Prisoners' triad is given in the same manuscripts, in *Culhwch and Olwen*. In the triads themselves, it has a different form. Mabon, son of Modron, is one, in common with *Culhwch and Olwen*, as is Gwair, son of Geirioedd, who might be the prisoner of *Preideu Annwfyn*. The third is an almost unknown figure, Llyr Lledyeith (half-speech?), prisoner of Euroswydd. In the late thirteenth-century manuscript, Mostyn 117, he features at the head of the genealogy of Arthur himself. This implausibly grafts the genealogy of Arthur in the Bruts back to Constantine onto the supposed genealogy of Dumnonia by identifying this Constantine with Gildas's tyrant.

According to the triad, Arthur was more exalted than these three, being 'three nights in prison in Caer Oeth and Anoeth, and three nights imprisoned by Gwen Pendragon and three nights in an enchanted prison under the Stone of Echymeint . . . and it was the same lad who released him from each of these three prisons, Goreu, son of Kustenin, his cousin' (Bromwich 1961). Nothing in any other source would lead us to believe that Arthur had ever been imprisoned, but we can see some possible antecedents. In *Culhwch and Olwen*, we have already suggested that Goreu has an anomalous role as giant-killer and erstwhile central character, and we can imagine him connected with other similar Arthurian tales which have not been preserved.

The *Stanzas on Graves* described Arthur's grave as 'Anoeth' and we remarked how this was used as a place-name in another verse. *Annales Cambriae* and *Historia Brittonum* linked Arthur with the span of three nights, in connection with his battles. The whole concept, however, is so different from any surviving Arthurian material that we can only suppose that the writer has a truly independent source, albeit one which does not help us any further with our understanding of the truth behind the legend.

The other triads in the White and Red Books expand on the material surrounding the battle of Camlann. These are particularly interesting as we know that the writer has read a *Brut* giving Geoffrey of Monmouth's version, as well as, presumably, the versions of *Culhwch and Olwen* and the *Dream of Rhonabwy* in the same manuscript.

One tells us that one of the three harmful blows of the island of Britain was that which Gwenhwyfach struck Gwenhwyvar 'and for that cause took place afterwards the action of the battle of Camlan' (Weith Kat Gamlan). These two appear in *Culhwch and Olwen*, as sisters, but not necessarily as feuding rivals.

An explanation of at least one of these characters is found in the triad of Arthur's great queens, 'Gwenhwyvar daughter of Guryt Guent, Gwenhwyvar daughter of Uthyr son of Greidiaul and Guenhuyvar daughter of Ocvran the Giant'. Although, as we shall see, there was material in circulation saying that Arthur's Guenevere was his second wife, this is unprecedented material. It may be intended to reconcile variant traditions on the parenthood of Guenevere, but it seems to be written here to lead into Arthur's convoluted marital situation. The next triad specifically linked with this one 'and his three mistresses were these: . . .' Whether the tradition of Arthur killing his own son derived from this sort of background we cannot say, but it does seem very different from Geoffrey's version which makes Arthur the wronged party. Arthur, Gwenhwyvar and Medraut are linked in another triad, but in an unexpected way: 'Three unrestrained ravagings of the island of Britain: the first occurred when Medraut came to Arthur's court at Celliwig in Cornwall, he left neither food nor drink in the court that he did not consume. And he dragged Gwenhwyvar from her royal chair and then struck a blow upon her. The second unrestrained ravaging when Arthur came to Medraut's court. He left neither food nor drink in the court.'

The motifs of Arthur, Medraut and a blow struck against Gwenhwyvar, suggest a variant tradition on the battle of Camlann. A Cornish location for Camlann would make sense for a return attack after one on Kelliwig, if Arthur and Medraut are considered to be neighbouring rivals. Another triad, the three unfortunate counsels, includes 'the threefold dividing by Arthur of his men with Medraut at Camlan', suggesting that they are on the same side. This makes sense of the ideas that Iddawg distorted the messages between them to start a battle, and that the whole thing was plotted by scheming underlings.

There is no way of sorting out the 'truth' from these versions. Their value lies in showing that the entry in *Annales Cambriae*, usually read in the way the story is presented by Geoffrey of Monmouth, could have various interpretations.

The Welsh tales and poems do not derive seamlessly from the historical materials which precede them. They have little in common with the *Historia* and *Annales*, still less with Gildas. It is inconceivable that these legendary materials are the source of the historical Arthur. *Gereint son of Erbin*, and possibly the *Stanzas on Graves*, may contain historical material, but the rest use Arthur as a convenient leader around whom unrelated heroes congregate.

8

LIVES OF THE SAINTS

Between 1100 and 1135, Arthur figured in the lives of several Welsh saints. The Norman lords of England and the Archbishop of Canterbury had been steadily encroaching on the churches and monasteries of Wales. Age-old lands and privileges, traditionally unchallenged, were threatened. The Anglo-Normans now required written proof or they would ignore them.

The Welsh monks responded by writing numerous 'ancient' charters in which kings of the sixth and seventh centuries bestowed land on their abbeys and cathedrals. Welsh saints, often commemorated solely in church dedications or local cults, were given detailed 'historical' *Lives*. These generally showed the saints, connected genealogically to local princely houses, humbling their relatives and extracting from them grants of land and custom to stand in perpetuity. For good measure, lest these rights should be challenged by Canterbury, charters were written up confirming the status of St David's as the Archbishopric of Wales. It was not that the monks were being consciously dishonest. They were committing to writing the customary practices and assumptions their predecessors had forgotten to record.

The saints' *Lives* were thus written with an axe to grind. Their denouements invariably involve the extortion of concessions from some hapless lord. Because these often involve land grants, territorial assumptions are those of the twelfth century, not the sixth. Britannia is thus often a synonym for Wales 'on the borders of Britannia and Anglia, near Hereford' (Wade-Evans 1944). The context of wars against the invading English is forgotten. The vindication of possession through military victory would do the Welsh writers no good, as it could equally be used by the Anglo-Normans. The temporal horizon of the saints' *Lives*, and the charters, is the sixth century. This parallels the Welsh secular material, which also concentrates on this period, often at the expense of older sources pointing to the later fifth century.

Arthur in *Historia Brittonum* and *Annales Cambriae* is presented as a paragon of Christianity, fighting against specifically pagan foes. The Celtic Church saw the fifth/sixth centuries as a heroic age, characterised by the activities of missionary saints. In both sources, Arthur's career is placed in a framework of such saintly activity.

When the saints' *Lives* came to be written, we should not be surprised to find Arthur in the company of these saints. What does surprise is that he is apparently their adversary. This lack of continuity, at least, is enough to call into question the evidence of the hagiographers.

All of this warns against the use of the saints' *Lives* to illuminate the actual history of sixth-century Wales. These warnings, however, have been ignored by Arthurian writers. John Morris makes great use of the *Lives* in *The Age of Arthur*. They form a cornerstone of Ashe's Riothamus theory and the Llandaff Charters have been given a recent outing in *The Holy Kingdom* (Gilbert, Blackett and Wilson 1998). It could be that these twelfth-century ecclesiastical materials contain actual sixth-century names, even pedigrees. However, these could have been gleaned from several non-historical sources, place-names, tombstones and intercessions on behalf of donors, for example. That they do not derive from written historical sources is obvious. If such sources existed, there would have been no reason to fake new ones in the twelfth century. Their origins are well-established, arriving at their later forms only in the late eleventh or early twelfth centuries. Where earlier versions exist, they make no Arthurian connections. These arise in later versions, composed when Arthur's fame was becoming established. However, as they present another possible interpretation, before Geoffrey of Monmouth came to dominate, it is worth examining what they say about Arthur.

The *Lives* of Sts Illtud, Cadoc, Carantoc and Padarn are from a single manuscript, Cotton Vespasian A14. This was written *c.* 1200, probably in Brecon or Monmouth Priory (Wade Evans 1944). It also includes *Lives* of St David and other non-Arthurian saints. The *Lives* themselves were composed in the early twelfth century, apparently uninfluenced by Geoffrey of Monmouth.

The Life of St David was written by Rhigyfarch, son of Sulyen, an eleventh-century Abbot of Llanbadarn Fawr/Bishop of St David's. Sulyen features in *Culhwch and Olwen*. If this is the same man, this points to an eleventh-century date for the tale. It is just one of several interconnections between *Culhwch* and the *Lives* (Bromwich and Evans 1992).

The shortest notice is in the Life of St Illtud (Iltutus). We have already encountered this saint in the *Mirabilia*, as the only other person connected to a wonder of Britain. That wonder was in south-eastern Wales, where the saint was the eponymous founder of the church at Llantwit Major. Iltutus has a successful career as a great soldier in Brittany. He hears of the magnificence of his cousin, King Arthur, a great victor, and sails across to Britain. Arthur is seen distributing largesse to a huge company of warriors. Iltutus joins them and is suitably rewarded.

This terse reference has nothing, other than Arthur's royal status, which could not have been inferred from the *Historia*. Arthur is a victorious warrior, a contemporary of Iltutus and a fellow denizen of south-west Wales. In accordance with hagiographic principles, the saint is his relative. His grandfather is Anlawd *Britanniae Rex*, who is also a grandfather of Culhwch in the tale, and, on this evidence, of Arthur as well.

The Life of St Padarn (Paternus), eponym of Llanbadarn, presents Arthur in a different light. The story is set at a time when Malgun, king of the northern Britons, is at war with the southern Britons, in whose lands Paternus lives. We easily recognise Maglocunus, in his role as overthrower of tyrants. Meanwhile, St David and his companions Paternus and Teliau return from Jerusalem, where Paternus has received a seamless tunic. Paternus is recovering from his journey in his church when Arthur, 'a certain tyrant who was passing through the neighbouring regions', comes to his cell. Arthur covets the saint's tunic but is told that it is only fit for a bishop, not for a man of such baseness as him. Furious, Arthur leaves but then returns, against the advice of his companions, raging and stamping the ground. On hearing this, the saint causes the ground to swallow him up, leaving only his head exposed. Arthur, chastened, admits his guilt and praises God and Paternus. Seeking forgiveness, he is released from the earth and receives absolution from the saint, imploring him 'with bent knees'. On receiving absolution, he takes Paternus as his eternal patron.

This story is not as contradictory of the earlier Arthurian material as it first seems. Arthur is localised in south-east Wales, as expected from the *Mirabilia*. That he is a tyrant is assumed from the career of Maglocunus and the *de Excidio* in general. The author may even have read the list of tyrants as sequential, with Vortiporius of Dyfed as one of Maelgwn Gwynedd's predecessors and victims. Arthur is not exactly shown as a tyrant, in contrast to his role as a Christian leader in the battle-list and *Annales Cambriae*. Rather, he is a redeemed tyrant, turned to God under the patronage of the St Padarn and no doubt ready to fight the good fight. By this means the author is able to make sense of the contradictions in the *Historia*, that Arthur is a Christian warrior who has also killed his son. The slaying of Anir could, in this model, have taken place before his conversion. The mention of Arthur's companions indicates a context of the brave men of Arthur suggested by the Welsh sources.

The Life of St Padarn is thus not such a departure from the Arthurian material. Aside from its miraculous element, it has nothing which could not be harmonised with the historical Arthur we have hypothesised. The stumbling block is, however, the historical context. The saints' *Lives* imagine Arthur as a (mid?) sixth-century contemporary of Maelgwn, Gildas and St David. Although some of these may have overlapped, it ignores Gildas's all-important point – that the victor of Badon Hill was a character from the previous generation. The war-leader of Maelgwn's era would be Outigirn.

There have been attempts to argue that the early to-mid-sixth-century southern Welsh Arthur is the 'real Arthur', erroneously displaced to the victory of Badon and the fifth-century British resistance. This misses the point. The character we are interested in is precisely the victor of Badon, the British leader of battles, a figure who must be real. It is unbelievable that he was completely replaced by a relatively insignificant South Welsh hero. It is more probable that the dating of the saints' *Lives* is in error. As far as we can tell, the writers intend us to recognise Arthur as the great warrior of the battle-list.

More detailed material on Arthur is given in the *Life of St Cadoc*. This was composed by Lifris who flourished around 1100. Cadoc is the son of King Gundleius, a minor ruler of 'the British region which is called Demetia', and Guladus, daughter of Brachanus, the king from whom Brecon takes its name. They elope when their marriage is opposed by Brachanus. He pursues them, and there is fierce fighting between his men and those of Gundleius, while the lovers seek sanctuary on the hill of Bochriucarn on the borders of the two kingdoms. 'Behold the three powerful heroes Arthur and two of his knights, that is Cei and Bedguir, sitting together on top of that aforementioned hill, playing at dice.' Arthur is presented without introduction, in contrast to the contextualising of Gundleius and Brachanus. He is later called 'king'. His knights are his companions from *Pa gur*, the best men in the world, with their description as 'three powerful heroes' perhaps hinting at a triad.

Arthur tells his friends that he is inflamed with lust for Guladus. The other two censure him for his evil thoughts and remind him that it is their custom to aid the poor and distressed. Arthur gives in with bad grace and sends them down to investigate. Being appraised of the situation, the three warriors rush down and scatter Brachnanus's army. The writer informs us that the countries of Brecheiniog and Gwynllwg take their names from the rival kings. Thanks to the rescue of his parents by Arthur, St Cadoc is born.

The genre of the *Life* is not the historiography of *Historia Brittonum*, and the presence of Kei and Bedwyr makes it obvious that this tale has more in common with *Culhwch and Olwen*. In the latter story, Arthur intervenes between Gwynn mab Nud, who has carried off the maiden Creiddylad, and her husband Gwythyr ap Greidawl. Gwythyr is pursuing them with his army and comes into conflict with Arthur's men.

Years later, St Cadoc crosses paths with his parent's rescuer. Ligessauc Lau Hiir (Long Hand), 'a certain very powerful leader of the Britons', has killed three soldiers (*milites*) of Arthur, the very illustrious King of Britain. It is not clear here what extent of Arthur's power is implied. Later, we discover that Mailgunus rules 'all Britannia', where Wales is almost certainly meant. Arthur may therefore be 'the most famous King of Britain/Wales', i.e. among others less famous, or conceivably is famous as king of the whole island.

That Arthur is dominant is made clear as he hunts Ligessauc everywhere and no one dares to shelter the fugitive. At last Ligessauc seeks sanctuary with St Cadoc in Gwynllwg (the area of Newport, Gwent) where Arthur tracks him down with a huge band of soldiers. The saint persuades Arthur to submit to arbitration. He summons Sts David, Illtud and Teilo, along with several other clerics and elders from '*totius Brittannie*' (all Britain/Wales). Their judgement is that Arthur receive three oxen or one hundred cows per man in compensation for those slain. Although Arthur agrees, he will only accept cows of two colours, red at the front, white at the rear. Presumably this ploy is intended to scupper the negotiations, but Arthur has reckoned without the power of the saint, who miraculously produces the parti-coloured animals from single-coloured ones.

The elders next determine that, according to custom, the animals must be handed over in the middle of the ford. Cei and Bedguur rush into the water to grab them but find the cows miraculously transformed into bunches of ferns. This transformation explains why the land, conceded to Cadoc by St Teilo, is known as Tref Tredinauc or Fern Homestead. Arthur, witnessing his power, begs forgiveness from Cadoc. Having taken council with his leaders, Arthur increases the terms of Cadoc's right of sanctuary. At this the ferns are changed back into cows. The treaty is later ratified by Arthur, Mailgunus and Rein, son of Brachanus.

Mailgunus is a king, also styled '*magnus rex Brittonum*' – great king of the Britons – who rules over all Britannia. He is later called 'King of the men of Gwynedd, that is, the men of Snowdon'.

Towards the end of the *Life*, Cadoc, digging in a certain fort on Mount Bannauc in Scotland, finds the collar-bone of an ancient hero, monstrous and of incredible bulk, through which a man can ride on horseback. Cadoc miraculously revives the giant, 'of huge stature and immense, altogether exceeding human size', who turns out to be Caur of Pictland, who later fathers Gildas!

Bromwich and Evans (1992) draw several interesting connections between the saints' *Lives* and *Culhwch and Olwen*. They suggest that the author of the tale actually had a copy of the *Life of St Cadoc*. Both feature Arthur, Kei and Bedwyr and the characters Caw of Prydyn, Samson, Sawyl Penn Uchel and Brys mab Bryssethach (an ancestor of Gladus). The *Life* explains the meanings of Bochriucarn and Rhyd gwrthebau, also explained in *Culhwch*, and both have the place-names Dinsol and Mount Bannauc. One indication that the author of *Culhwch* is simply taking names from an existing text is his lack of knowledge of where they are. Dinsol is St Michael's Mount in the *Life*, but is placed in the north in *Culhwch*, for example.

There is little of historical value in this *Life*, beyond, perhaps, the general Gwent milieu. The status of the kings is confused, though the chronological setting, with Arthur having a long career beginning many years before the reign of Maelgwn, who in turn is older than Gildas, is more plausible than that in the other *Lives*.

The remaining *Life* in the manuscript is that of St Carantoc. He is an older relative of Cadoc, living thirty years before the birth of St David, a native of Ceredigion. Carantoc receives a miraculous altar from heaven which he takes down to the Severn estuary and throws into the sea. It floats off to where God willed the saint to go, and Carantoc follows in his boat. 'In those times, Cato and Arthur were reigning in that country, living in Dindraithou. And Arthur came wandering in search of a most powerful serpent, huge and terrible, which had devastated twelve parts of the fields of Carrum. And Carantoc came and greeted Arthur, who rejoicing received a blessing from him' (Wade-Evans 1944).

In return for news about his altar, the saint miraculously tames the serpent. They bring it back to Cato in the fort where the saint is welcomed.

Although the people are keen to kill the serpent, Carantoc prevents them, because the beast is an instrument of God, sent to destroy sinners in Carrum.

Arthur gives back the altar, which he had tried to make into a table, but anything put on it was cast off. The king, apparently the writer means Arthur, grants the saint Carrum 'forever, by written deed' and Carantoc builds a church there. Later, Carantoc throws the altar into the sea again and sends Arthur and Cato to look for it. It has washed ashore at the mouth of the Guellit. 'The king' gives the saint twelve parts of the fields where the altar was found. 'Afterwards Carantoc built a church there, and it was called the city of Carrou.'

This provides the most detail about Arthur of any of the *Lives*, but it is difficult to reconcile it with what we have already deduced. The locations of Dindraithou and Carrum are unknown. It seems that the saint has crossed the Severn estuary, and that therefore we are in the West Country. Cato might be Cadwy, the son of Gereint, but this would be at variance with the chronology of the secular Welsh sources, with Gereint and Arthur contemporaries, or Arthur as the elder. In the *Life* he seems to be junior to Cato.

It is also unlikely that the *Life* is laying claim to land in Devon and Cornwall, long lost to English dioceses. The idea of the *Lives* is to justify existing holdings (presumably in this case bolstered by a copy of the king's written charter), not to lay claim to new ones outside Wales. It is most plausible that the writer intends the locations to be Welsh areas adjacent to the Severn estuary, which would fit with the geography of the other *Lives*.

These linked saints' *Lives* share a South Welsh viewpoint, which is as expected. They are not consistent on when Arthur flourished. For some, Sts David and Maelgwn are older or his contemporaries, which seems too late. The wars against the Saxons are completely absent. The *Lives* agree that Arthur is a king, either a local one or a more powerful British monarch. This is in a context of both royal and non-royal leaders like Ligessauc. The idea that Arthur is a tyrant, in contrast to his heroic image elsewhere, has been over-played. The *Lives* all leave Arthur chastened and reverential, and can be seen as prequels to his Christian career. They have much in common with the Welsh legends, a context in which Arthur's companions, specifically Kei and Bedwyr, are prominent, in which miracles abound and etymology derives from such incidents. Once again, Arthur is not derived from stories such as these. He is a pre-existing historical figure, grafted on to the newly composed saints' *Lives* to add to their credibility.

The *Life* most influential on the development of the Arthurian legends is that of St Gildas himself. It appears in a different manuscript, called CCCC 139. It was written by Caradoc of Llancarfan, *c.* 1130. A previous *Life of St Gildas* had been composed, about a century earlier, by a monk from Ruys in Brittany, which claimed his tomb. This, however, was of little use to the monks of South Wales, hence the need for a new version.

Neither *Life* helps us interpret the actual life of the writer of *de Excidio*. What we learn from them, for example that Gildas was the son of a Pict called Caw and studied under St Illtud in southern Wales, is belied by his ignorance of northern geography and his familiarity with the classical Latin of formal schools. Details such as the idea that he and Maelgwn Gwynedd were pupils together can be inferred from *de Excidio*, and need not derive from any independent tradition.

'The most holy man Gildas was the contemporary of Arthur, king of the whole of Greater Britain', Caradoc starts. Although Gildas loved and obeyed Arthur, his twenty-three brothers, led by the eldest Hueil, constantly made war against him, launching attacks from Scotland. Arthur pursued Hueil, described as a 'very famous soldier, who submitted to no king, not even Arthur', finally cornering and defeating him on the island of Minau (Man, or possibly Anglesey).

Caw's large family features in *Culhwch and Olwen* (Caw is spelled incorrectly 'Cadw' in both *Culhwch* manuscripts). The story of the feud between Arthur and Heuil, son of Caw, 'Who never submitted to a lord's hand' is also mentioned: 'Gwydre son of Llwydeu by Gwenabwy daughter of Caw (his uncle Hueil stabbed him and the wound was the source of the feud between him and Arthur)'.

Gildas was at this time preaching in Ireland, but hearing of his brother's death he returned to Britain, lodging with St Cadoc in Llancarfan. Gildas prayed for Arthur and summoned the bishops to grant him formal absolution. 'With this done, King Arthur, lamenting and grieving, received his penance from the bishops . . . and corrected himself in what way he could, until his life was completed.' In common with the previous *Lives*, Arthur, though initially a practitioner of civil war, leaves his encounter with the saint ready to take up the Christian role assigned to him in the *Historia*. The war in northern Britain, with opponents coming from Scotland and fighting in woods and battlefields, is derived from the *Historia*. Robbed of a Saxon context, it becomes a civil war between Britons.

By the end of the twelfth century, Hueil's death was being cited as the reason why Gildas left no reference to Arthur in his writings. Whether Caradoc intends us to understand that Gildas, 'Historiographer of the Britons', has deliberately removed those references is not clear. Generally, Arthur and Gildas seem to be on good terms.

The next episode takes us to territory which would dominate the Arthurian legend, signalling radical departures from the material we have seen so far. Gildas, after a spell in the Orkneys, comes to Glastonbury, where he writes the histories of the kings of Britain (*de Excidio Britanniae*, or possibly the Gildasian Recension of *Historia Brittonum*). Glastonbury, an ancient ecclesiastical centre in the *civitas* of the Durotriges, rather surprisingly fits all the clues in *de Excidio* for its place of composition, as both Dark and Higham have to admit embarrassedly. It is conceivable that Caradoc has genuine tradition to back this up. However, he has a high miss rate, Llancarfan, Armagh, Pictland and Orkney all being implausible locations with which Gildas should be familiar.

Caradoc tells us Glastonbury's actual name was *Urbs Vitrea*, City of Glass in British. He may be doing nothing more than interpreting the 'Glass' element in English, but we should also recall the *Caer Wydyr*, the glass fort or city of *Preiddeu Annwfyn*. It is, says Caradoc, in the summer country '*in aestiva regione*', which may again be nothing more than an interpretation of the English 'Somerset'. Remember, though, that the summer country, *Gwlat yr Haf*, is an enigmatic region from which Arthur summons troops in *Culhwch and Olwen*. At this time, King Meluas was ruling the summer country. He violates and carries off Guennuuar, wife of 'the tyrant Arthur' and hides her in Glastonbury, all but impregnable behind its rivers, reeds and marshes. It takes the rebel king (Arthur) the whole cycle of a year to find where his wife is held. He then raises the armies of Devon and Cornwall to besiege the city.

The Abbot of Glastonbury, with Gildas and other clerics, steps in to make peace, persuading Meluas to restore Guennuuar to her husband. The story ends in the expected way (for a saint's *Life*): the two kings give the abbot many territories and swear reverently to obey him and 'not to violate the holiest part or even the lands bordering on the Abbey's land'.

All the major participants – Arthur, Meluas, Guenevere and Gildas – together with the motif of the abduction of a wife and a contest for her linked to the annual cycle, are found in *Culhwch and Olwen*. In the tale, the contestants who fight annually for the hand of abducted Crieddylad, are Gredawl and Gwynn mab Nud. Another *Life*, that of St Collen, has Gwynn as a supernatural adversary of the saint, with a palace on top of Glastonbury Tor. Caradoc has, however, presented them as historical characters and events, linked to the rights and privileges of the ancient church at Glastonbury. Are his assumptions on the historicity and geography of the tale right, through lucky guesses or the result of established tradition? That the earlier *Life of Gildas* had none of these elements points to their addition from a burgeoning corpus of Arthurian legend. We have to acknowledge, however, that the picture is not implausible. The action accords with the marital and martial strife recorded in Gildas; the location is at least plausible (finds of Tintagel ware demonstrate high-status sixth-century occupation of Glastonbury Tor), with Somerset (the Durotriges) a kingdom at war with the *civitas* of Dumnonia. However the lack of any provenance for the material raises suspicions that only lucky guesswork has brought Caradoc to such a plausible scenario.

THE SAWLEY GLOSSES

Corpus Christi College Cambridge Manuscript 139 (CCCC 139) reminds us that the manuscripts relating to the Dark Age history of Britain are no chance survivals. They are careful preserved by groups with an interest in passing on the information in them. In the case of CCCC 139, these were monks from the Abbey of St Mary at Sawley, Yorkshire. The textual history has been established by Dumville (Dumville 1990), suggesting that the scribes responsible included members of the Welsh immigrant community in the area. The manuscript's origin is established by various features, including an *ex libris* inscription.

The manuscript was compiled on the years immediately preceding 1166. It includes a version of *Historia Brittonum* immediately followed by the earliest surviving version of Caradoc's *Life of Gildas*. The monks of Sawley received their *Historia Brittonum* in the Gildasian Recension, the most common version in the twelfth century, attributed to Gildas and often then assumed to be the actual *de Excidio Britanniae*. By 1164, the monks had acquired two pieces of evidence that convinced them otherwise. One was the *Life of Gildas*, describing him as a contemporary of Arthur. The other was a manuscript giving what they took to be the actual identity of the author – Nennius. They annotated their own version of the *Historia* with material from this example of the Nennian Recension, including that famous prologue: 'I have therefore made a heap of all that I found . . . .'

Work did not finish on the manuscript in 1166. New glosses were added through to the early years of the thirteenth century. Some of these 'Sawley Glosses' relate to the Arthurian material. Their late date makes them suspect as primary evidence, but their different interpretation of the Arthurian material is interesting. The first Arthurian gloss appears in the margin of the battle-list, by the description of Arthur at Mount Badon. 'Mabutur [later glossed 'in British'] that is 'horrible son' [glossed 'in Latin'] since from his boyhood he was cruel. Arthur, translated into Latin means 'horrible bear' or 'Iron hammer', with which the jaws of lions were broken.' This gloss reveals the author's interest in Welsh etymology. *Mab uthr* could mean 'horrible son' and *arth uthr* is the Welsh for 'horrible bear'. Most writers agreed that Arthur does indeed derive from *Arth*. The Welsh for hammer *ordd* is less plausible and has not found favour.

By the time the gloss was written, Arthur was known among Welsh speakers with the name Map Uthyr. This is a relatively recent, Middle Welsh patronymic, meaning son of Uthyr. The 'official' version of Arthurian history following Geoffrey of Monmouth had established that Arthur was the son of Uther Pendragon, a character mentioned in *Pa gur*. The form in the gloss is not old and there is no reason to think the writer found it in an earlier source. It is surprising, given his obvious interest in the subject, that he has not heard the canonical explanation for the name or wanted to pass it on.

Significantly, the glossator considers Arthur to have been congenitally cruel. This ascription of ingrained cruelty to Arthur places the author in the tradition of the saints' *Lives* – the sixth century was a time of tyrants and Arthur must have been one such man.

The 'iron hammer' alternative points us towards *Pa gur*, where Kei fought lions, perhaps including the man-eating Palug's cat. By the thirteenth century, continental romances were making Arthur an opponent, even a victim, of the monstrous cat. The gloss does not suggest that any ancient source provided the information.

The same writer provides another gloss in the bottom right-hand corner: 'For Arthur travelled to Jerusalem. And there he made a cross to the same size as the Cross of our Salvation, and there it was consecrated. And for three days continuously he fasted and kept vigil and prayed in the presence of Our Lord's Cross, that the Lord should grant victory to him over the pagans, through this sign, which was done. And he carried with him an image of St Mary, fragments of which are still preserved at Wedale, in great veneration.'

The writer here takes a guess at the nature of the image of the Virgin Mary carried by Arthur at Castellum Guinnion, in this case a separate image whose pieces still exist in St Mary-at-Stow in Wedale (Lothian). The writer makes a conflation that has become common in modern works, that of the image the *Historia* says Arthur bore on his shoulders at Castellum Guinnion, and the cross he carried at Badon. As the latter is not actually referred to in the *Historia*, it shows a familiarity with *Annales Cambriae* which do not feature in the manuscript.

As we have seen, the twelfth century was the great age for ecclesiastical 'forgery'. We need suspect no more than that Wedale had a fragmentary image of the Virgin, which the writer has tied to the *Historia* to create a respectable pedigree. The true cross and Arthur's journey to Jerusalem are also suggestive of a twelfth-century date. The Crusades to conquer, defend and reclaim Jerusalem must have been on everyone's lips, especially the recent journey of Richard the Lionheart to the Holy Land and the church campaign to raise money for it. In this atmosphere, the *Annales* 'Cross of our Lord Jesus Christ' has become in the writer's mind the True Cross in Jerusalem.

The Sawley glosses thus hardly indicate existing variant traditions or even sources. They are the deductions of enthusiastic historians.

ARTHUR'S PALACE

Another source looked at by Dumville is Lambert of St Omer's historical collection *Liber Floridus* (*c.* 1120). For early British history, Lambert used the Harleian Recension of *Historia Brittonum*, augmented by other sources, such as Bede and the Anglo-Saxon Chronicle. These materials reached him from a Kentish source, most likely Christ Church, Canterbury.

Lambert used the Arthurian battle-list to expand on the references to Arthur in the *Mirabilia*. He appends four additional wonders to the list, two in the Gloucester region, one in Ireland and one in Scotland, a similar distribution to that in the Harleian Manuscript. Only one is connected with a named individual, and that individual is Arthur the Soldier, exactly as we would expect. This time, however, it is not one of the Gloucester-area wonders which bears his name, but the one in Scotland: 'There is a palace in Britain in the land of the Picts belonging to Arthur the Soldier, made with wonderful art and variety, in which can be seen sculpted all his deeds and battles.' Our examination of *Historia Brittonum* led us to conclude that South Welsh,

Kentish and northern sources had been combined in the Arthurian section. In Lambert, this new northern material from an apparently Kentish source seems almost too good to be true!

Where was this incredible palace which, if real, would answer our questions at a stroke? The only large stone building in Scotland ascribed to Arthur was a circular domed construction called Arthur's O'on or Oven. This stood in the Carron valley in Stirlingshire until it was demolished in 1742–3. It was known as Arthur's Oven (*furnum arthuri*) as early as 1293 (XII in Dumville 1990). From what we know of the building, it was not carved with battle scenes and we do not know whether it had an Arthurian connection as early as Lambert's time. One indication that it did not can be found in manuscript CCCC 139. In this, a writer (*c.* 1200) added at the point where the Romans build a wall across the island: 'Later the Emperor Carutius rebuilt it . . . and constructed a round house of dressed stone on the banks of the river Carun (which got its name from his name), erecting a triumphal arch in memory of his victory.'

This rotunda is clearly the building which less than a century later would be called 'Arthur's Oven'. Not only does it stand in the same location and have the same shape, it is also possible that the similarity between the word *fornix* (arch) in the Sawley description and *fornum* (oven) is not entirely fortuitous. If 'Arthur's Oven' and 'Arthur's Palace' are the same, then we would have to accept that, in the half-century between Lambert and the Sawley writer, the Arthurian identity was lost in favour of an uninspiring etymology from the 'Carutius'. This seems unlikely, given that the Sawley school were interested in passing on Arthurian material, and that the Arthurian name resurfaced anyway.

If we suppose that Arthur's palace was more than a figment of the imagination, what kind of a building could it have been? Large stone structures were still being erected in Europe during the early sixth century. The rotunda built for Theodoric the Ostrogoth can still be seen in Ravenna, for example. Rich pictorial decorative schemes, more often in mosaic than carvings, were also a feature of royal and imperial buildings of the period. Needless to say, nothing of the kind has survived in Britain. There are figurative carved stones in Pictish territories, but none incorporated in the decoration of a building as distinctive as this 'palace'. The only reasonable conclusion is that the *Mirabilia* intended some real or imagined Roman building. More significant, however, is the idea that Arthur the Soldier owned any kind of palace at all.

Lambert writes:

> At that time the Saxons increased in number and grew in Britain. On the
> death of Hengist, Octha his son came down from the northern part of
> Britain to the kingdom of the men of Kent, and from him are descended
> the kings of Kent. Then Arthur, leader of the Picts was ruling the
> kingdoms of the British interior. He was mighty in strength and a fearsome
> soldier. Seeing that England was being attacked in this way, and that
> wealth of the land was being despoiled and many people captured and
> ransomed and expelled from their inheritances, he attacked the Saxons in a
> ferocious assault, with the kings of the Britons, and rushing against them
> fought manfully, being *dux bellorum* twelve times as written above.

Lambert is alone among the Dark Age and medieval writers in reading the
phrase '*cum brittonum regibus*' not as 'with the *kings* of the Britons', i.e. that
he was not a king, but as 'with the kings of the *Britons*' because he, though a
king, is not British. Although Lambert may have had other, Kentish-derived
material, saying Arthur was a Pict, Occam's razor leads us to the conclusion
that we already know what is his source – the Wonder of Arthur's Palace in
Pictland. It could be an inference from this alone that Arthur was a native of
Pictland. Lambert may have had no idea where the regions of Buelt and
Ercing were, but Pictland would have been comprehensible to him.

As far as we can ascertain, Lambert is the first writer to say that Arthur is
the King of Britain. This is no longer a surprising image, as it has been the
standard interpretation of Arthur's position in fiction since the late twelfth
century. However, for a historian in 1120 to make such a claim is remarkable.

Lambert's view of Arthur, as a warleader against the Saxons and as King
of Britain, is an extension of the historical line we have been following. The
other ecclesiastical materials diverge in the same way as the Welsh vernacular
ones. In them, Arthur inhabits a world of giants, monsters and miracles. His
armies and royal allies are reduced to small bands of heroes, with Kei and
Bedwyr named among them. A concentration on south-east Wales is in
keeping with the *Mirabilia*, but is combined with a shift towards a later
historical position as a contemporary of Maelgwn and Gildas.

Both strands of twelfth-century opinion are brought together in the
major Arthurian work of the period, Geoffrey of Monmouth's *History of the
Kings of Britain*.

9

GEOFFREY OF MONMOUTH

Early in the 1130s, Geoffrey of Monmouth was thinking about the history of Britain. It seemed strange to him that, apart from the brilliant works of Gildas and of Bede, so little had been written about the early kings of Britain, 'or indeed about Arthur and all the others who followed on after the Incarnation'.

It was then that Walter, Archdeacon of Oxford, presented Geoffrey with a very ancient book in the British language, brought, according to some versions, 'from Britannia'. This book 'attractively composed to form a consecutive and orderly narrative, set out the deeds [of the Kings of Britain] from Brutus, the first king of the Britons down to Cadwallader son of Cadwallo'. At Walter's request, Geoffrey of Monmouth translated the book into Latin. That was, according to him, the origin of the book *Historia Regum Britanniae* – 'The History of the Kings of Britain', which appeared under his name.

The book tells the story of ninety-nine British kings, the majority pre-Christian and, before Geoffrey, pre-historic. As the introduction hints, Arthur is the central figure in the History. The book was an instant hit. The historian, Henry of Huntingdon, seeing a copy for the first time in 1139, wrote approvingly to a colleague. At least fifty manuscripts survive from the twelfth century alone, outweighing all the manuscripts of all the earlier Arthurian sources put together. By the end of the century, translations into French, English and Welsh had spread Geoffrey's version even further afield.

Later in the twelfth century, William of Newburgh wrote critically

In our own day, a writer of the opposite tendency [to the truthful Gildas] has emerged. To atone for these faults of the Britons he weaves a laughable web of fiction about them. . . . This man is called Geoffrey, and bears the soubriquet Arthur, because he has taken up the stories about Arthur from the old fictitious accounts of the Britons, has added to them himself and has cloaked them with the honourable title of history. . . . It is clear that

Geoffrey's entire narration about Arthur, his successors and his predecessors after Vortigern, was invented partly by himself and partly by others. The motive was either an uncontrolled passion for lying, or secondly a desire to please the Britons.
(Walsh and Kennedy 1986)

This passage is often quoted to show how even contemporaries saw through Geoffrey's fiction. This is misleading. William of Newburgh, writing forty years after Geoffrey, was in a minority condemning everything in the book as a lie. Although most of the kings are unknown before Geoffrey, the bulk of the book is dedicated to characters such as Brutus, Brennius, Cassivelaunus, Constantine, Cadwallo and of course Arthur, who were already known from earlier sources.

That is not to say that we can take Geoffrey at face value. Much of his work is fiction, or at least fictionalised. One of the major distorting factors can be found in the title, 'The History of the Kings of Britain'. All the major characters are made 'kings of Britain'. As Geoffrey understands the term, they are actually kings of England and rightful overlords of Scotland, Wales and Cornwall, a concept derived from the aftermath of the Norse invasions. There is no question of it being a fifth/sixth-century reality. Thus Cadwallo, Gildas's tyrants, Constantine the Great, Cassivelaunus and Brenn(i)us, the Celtic chieftain who sacked Rome, are all kings of Britain. It is no surprise, therefore, to find that Ambrosius and Arthur are kings of Britain too.

As Geoffrey begins his History with a claim to a unique source, it is reasonable to investigate this first. The idea of an orderly and consecutive narrative of kings immediately raises the possibility of a kings' list or genealogy. The work is light on dates, pointing away from an annalistic or chronicle work. Piggott (1941) showed recurring patterns of names, suggesting several genealogies of related or supposedly related persons, similar to those in the Harleian Manuscript. He argued that a Welsh-style genealogy, ordered A, son of B, son of C, with A being the modern descendant of an ancestral C, has at some point been confused with a biblical-style genealogy, A begat B begat C, in which C is modern and A ancient. This simple mistake would transform a fairly conventional genealogy leading back to Caswallaun (perhaps Maelgwn Gwynedd's 'father' from the Harleian Genealogies), into a bizarre list culminating in Julius Caesar's 55 BC adversary Cassivelaunus and thus consisting of pre-Roman rulers.

This theory explains why we find Dark Age names such as Cunedagius, Urianus, Gerennus and his son Catellus (Gereint and Cadwy) in the story of ancient Britain. Such genealogies could have formed a framework by which a British author could have ordered a history.

Unfortunately, genealogies cannot form the basis of Geoffrey's Arthurian section. This begins with Constantine, a scion of the Breton royal house, not immediately connected with the previous rulers of Britain. The succession goes to his eldest son Constans, then to Vortigern and his son, then back to two of Constantine's sons, then to his grandson Arthur, then to the peripherally connected tyrants before ending in Cadwallo and Cadwallader. These are not treated as a genealogical succession, nor can they plausibly derive from one. The genealogy of Cadwallo, which does not include any of Geoffrey's Dark Age kings except Malgo/Maelgwn, was long established. Cadwallo actually recites it in the book. The 'kings' of this period are all from known sources, but had never been connected before.

Geoffrey's 'Arthurian' section incorporates material from various sources. He quotes directly from Gildas's *de Excidio*, using the Latin version, not translating from a Welsh intermediary. This would imply that the 'very ancient book' did not offer a detailed context for the Arthurian period. The framing passages showing the period as following Agitius and preceding the tyrants of *de Excidio* must be Geoffrey's editorial additions.

Without the material derived from Gildas, the 'very ancient book' looks like a relatively disjointed history of Britain, with separate episodes about Dark Age kings, genealogies without historical context, and undated lists of events. Such a work is not hard to imagine: we have already encountered one, the Harleian Manuscript. Is it possible, therefore, that Geoffrey had such a composite work? The Harleian Manuscript has as its basis *Historia Brittonum* and it is obvious that Geoffrey has this too. *Historia Brittonum*, like *Historia Regum Britanniae*, is a history beginning with Brutus the first king, arriving at Cadwallo by way of Arthur.

This presents us with two possibilities. The first is that Geoffrey simply has a Latin copy of *Historia Brittonum*, which he uses along with *de Excidio* to supplement his 'very ancient book'. If so, the ancient book would have contained very little indeed. Once Gildas, *Historia Brittonum* and other known Latin sources are removed, there is little potentially British-derived material, and none of that orderly and consecutive narrative. The second possibility is that the 'very ancient book' is a British translation of the *Historia*. This is by no means inconceivable, though no such work exists for comparison.

Another approach is to investigate just how ancient such a source book could be. At its earliest, it must post-date the late seventh-century reign of Cadwallader. If it incorporates *Historia Brittonum*, this brings it forward to the early ninth century. Some features, such as the use of the form 'Urianus' for the *Historia*'s 'Urbgen' point it forward from this, while others such as *Camblan* for the *Annales*' *Camlann*, and the early names of Arthur's equipment suggest something in the early tenth century. This is supported by the reference to Athelstan (reigned 924–40) as king of England at the end of the book.

The most generous hypothesis is that Geoffrey's very ancient book is a tenth-century British manuscript, perhaps an expanded version of *Historia Brittonum*. Most commentators would not even grant this. It is possible that Geoffrey combined material from known (Latin) sources with disparate British legends unconnected before *Historia Regum Britanniae*. Geoffrey lets slip that these legends exist in unwritten form: 'these deeds were handed down joyfully in oral tradition, just as if they had been committed to writing, by many peoples who had only their memory to go on.'

The ancient book is not cited throughout as a source. It appears in the introduction, and serves the purpose of validating the author's work while at the same time distancing him from its content. Geoffrey might want to conceal his own authorial voice, given the dangerous times he lived in. The men to whom different manuscripts of *Historia Regum Britanniae* are dedicated were contenders in the Anarchy, the civil wars raging in England, and political points could easily be inferred from the book.

The principal dispute in the Anarchy was whether a woman could succeed to the throne or pass the throne to her son. This was unprecedented in the actual history of England, but Geoffrey shows it happening several times. Readers might also see Modred's treachery to his uncle, Arthur, as reflecting the political situation. King Stephen had broken his oath to his uncle Henry I and usurped the kingdom of Queen Mathilda. In fact, Modred's usurpation is the only point where Geoffrey cites the ancient book as his authority: 'About this particular matter, most noble Duke, Geoffrey of Monmouth prefers to say nothing. He will, however, in his own poor style and without wasting words, describe the battle which our most famous king fought against his nephew . . . for that he found in the British treatise already referred to.'

Geoffrey's obvious sources are not confined to British history. His Latin sources include Jerome and Bede for synchronism, Orosius for Roman history and Roman epics for stylistic and verbal features.

GEOFFREY AND GILDAS

While Geoffrey cites the 'very ancient book' once, he makes frequent references to Gildas. Some of this is to the real Gildas of *de Excidio*, some to the writer of the Gildasian Recension. Most are less clear and may give another clue to his source. Geoffrey clearly knows Gildas's *de Excidio Britanniae*. Cadwallo, while denouncing his countrymen, says 'As the historian Gildas tells us . . .' before quoting directly from it. This is the lone example of Geoffrey using Gildas's name in connection with his actual work. Every other citation is problematic. When Geoffrey says that Gildas has said sufficient about the dispute between King Lud and his brother Nennius over the renaming of London, we may be invited to share his joke that Gildas says nothing about it. When we read that King Alfred's Laws are only English translations of the prehistoric Laws of Dunwallo Molmutius, a character from the Harleian Genealogies, via a Latin translation by Gildas, this may derive from an impression that laws are the sort of thing Gildas wrote. However, Geoffrey's other references to Gildas are not so explicable.

Geoffrey reports the evangelisation of Britain before AD 156, the death of the first Christian king, Lucius. This information is derived from Bede, who received a mistaken report to this effect from Rome. Faganus and Duvianus lead the missionary work, but are later accompanied by a great number of other religious men: 'Their names and deeds can be found in the book which Gildas wrote about the victory of Aurelius Ambrosius. All this Gildas set out in a treatise which is so lucidly written that it seemed to me unnecessary that it should be described a second time in my more homely style' (HRB IV.20, Thorpe 1966:125).

Geoffrey asserts that Gildas writes about the deeds of the saints again: 'It was at this time that St Germanus of Auxerre came and Lupus, Bishop of Troyes, with him, to preach the word of God to the Britons . . . through their agency God performed many wonders which Gildas has described with great literary skill.' Here Geoffrey may have written 'Gildas' by mistake – it is Bede who covers the deeds of these two saints in detail. However, both references together suggest that Gildas produced hagiography. This is very strange. The

account of the conversion of Britain is not found in any work attributed to
Gildas, nor can any of his works be called 'about the victory of Aurelius
Ambrosius'. Geoffrey does not read *de Excidio* as ascribing victory to
Ambrosius. Even if *de Excidio* were the work intended, it only names three
saints, not a great number, not Faganus and Duvianus, and not as mission-
aries, but as martyrs. Whatever book Geoffrey is thinking of, it is not *de Excidio*.

On the other hand, Geoffrey clearly knows *Historia Brittonum*. The story of
Vortigern and Vortimer derives directly from it. Geoffrey, however, never
recognisably cites this work. If he knew it in the Gildasian Recension, the
most common at the time, then he specifically distinguishes material therein
from that found in the ancient book. Until he receives the book, he has hardly
any British material 'apart from such mention of them as Gildas and Bede
had each made in a brilliant book on the subject'. As he only refers to one
book by Gildas, and it must include *de Excidio Britanniae*, we can only assume
that Geoffrey must be using a version of Gildas supplemented by
hagiographical material and extended treatment of Ambrosius, and perhaps
the whole of the Gildasian *Historia Brittonum*. If his 'Gildas' is extended in this
way, then there is even less material additional to it which we would have to
assign to the 'very ancient book'.

There is one more factor in the equation, Geoffrey's own contribution as
author. To find out what this might have been, we need to consider him in
relation to other historians of his own time.

GEOFFREY AND THE HISTORIANS

It is about this Arthur that the Britons tell such trifling stories even today.
Clearly he was a man more worthy to be extolled in true histories, as the
leader who long preserved his tottering homeland and kindled an appetite
for war in the shattered minds of his countrymen, than to be dreamed of
in fallacious fables. (William of Malmesbury, *The Deeds of the Kings of the
English c.* 1125.)

At the end of some manuscripts of the *Historia Regum Britanniae*, Geoffrey
refers pompously to three historians. 'The task of describing [the] kings who
succeeded from that moment in Wales, I leave to my contemporary Caradoc of
Llancarfan. The kings of the Saxons I leave to William of Malmesbury and
Henry of Huntingdon. I recommend these last to say nothing at all about the

kings of the Britons, seeing that they do not have in their possession the book in the British language which Walter, Archdeacon of Oxford brought from Britannia' (after Thorpe 1966).

Although William and Henry are told to avoid the Britons, this warning does not extend to Caradoc. But for the survival of his *Life of Gildas*, we would have no idea of Caradoc's output and would have to take on trust that he was working on or capable of working on the history of Welsh rulers from the eighth century onwards. His surviving work, however, bears no affinity to Geoffrey's. If Geoffrey knew of Caradoc's work, we have to wonder why he does not incorporate anything of it in his book. The key Arthurian episode in the *Life of Gildas*, the abduction of Guenevere, does not appear in Geoffrey. Their works show that they have fundamental differences in approach. For Geoffrey, the churchmen of Britain are loyal subordinates of the kings. They are not, as Caradoc and the other saints' *Lives* have it, mediators to whom the kings must turn for help or absolution. Geoffrey specifically says of the monk-king Constans (Arthur's 'uncle'), 'What he learned in the cloister had nothing to do with how to rule a kingdom'.

The early twelfth century saw an upsurge of interest in national history. The Normans and the Angevins had their national histories. Henry of Huntingdon reports Henry I's enquiries into the origins of the French and his discovery that they were descended from the Trojan Antenor. England was particularly well off for ancient, Anglo-Saxon, sources. The Laud Manuscript of the Anglo-Saxon Chronicle, for instance, was written 1121–54. These provided material for William of Malmesbury, who began his *Gesta Regum Anglorum c.* 1125 and Henry of Huntingdon, starting his *Historia Anglorum* in 1133. This is the background which inspired Geoffrey's work.

All the historians incorporate etymology, showing how familiar place-names or words derived from history or ancient languages. Geoffrey and William of Malmesbury both give the pagan meanings behind the English days of the week, for instance.

The idiom in which all the writers worked used what we would describe as imaginative reconstructions or historical fiction. This included inventing 'direct speeches', spicing up accounts of battles with troop dispositions and single combats, and relaying anecdotes of a moral or simply entertaining nature. Henry of Huntington includes the story of King Canute trying to turn back the tide in his Chronicle-derived account of the Danish conquest. Geoffrey's tale of King Bladud, who tried to fly and crashed on to the temple of Apollo in London is no more outlandish than William's account of Eilmerus, the flying monk of Malmesbury.

It is not surprising, therefore, to discover that Arthur's campaigns in Geoffrey are similar to those William records for Athelstan or Canute. The court of William the Conqueror is reflected in Arthur's court at Caerleon. Geoffrey has the tale of the fatherless wonderchild, Merlin, similar to the story of St Aldhelm in William's *Gesta Pontificum.* This is not to say that Geoffrey parodied the other historians – in this case he took the story from *Historia Brittonum* – but that all worked in the same idiom.

The similarity of their works is not surprising, as the historians often shared the same patrons. William's *Historia Novella* is dedicated to Robert of Gloucester, one of the dedicatees of Geoffrey's work. Geoffrey's Prophecies of Merlin and Henry of Huntingdon's work are dedicated to Alexander, Bishop of Lincoln. Once the writers found an idiom which pleased these powerful patrons, they were wise to stick with it.

Where Geoffrey worked in the same intellectual sphere as the secular histories, he gently contradicts the ecclesiastical material produced by Caradoc, William of Malmesbury and others. The pretensions of Llandaff are given short shrift. The fictitious Archbishopric of Caerleon, with primacy over all Britain, precedes St David's with its claims over Wales. Caerleon is granted the Apostolic legation centuries before it was given to Canterbury, mentioned only as a place frequented by the wicked Vortigern. William of Malmesbury's beloved Glastonbury is not mentioned at all.

Geoffrey of Monmouth's perspective

Geoffrey's own perspectives are usually obvious. We mentioned his conviction that all the great characters of British history were 'kings of Britain', often linked dynastically. The succession of kings of Britain from Constantine to Ambrosius and Uther Pendragon, his sons, to Uther's son Arthur, to Arthur's cousin Constantine, then to Constantine's nephew Aurelius need not have any source before Geoffrey.

Although Geoffrey's geographical scope is broader than any previous Arthurian material, regional bias is clear. With a writer who identifies himself as 'of Monmouth', south-east Wales and adjacent Gloucestershire feature prominently. Strangely, although Geoffrey knows the *Mirabilia* – King Arthur discusses them with King Hoel – he makes no reference to the Arthurian wonders. Ercing is just a refuge of Vortigern. Similarly, although Geoffrey gives Caerleon as 'City of the Legions' he does not equate this with the similarly named battle-site in *Historia Brittonum*.

We cannot tell whether Geoffrey made use of Arthur because he was already famous in the region or if the connection derived from his own regional bias. There is only one pre-existing south-eastern Welsh tradition with an identifiable link – that to St Dubricius. Geoffrey makes this Welsh saint the Archbishop of Caerleon, Primate of Britain and Arthur's right-hand cleric. It is Dubricius who crowns Arthur. The pre-Geoffrey *Life of St Dubricius* does not make any of these claims and knows nothing of Arthur. However, we saw how Davies was able to make a reasonable case defining the area of Ercing, the sub-kingdom associated with Arthur, by church dedications to St Dubricius.

The magnification of Caerleon is Geoffrey's invention, doubtless based on the Roman remains visible there, familiar to a native of Monmouth. Any ancient book which he possessed would have to be transmitted by clerics. It is inconceivable that an ecclesiastical writer from elsewhere would so aggrandise a rival see. None of the abundant twelfth-century South Welsh material supports the claims of Caerleon. For the church historians of twelfth-century Wales, Llandaff or St David's are the key locations. Geoffrey contradicts these claims. Teilo, first Bishop of Llandaff is just a priest, and St David's is a foundation of St Patrick.

This predictable regional bias is not the only one found in Geoffrey's work. Towards the end of the book, Cadwallo, exiled from Britain, arrives at the court of King Salomon of Brittany. Salomon launches a verbal attack on the Welsh, compared with the earlier kings of the Britons: 'a series of weaker men succeeded them as their heirs, and these lost the island once and for all when the enemy attacked. That is why I am so distressed at the feeble behaviour of your people, for we come from the same stock and we bear the name of Britons just as the men of your kingdom do, and yet we manage to protect our fatherland, which you see around you, when it is attacked by any of our neighbours.'

Strangely, Cadwallo agrees with him: 'When you said it was extraordinary that my people could not maintain the proud position of their ancestors once the Britons had migrated to these lands, I myself really find nothing to be surprised at. The nobler members of the whole community followed the leaders [to Brittany] and only the baser sort remained behind and took over the lands of those who had gone' (HRB XII.6, Thorpe 1966:275). He then piles more invective on the insular Britons than his host has done.

Later, the Voice of God, confirmed by all written oracles and prophesies, informs Cadwallo's son that his people will never more rule the island. The remaining insular Britons continue to degenerate so much that even their ancient name is lost, and they become known as the Welsh, perhaps, Geoffrey suggests, because they are so barbarous.

This Breton bias is evident throughout the history. Every major ruler, Arthur included, has military exploits on the continent, in the lands bordering Brittany. Arthur's family is from the Breton royal house, and his victories are only accomplished with Breton military might.

There is no convincing twelfth-century reason for this. Neither Geoffrey nor his dedicatees are Bretons. The only real explanation is that he is using a Breton source. He tells us specifically that he has a book about Breton history. As Gormund, King of the Africans, devastates seventh-century England, 'many priests fled in a great fleet to Armorican Brittany . . . I shall describe these happenings elsewhere when I come to translate their Book of the Exile'. There are clues that Geoffrey's very ancient book in the British language is also a Breton work. When Geoffrey uses the word *Britannia* in his book, he either means Britain or Brittany. As there is no indication that he is writing outside England (indeed, he was witnessing charters in Oxford at the time), the only explanation for his claim that Walter the Archdeacon brought him the book 'ex Britannia' is that it came from Brittany. As we will discover, the only major parts of Geoffrey's story of Arthur which cannot be extrapolated from known sources are those dealing with his exploits in France. We have thus some pointers towards Geoffrey's unknown source.

THE HISTORY OF THE KINGS OF BRITAIN

Although Geoffrey's work runs from the aftermath of the Trojan War to the end of the seventh century AD, half of it focuses on the hundred years *c*. AD 450–550. Geoffrey's passages which begin and end the period are those from Gildas which I have chosen to define the Arthurian era. Geoffrey simply quotes Gildas describing the Roman withdrawal from Britain. He includes the appeal to Agitius with no guess at who he might be.

We are back on familiar ground at the end when we meet Gildas's tyrants Constantine, Aurelius Conanus, Vortiporius and Malgo. The indications are that Cuneglassus was also in Geoffrey's original version. His reign had earlier been predicted by Merlin. However, at a very early stage in the manuscript transmission, he must have been dropped accidentally as a scribe moved from one similar passage to another. Each of the reigns begin with the same words, '*cui sucessit*' (to whom succeeded), so such a mistake would be easy to make.

The tyrants are consecutive rulers of all Britain. Although readers can detect a light-hearted air to Geoffrey's work, it is not justified to say that the work is a knowing parody. No contemporaries 'got' Geoffrey's jokes and he never draws attention to them as would be expected from a writer of the time. We cannot say, therefore, that his consecutive reigns of reasonably good kings are a humorous distortion of Gildas's contemporary bad ones. He may genuinely have understood Gildas as saying they were a succession of kings of the whole country. Gildas never states explicitly when or even if Britain has fragmented into small regional kingdoms. This is something we have established from external evidence. Geoffrey, on the contrary, might fully appreciate his difference from Gildas, and consider he is setting the record straight. Whatever Geoffrey's intention, he does not know anything about these rulers other than what is contained in Gildas. He embellishes and glosses this material but does not add to it significantly.

The sequence begins with the reign of Constantine, according to Geoffrey the son of Duke Cador of Cornwall and a cousin of Arthur. Geoffrey synchronises his reign to the deaths of Daniel, Bishop of Bangor, and St David. As they do not feature in Gildas, they must derive from a separate source. David is buried in Menevia (St David's) on the orders of Malgo, King of the Venedotians, with no indication that this is the same man who appears a few years later as 'Malgo King of Britain'. He is, of course, Maglocunus of *de Excidio*.

Unlike the previous sources we have been studying, the problem with analysing Geoffrey's History is the huge number of copies (at least 200) which survive. The current editor, Neil Wright, is working on a detailed textual history, but until that is completed it is difficult to say which manuscripts give the best witness to Geoffrey's intentions. Modern editors of Geoffrey's work have used different criteria for which variant readings they prefer.

Malgo is a case in point. 'Mabgo', King of the Venedotians, appears in Cambridge University Library MS Ii.1.14 (1706) as edited by Griscom, the source of Thorpe's popular translation. Griscom, however, had only the Bern Manuscript for comparison, which does not say anything about the king who ordered St David's burial. Meanwhile, Faral's edition of Cambridge, Trinity

College MS 0.2.21 (1125), combined with nine others, opts for Malgo, King of the Venedotians. Presuming this is the original reading, Geoffrey must recognise that Malgo of the Venedotians and Malgo, King of Britain, are the same person. Cadwallo gives his genealogy going back to Malgo, specifically stated to be the fourth ruler after Arthur. This is essentially the Harleian genealogy of Gwynedd, and Cadwallo's father Cadvan(us) has been described as King of Gwynedd. This suggests that Geoffrey does associate Malgo King of Britain with North Wales. He would begin as King of North Wales in the time of Constantine, rule through the three years of Aurelius and the doubtless short reign of the, according to Gildas, aged Vortiporius, before becoming King of Britain. This neatly combines Maelgwn's traditional location with Maglocunus's wide power in Gildas.

The only incident of Constantine's life which Geoffrey covers is his killing of the two royal youths in a church. According to Geoffrey, these are the sons of Arthur's adversary, Modred, defeated in a civil war and pursued to monasteries in Winchester and London. More discreditable aspects of the story, such as Constantine's oath not to use his wiles on the Britons, his 'disguise' as a holy abbot and the presence of the youths' earthly mother, described by Gildas, are glossed over. The killings in church are, however, punished four years later by God. Constantine is buried at Stonehenge.

Constantine is succeeded by his nephew, Aurelius Conanus. I have suggested a family relationship between them, too, but in this case Geoffrey could equally well be guessing at a dynastic link. The other lion's whelps, in Gildas the uncle of Maglocunus and his men, are transposed to Aurelius's story. In Geoffrey's version, Aurelius defeats his uncle, presumably Constantine's brother, who should have ruled after him, and kills his sons. This replaces the untimely death of Aurelius's father and brothers in Gildas. Aurelius's involvement in civil wars is considered by Geoffrey as the one blot on the career of this 'extraordinarily brave' and 'worthy' king of the whole island of Britain. Aurelius comes to the throne a young man and dies just three years later, fulfilling Gildas's suggestion that he will not live to see his descendants. Geoffrey's version of his name 'Aurelius Conanus' is rather more likely than Gildas's (punning?) Caninus.

Little is said about Aurelius's successor, Vortiporius. He is a successful fighter against the Saxons, but none of the information from Gildas, not even his Demetian origin or his royal father, is given. He simply 'governed the people frugally and peacefully'.

The detailed condemnation of Maglocunus is disregarded by Geoffrey, who paints the king in the best possible light: 'He was the most handsome of almost all the leaders of Britain [the tallest, in Gildas], and he strove hard to do away with those who ruled the people harshly [the tyrants Gildas says he dispossessed]. He was a man brave in battle, more generous than his predecessors [even Gildas acknowledges this] and greatly renowned for his courage.' Geoffrey interprets his epithet 'insular dragon' with the greatest hyperbole. Not only is he 'ruler of the entire island [of Britain]', he also conquers the six neighbouring islands of Ireland, Iceland, Gotland, the Orkneys, Norway and Denmark! The only bad thing Geoffrey finds to say about him is that he was 'given to the vice of sodomy', a probably over-literal interpretation of Gildas's description of him behaving like 'a man drunk on the wine of the sodomitic grape'.

These passages are no more than Geoffrey's variations on Gildas's themes. Apart from the synchronism with Constantine, Mabgo and the saints, there is no indication of any outside source. Geoffrey clearly knows no more than we do about Gildas's tyrants. The other characters, like Maglocunus's wives, Vortiporius's father, the royal youths' mother, are not even hinted at. Malgo and Agitius are no more than characters from Gildas, framing the story of the Saxon revolt and British recovery.

THE HOUSE OF CONSTANTINE

The story starts with the reign of Constantine 'King of Britain'. This is the usurper Constantine III, discovered in Orosius's history and played out to Geoffrey's various distortions. Gildas had assigned the end of Roman rule in Britain to Maximus, and described the era which followed as being given over to kings of Britain, deposed by yet more cruel successors. It was reasonable for Geoffrey to conclude that Constantine III, who ruled later than Maximus, was one of those kings. Geoffrey shares Gildas's view that Romans are a continental people, distinct from the inhabitants of Britain, so if Constantine is a Roman, he must come from overseas. In keeping with the detected bias, he is a Breton, brother of King Aldroenus of Brittany.

Geoffrey has little use for Constantine who briefly fights 'the enemy' before being murdered by a Pict. Vortigern, duke of the Gewissei, seizes power in the name of Constantine's monk son, Constans, whom subsequently he has murdered. In this, Vortigern plays the role of Constantine III's treacherous

British lieutenant, Gerontius. Vortimer is briefly 'King of Britain' in keeping with Geoffrey's view that all the major characters hold this rank.

Ambrosius is the son of King Constantine and his British bride, 'born of a noble family'. This explains Bede's description of them as 'of royal rank and title'. On his father's death (before the Saxon revolt rather than, as Gildas tells us, during it), Ambrosius and his brother are whisked off to Brittany while still infants. Vortigern is preoccupied about their possible return, explaining how in *Historia Brittonum* he can fear Ambrosius, even though he is still a child.

Geoffrey does not have an explicit chronological framework at this point. Without any idea of the identity of Agitius, he has nothing compelling him to place these events in the second half of the fifth century. If he has a plan, it is that the arrival of the Saxons corresponds with the early date (420s) in the *Historia*, synchronised to the early visit of St Germanus. This scheme, Constantine before 410, Vortigern and the Saxons 420, first generation of the Saxon wars under Ambrosius and his brother (450–60?) and final victory by Arthur (460–70?) is maintained with an insistence that Leo (470s) is the eastern Roman emperor at the time of Arthur's post-Badon career. Gildas would, on this assumption, be writing *c.* 510 and Badon could equally well be forty-four years after a Saxon arrival as Bede has it, albeit one in the 420s.

Ashe argues that these are the 'real' dates, somehow preserved by such synchronisms as the reign of Emperor Leo (Ashe 1982). This is to read the information the wrong way round. Geoffrey had all the sources available to construct this chronology for himself, based only on the knowledge that Constantine III reigned before 410. It comes completely apart at the other end, when Arthur fights his last battle in 542. Geoffrey gives some exact lengths for parts of Arthur's reign. Arthur is at least forty when he dies, after a reign of not much more than twenty-four years. Geoffrey must therefore imagine his reign starting *c.* 517, with Uther starting his reign *c.* 500.

Gildas cannot be writing until after the insular conquests of Malgo. Geoffrey tells us Constantine of Cornwall reigned for four years after killing the royal youths and that Aurelius ruled for three years in total. Vortiporius seems to have ruled for a reasonable amount of time. Gildas therefore can hardly have been born at the time of the battle of Mount Badon, as Geoffrey knows he must be, if this battle is in the 460s. It is this discrepancy which surely compels Geoffrey to gloss over the details of the earlier chronology, when no AD dates are given although he could easily have added them to his narrative.

The proof that the early dating is not 'right' is the appeal to Agitius. Geoffrey has no idea when or to whom this was sent. Yet this appeal was made in the second quarter of the fifth century, at the earliest. It cannot possibly pre-date the reign of Constantine III and Constans.

Geoffrey continues the story with the massacre of the British by the Saxons at their peace conference, following *Historia Brittonum*. Vortigern flees to Wales and tries to build a castle which keeps collapsing. At this point, we are introduced to Geoffrey's major innovation, the figure of Merlin.

Although Geoffrey did not know this at the time, the Welsh prophet Myrddin (his Merlin) had acquired quite a legendary history. He was connected to the late sixth-century British kingdoms of the north and was famous for his prophecies. Several poems in the *Black Book of Carmarthen* are attributed to him. Geoffrey subsequently learnt more about him and incorporated it in his *Vita Merlini (Life of Merlin)* some twenty years later.

Geoffrey had access to the prophecies of Merlin in the British tongue, so he says. While he was writing the history, there was much interest in the prophecies, so Geoffrey 'translated' them into Latin. He attached them to the History crudely, at the point in *Historia Brittonum* where prophecy was mentioned, that of the boy about to be sacrificed at Vortigern's tower. In *Historia Brittonum* the denouement is that the prophetic boy is Ambrosius. Here it is Merlin 'also called Ambrosius'.

The prophecies of Merlin were originally independent of the History. They have their own dedication. They allude to Arthur as 'The Boar of Cornwall'. This image is not carried through to the History, where Arthur uses a golden dragon as his symbol. When Arthur has a dream about a *bear* fighting a dragon, his advisers connect him with the dragon while he and Geoffrey seem to think he is actually the bear.

The epithet 'of Cornwall' is also odd. According to Geoffrey, Arthur was conceived in Cornwall and is related by marriage to the rulers of Cornwall. This seems hardly sufficient to warrant describing him as 'of Cornwall'.

'The end of the Boar will be shrouded in mystery', we are told. Although, as William of Malmesbury confirms, legends were circulating that Arthur would return, or that his grave was unknown, or a mystery, Geoffrey does not make this explicit. In his version, Arthur goes to the Isle of Avallon to have his mortal wound treated. He then disappears from the story. Perhaps Geoffrey later decided he had been too coy, for the version given in the *Vita Merlini* is more mysterious than the account in the History.

Merlin prophesies that 'six of the boar's successors shall hold the sceptre, but after them 'the German Worm' [the Saxons] will return' (HRB VII.3). Thorpe translates this as Arthur's 'descendants', though it is perfectly clear that he has none, or at least that his successors are not among them. The successors are Constantine of Cornwall, Aurelius Conanus, Vortiporius, Malgo and Keredic. As suggested, the fact that there are only five of them indicates that, at some early stage, the reign of Cuneglassus was dropped accidentally.

AMBROSIUS

By allocating the prophetic role from *Historia Brittonum* to Merlin, Geoffrey can tell the story of Ambrosius in a generally realistic fashion. Ambrosius begins by overthrowing Vortigern's government, as we have inferred earlier. 'The Britons counselled an immediate attack on the Saxons, but [Ambrosius] persuaded them against it, for he wanted to hunt down Vortigern first.' Vortigern is defeated and burnt in his castle in Erging.

Next, Ambrosius turns his attention to Hengist. The terrified Saxons have retreated north of the Humber and fortified cities there. They are strengthened by the proximity of Scotland, 'for that country had never missed an opportunity of making matters worse whenever the Britons were in distress. It was a land frightful to live in, more or less uninhabited, and it offered a safe lurking-place for foreigners' (HRB VIII.3, Thorpe 1966:189). Although *Historia Brittonum* supports a northern location for some of these wars, this derives primarily from the political situation in Geoffrey's own time. In the early twelfth century, England and Scotland were hostile kingdoms, warring in the debatable land which separated them. It was therefore a natural battleground in the British Isles, easy for Geoffrey and his readers to imagine as a scene of past conflict.

Ambrosius's forces consist of Britons (Geoffrey means people from England), Bretons and Welsh. They defeat Hengist at the battles of Maisbelli and Kaerconan (Conisbrough), after which Hengist is executed. His son Octa surrenders at the siege of York and is settled in lands near Scotland. After this Ambrosius 'was devoted to restoring the realm, rebuilding the churches, renewing peace and the rule of law, and administering justice'. He was eventually assassinated by a Saxon, on the orders of Vortigern's son, Pascent.

There is little in Geoffrey's account of Ambrosius which cannot be put down to imaginative linking of material from Gildas, Bede and *Historia*

Brittonum. The only additional aspects are the names of the battles. The only major part of the story of Ambrosius which has no known antecedents concerns Merlin, Stonehenge and Uther Pendragon.

Ambrosius decides to build a memorial at Mons Ambrii (Amesbury) to the Britons killed at the council. On Merlin's advice, Ambrosius decides that the monument will be the Giants' Dance, a stone circle with magical properties in Ireland. Ambrosius's brother, Uther Pendragon, Merlin and 15,000 men go to Ireland to take it back. Only Merlin is capable of the engineering feat of dismantling the stone circle and re-erecting it at Mons Ambrii, where it now stands, known, as we later discover, as Stonehenge. It serves as the burial place of Ambrosius, Uther Pendragon and Constantine of Cornwall. The disgruntled Irish, meanwhile, make a league with Pascent and the Saxons. They invade and fight Uther Pendragon near St David's.

During this campaign, a star appears, in the form of a dragon with two beams of light issuing from it. Merlin interprets this as meaning that Ambrosius has died and that Uther Pendragon is now King of Britain. The star symbolises him and the rays are his son (Arthur) and his daughter, whose sons and grandsons will one day rule Britain.

When Uther returns to his coronation in Winchester, 'mindful of the explanation given by Merlin of the star . . . he ordered two dragons to be fashioned in gold, in the likeness of the one which he had seen in the ray which shone from that star'. He gave one to Winchester Cathedral. 'The second one he kept for himself, so that he could carry it round to his wars. From that moment onwards he was called Utherpendragon, which in the British language means "a dragon's head". He had been given this title because it was by means of a dragon that Merlin prophesied that he would become king' (HRB VIII.17, Thorpe 1966:202).

Many odd features of this story suggest that Geoffrey is dealing with an outside source. His explanation of Uther's name makes no sense. A dragon's head has never been mentioned, nor any convincing reason why Uther should take this surname. In fact, Geoffrey has called him Uther Pendragon since birth. The prophecy Merlin gives on the star is not carried forward into the rest of the narrative, nor are the two dragon figures and Uther's motive for making them. Only one dragon, with two rays of light, is seen in the sky.

Geoffrey did not understand that the meaning of Uther's surname is not 'Dragon's Head' but rather 'Head Dragon'. As we saw, early Welsh only knew *Dragon* as the title of a ruler or military leader. Uther's surname is therefore 'Chief Warlord'. It is similar to Maglocunus's epithet '*insularis draco*', warlord of Britain.

The Stonehenge episode sits oddly in context. Although Ambrosius is the King of Britain, it falls to Uther Pendragon to go to Ireland to capture the stone circle. Likewise, when the Irish attack Britain to take it back, Uther has to defend the island. The story, involving Uther Pendragon's journey to Ireland to bring back a mystical artefact, need not originally have involved Ambrosius at all. Uther is later buried at Stonehenge.

Uther Pendragon was known before his incorporation in Geoffrey's history. He is mentioned in *Pa gur*, where Arthur's companion, Mabon, son of Modron, is called his servant. This Mabon is clearly a mythological figure, which must raise questions about the historicity of Uther. One of the triads, the three great enchantments, refers to the enchantment of Uther Pendragon. Readers of Geoffrey would see this as a reference to the enchantment whereby Uther changed his appearance to sleep with Ygerna. Yet, as Geoffrey reports it, this is an enchantment of Merlin, not of Uther. All three of these great enchantments are skills which the named characters teach to other famous enchanters. Thus, Uther Pendragon teaches his enchantment to Menw, Arthur's shape-shifting enchanter in *Culhwch and Olwen*. He is clearly its caster, not someone affected by it. This suggests that Merlin's name has been attached by Geoffrey to a famous magical incident concerning Uther alone. Of most significance is Geoffrey's idea that Uther is the father of Arthur. Nothing until this point has suggested that there was any tradition of Arthur's father.

We can identify Uther and the unexpected episodes he is connected with as deriving from external sources. Whether, before Geoffrey, Uther Pendragon had been seen as a Saxon-fighting fifth-century king of Britain or Arthur's father will be discussed later. We can say that the tales of Stonehenge and enchantment are unlikely to derive from Dark Age reality.

Uther Pendragon becomes King of Britain after Ambrosius. His military career seems to be derived from the Arthurian battle-list. Thus, Hengist's son Octa comes down from the northern part of Britain, destroying all the towns down to York, which he besieges. Geoffrey once again recasts the Saxon wars into the familiar pattern of conflict between England and Scotland. Uther tries to raise the siege of York but is driven back to a defensive position on Mount Damen. On the advice of Duke Gorlois of Cornwall, Uther makes a surprise night attack on the Saxon camp and captures Octa. This Mount Damen is the nearest Geoffrey comes to a battle of Mount Agned. This is strange as he is aware of Mount Agned and does refer to it earlier in his History. In pre-Roman times, it is founded by King Ebraucus, who also founded York. Geoffrey affirms that it is now called the Castle of Maidens. Other twelfth-century sources called Edinburgh the Castle of Maidens, but the identification is not explicit in Geoffrey.

Uther defeats Octa and enters Alclud (Dumbarton) as victorious king of all Britain: 'Then he visited all the lands of the Scots and reclaimed that rebellious people from their state of savagery; for he administered justice throughout the regions in a way that none of his predecessors had been able to do.' He returns in triumph to London.

It is at the victory celebrations that Uther first sees Ygerna, wife of Gorlois, and falls in love with her. Angered, Gorlois withdraws to Cornwall, and Uther, inflamed by lust, pursues him. Ygerna is placed for safety in the fortress of Tintagel. There was nothing for it but to summon Merlin, who transforms Uther into the likeness of Gorlois to gain entry to the castle. While Gorlois is being killed in an unwise sally from a nearby fortress, Arthur's parents, Uther and Ygerna, are united. 'That night she conceived Arthur, the most famous of men, who subsequently won great renown by his outstanding bravery' (HRB VIII.19, Thorpe 1966:207).

DIGGING UP ARTHUR I – TINTAGEL 1998

It was a broken stone, used to cover a drain. It was a piece of slate, poorly etched with Dark Age British names. It was also 'the find of a life-time'; 'an extremely exciting discovery'; an artefact where 'myth meets history'; so said Dr Geoffrey Wainwright of English Heritage. Professor Christopher Morris described the physically uninspiring piece of stone as 'priceless' and 'very exciting'.

Professor Morris clarified that his 'excitement' was based on the evidence the slate provided 'that skills of reading and writing were handed down in a non-religious context and that [one of the men mentioned on it] was a person of considerable status'. This was slightly disingenuous, as the 'context' of the object was re-use as a drain cover and the inscription itself hardly a high-status work. The press interest was not prompted by the inherent value of a Dark Age inscription. Dr Wainwright obliged with the connection the journalists were seeking: 'It is remarkable that a stone from the sixth century has been discovered with the name of Arthnou [*sic*] inscribed upon it at Tintagel, a place with which the mythical King Arthur has long been associated' (Smith 1998).

The stone was found during excavations at Tintagel. The spectacular site is dominated by the ruins of 'King Arthur's Castle', actually Earl Richard of Cornwall's thirteenth-century fortress, built perhaps to hark back to the legends. When archaeologists turned up large amounts of high-status sixth-century material, Tintagel was at first described as a monastic site (Ashe 1968). This theory eventually had to yield ground, as no other monastic features could be discovered, while at the same time similar luxury goods, including the distinctive imported pottery dubbed 'Tintagel ware', were unearthed at other clearly secular sixth-century locations. It is now accepted that Tintagel was a major secular centre for the Kingdom of Dumnonia, much as Geoffrey of Monmouth describes it.

Tintagel's undoubted importance during the reign of Arthur, one of the locations where we might expect to find traces of the tyrant Constantine which might clarify much of Gildas's world, has been utterly obscured by the site's supposed Arthurian connections. The slate, described by its discoverer Kevin Brady as 'a red herring' and 'a very tenuous link at best', does not mention Arthur at all. The fragmentary inscription appears to read:

Patern . . .
Coliavificit
Artognov . . .
Col . . .
Ficit . . .

Professor Charles Thomas offered a tentative translation as 'Artognou, father of a descendant of Coll has had this made'. This translation seems based on a partial transcription of the text, omitting the second part and unaware of the 'n' which appears at the end of 'Pater'. I follow Andrew Smith's proposed translation, in which both Patern and Artognou are named as donors (Smith 1998).

The most striking feature for most commentators was the name 'Artognou', seen as very similar to that of Arthur. In fact, its only similarities are its first three letters, presumably derived from the same Celtic root. The names are not the same and there has never been any question that 'Arthur' was a garbled version of the hero's real name. In all the sources we have studied, the name has been given only as 'Arthur'. These sources are independent and none of them gives any hint in all their manuscript variants that a slightly different 'Art . . .' name lay behind that of Arthur. The only name which we can reasonably expect to find on any sixth-century inscription relating to Arthur is Arthur itself, or accepted Latin versions of the same. Whoever he might have been, Artognou was not Arthur. Even if the name had actually been 'Arthur', the 'traditions' and 'coincidences' linking him to Tintagel do not feature him as the 'father of a descendant of Coll'.

Smith suggests a more plausible reading of the stone, which does give a vague Arthurian connection. 'Patern . . .' is readily recognisable as the name Paternus, Padarn in Welsh, the name of, for example, the sixth-century saint we encountered previously. The following line reads not 'of a descendant of Coll', but 'of Grandfather Coll'. Now, if Paternus has anything to do with Grandfather Coll, then the likelihood is he is his grandson. The inscription would then read 'Paternus, descendant of Grandfather Coll made it'. The reappearance of 'Col . . . Ficit' at the bottom suggests that the inscription continued 'Artognou, descendant of Grandfather Coll made it', a joint dedication by two members of the same clan.

Interestingly enough, a legendary Cornish figure named Coll appears in two triads we have already noted. He is one of the powerful swineherds tending pigs in Cornwall. According to the triad, one of his pigs gave birth to Palug's cat, killed by Kai in *Pa gur*. Coll is also one of the three enchanters and appears in the 'Triad of the Three Great Enchantments', along with Uther Pendragon.

Wainwright made much of the 'coincidence' of the Artognou name and Tintagel. A slightly more intriguing coincidence is that of Tintagel, Coll and Uther Pendragon, featuring in local tales of enchantment.

We should reconsider the evidence on which 'the find of a lifetime' was lauded in the press. The general discrediting of historical Arthurian material has the effect of 'if every source is equally suspect, then every source is equally permissible'. Even respectable academics like Dr Wainwright were quoted in the press as describing Tintagel as 'a place with which the mythical King Arthur has long been associated' and that Arthur was 'a rough tough leader of men'; 'a tough little Celt . . . given command of a number of Celtic Warbands . . . killed at the battle of Camlan in 510 BC'. Professor Morris on the other hand raised the objection that 'Arthur is a figure who first enters the historical domain in the twelfth century', all exceedingly debatable statements. We have to remember that the connection between Arthur and Tintagel is hardly founded on historical material. There is nothing in all the sources before Geoffrey to lead us to suspect that Arthur was connected with Tintagel, and all later references derive from Geoffrey. Geoffrey's account of Uther's seduction of Ygerna at Tintagel is by far the most legendary, magical episode in his history of Arthur. It seems unjust that one of the few things permissible for academics to say about Arthur is that a longstanding tradition connects him with Tintagel.

Even if every word which Geoffrey wrote about Tintagel was to be proven as historical (a very unlikely supposition) then he still gives no connection between Arthur and Tintagel other than as the place of his conception. Arthur is not even said to have been born there. Nothing in Geoffrey or the romances indicated that Arthur lived at Tintagel or had any reason to dedicate a slate slab at the site. It is unlikely that a historical connection existed between Arthur and Tintagel, and even if it did, Geoffrey does not document it.

THE REIGN OF UTHER

The story of Uther fizzles out after the Tintagel episode. With Gorlois killed, Uther and Ygerna marry and have two children, Arthur and Anna. The daughter, foretold by Merlin as the progenitor of future kings of Britain, is a source of confusion in the text. She is married to Loth of Lodenesia and is the mother of Gualguanus and Modred, Arthur's nephews. Later she is described as the wife of King Budicius of Brittany and mother of Arthur's ally, King Hoel. This cannot work in Geoffrey's chronology, since Hoel is a grown man only fifteen years after the birth of Arthur.

Romance writers gave Arthur multiple stepsisters to account for all his adult nephews. There is no suggestion of this in Geoffrey. Thorpe compounds the problem by misreading Loth's wife as 'Ambrosius's sister', then clearing the 'confusion' by making Hoel *Ambrosius*'s nephew! There is nothing to warrant this. Geoffrey shows no confusion over Hoel's parentage; he is the son of Arthur's sister. His descendants do continue to rule Brittany at least to the end of the seventh century, giving some vindication of Merlin's prophecy.

Many years pass, Uther becomes ill and Octa escapes to gather the Saxons. Predictably, they invade Scotland and the 'English' Britons have to repulse them. Loth, acting as general and regent during Uther's sickness, fights unsuccessfully against them. Uther sets out in a litter to lead the defence, but finds the Saxons have taken St Albans in their first appearance in south-east England since the days of Vortigern. Octa is killed and Uther recaptures the city. The Saxons retreat to the north but some of their spies succeed in poisoning Uther. The stage is set for the long-awaited reign of Arthur.

Loth features in the *Life of St Kentigern,* as the saint's grandfather. Geoffrey subsequently used Kentigern-related material in *Vita Merlini.* The *Life* further adds that Lothian was named after Loth, an etymology which Geoffrey surprisingly does not give. This may be correct. Soon after the expedition to Catraeth, the lands of the Gododdin became known as Lothian, presumably derived from a personal name. This process of Dark Age leaders giving their names to kingdoms is identifiable in the case of Ceredigion and Glamorgan. Loth's name is Lleu in Welsh (the *Life* uses the form Leudo), and Gododdin is called Lleu's country in the poem.

Geoffrey's pre-Arthur story incorporates two different types of material. The first derives from and embellishes sources which we already know. The root is magical material surrounding the figures of Merlin and Uther Pendragon. Although Merlin was to become one of the major figures in the Arthurian legends, he is clearly intruded into the History. Geoffrey has simply connected the late sixth-century prophet Myrddin to the most famous incidence of prophecy in *Historia Brittonum.*

Merlin may similarly have been attached to the stories of Uther Pendragon. These can function just as well without him, especially if Uther is himself an enchanter. If Uther and Merlin were connected before Geoffrey, it is odd that we do not find the connection in other Myrddin material or in *Vita Merlini.* If Geoffrey did find Uther and Merlin connected in a source, this would imply that Geoffrey alone is responsible for placing Uther Pendragon in the generation after Vortigern. This depends on Geoffrey's conflation of the apparently late sixth-century Merlin with the much earlier (fifth-century?) Ambrosius. If Uther was already associated with Merlin, then his 'true' chronological position is after the reign of Arthur, and he cannot possibly be his father.

It is difficult to give credence to Uther's status as King of Britain and member of the dynasty of Constantine III and Ambrosius. His name, Uther,

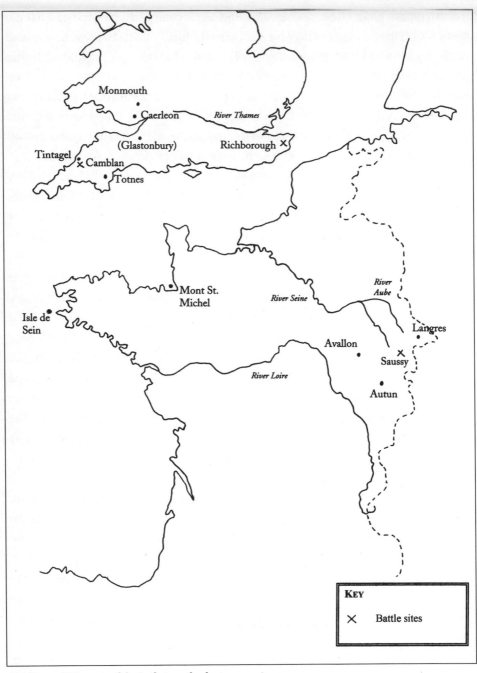

Geoffrey of Monmouth's Arthur – the last campaigns.

and surname 'Chief Dragon/Warlord' seems to give him more affinity to the other 'Celtically' named figures, Arthur the Leader of Battles and Maglocunus, Dragon of the Island, than with the last of the Romans. The stories told of him are just as legendary as those about Ambrosius in *Historia Brittonum*, but whether, like them, they conceal a historical reality is impossible to determine.

Loth is the brother of Urianus and Auguselus, 'sprung from a royal line' *regali prosapia orti* (HRB IX.9), presumably of Scotland, though Loth is later shown as related to the King of Norway. Urianus is Urien of Rheged of the Taliesin poems, another late sixth-century figure. Geoffrey later mentions Urianus's son, Hiwenius, the historical Owain, son of Urien Rheged. Loth and Urianus are linked in the same generation in the *Life of St Kentigern*, in which Urien's son and Loth's daughter are Kentigern's parents.

Urien was known to the Welsh as the son of Kinmarch, so post-Geoffrey Welsh sources made all the brothers sons of Kinmarch. Geoffrey had heard the name. He uses it for an ancient king of Britain and, under variant spellings, for the duke of Canterbury and a Welsh leader at Arthur's court. He makes no connection with it and the three northern 'brothers'.

The synchronism of Uther, Merlin, Urianus and Loth fractures Geoffrey's link with *Historia Brittonum*, in which Urbgen (Urien) lives after Arthur's victory at Badon. Geoffrey's chronological scheme, with Malgo ruling after three other 'tyrants' ought, if anything, to push Arthur and Urianus even further apart.

For Geoffrey, Urianus and Hiwenius have little role to play in the events of Arthur's reign. We might speculate that they have become enmeshed in the Arthurian cycle because they are connected with Loth of Lodenesia. Loth is connected with Uther Pendragon, who is connected with Merlin, who is a late sixth-century figure, as is Urien. If Geoffrey's source connects some or all of these characters, then they have been displaced in time either by Geoffrey's equation of Merlin with Ambrosius, or by making Uther Pendragon Arthur's father. Geoffrey seems to be trying to assimilate existing material into a framework which does not precisely accommodate it. This suggests that Uther, Urien and Loth share a source, relating to the late, not the early, sixth century.

10

ARTHUR, KING OF BRITAIN

Geoffrey of Monmouth's story of Arthur falls into two uneven parts.
The first follows the expected line: Arthur is a king who fights wars
against the Saxons, in the company of other kings of the Britons,
wins the battle of Badon but dies in a civil war at the battle of Cam(b)lan. It
is a fictionalised account extrapolated from surviving sources. It is little
different from the romanticised versions of the lives of Anglo-Saxon kings
spun out by William of Malmesbury and Henry of Huntingdon.

The larger part is almost completely unexpected. It tells how, after his
victories over the Saxons, Arthur crossed to Brittany to embark on a series
of overseas conquests. Having conquered northern France, he takes on the
Romans and is only prevented from making himself emperor by the revolt
of Modred.

It was these continental wars, with the attribution to Arthur and his men
of French territories which gave the legends a new lease of life among the
French aristocrats. They featured in all subsequent retellings of the story,
even at the expense of the Saxon campaigns and Mount Badon. They were to
be the prime cause of the destruction of Arthur as a historical character.

When renaissance scholars reviewed the Arthurian material, they were not
put off by the legendary aspects. No one argued that Arthur was not
historical because he was associated with the Holy Grail, the Round Table and
Avalon. They drew attention to the fact that the wars in France had no
support in any continental source.

When Arthur (supposedly) left these shores, in the late fifth or early sixth
centuries, he would have been leaving a land caught in the darkest of Dark
Ages. Literary sources, bar the writings of Gildas and Patrick, had dried up.
Large parts of the island were overrun by illiterate pagans.

None of this was true across the Channel. The literate Catholic Church
continued to thrive in the old Roman urban centres. The Empire itself existed,
centred on Byzantium but, by the reign of Justinian, with Italy and some of

southern France under its sway. Even the barbarian conquerors were Christian and were quick to use the framework of laws and legal tenure to bolster their positions. It was not a milieu where details of Arthur's battles and conquests could be lost.

The work of the sixth-century historian Gregory of Tours survives, preserving the work of still earlier historians. There is nothing in it to suggest that late fifth/early sixth-century Paris was ruled by the Tribune Frollo on behalf of the Emperor Leo, still less that Frollo was a gigantic man killed in single combat by Arthur, King of Britain. The western Emperor Lucius Hiberius, Procurator of the Roman Republic and ruler of Rome, makes no appearance in the annals of Rome or Byzantium. Ashe argues that Arthur does appear in the continental sources, under the name of Riothamus (Ashe 1982). We have to say, though, that even if that was the case, apart from the bare facts of fighting in France, there is no connection between the military exploits of the two leaders. The nearest Geoffrey comes to acknowledging the historical campaigns fought by Britons/Bretons in the fifth century are some minor wars of Arthur's ally, King Hoel of Brittany. We shall return to this continental material, but first we shall consider the material which draws on known sources.

On the death of Uther Pendragon, Arthur was declared king by an assembly of Britons convened at Silchester. Although he was only fifteen, his candidature was urged by Archbishop Dubricius of Caerleon as the only response to the renewed threat of the Saxons. That Arthur should peacefully succeed his father as King of the Britons is very much in Geoffrey's idiom. Nothing we have read so far suggests that Arthur was hereditary king of all Britain. The choice of Silchester is strange. It is hard to imagine any genuine tradition passing this on, especially as Geoffrey preserves no British or Latin name for it. It may just have been knowledge of the Roman remains there which prompted it.

Although Arthur's military campaign is against the Saxon leader Colgrin, it follows a familiar pattern. The first battle is on the banks of the River Dubglas, somewhere near Saxon-held York, which Arthur then proceeds to besiege. Cador of Cornwall accompanies Arthur in the siege. Later we discover that Constantine of Cornwall, Arthur's successor, is the son of Cador, and Arthur's cousin. We can infer that Cador is an uncle of Arthur. St David is also called Arthur's uncle.

The siege is unsuccessful, as a new influx of Saxons led by Cheldric arrives from Germany and seizes Scotland. Having killed off Octha in the previous generation, Geoffrey fills the gaps with fictitious Saxons. Cheldric may owe his name to Cerdic of the West Saxons, but at this point is located in Scotland.

Arthur returns to London to take council. Geoffrey knew perfectly well from *Historia Brittonum* that Arthur fought with the *Reges Brittonum*. However, for him, Britain (England, that is) is not fragmented into separate kingdoms. Arthur is the sole King of Britain. To resolve the paradox, Geoffrey has Arthur send to Brittany to his sister's son, King Hoel. Hoel arrives in Southampton with 15,000 Breton warriors, who join Arthur. Arthur therefore, literally, does fight with the king and soldiers 'Brittonum', here read as 'of the Bretons'.

The combined forces set off for the rest of *Historia Brittonum*'s battles on the Dubglas. They fight the Saxons in the Lindsey (Linnuis) region, raising the siege of Lincoln. Geoffrey has a list of British towns, similar to that in *Historia Brittonum*, which he uses to give authenticity to his claim that his source book is in British. However, many of his identifications are incorrect and seem to originate with him. For instance, he gives Paladur as the ancient name of Shaftesbury, as it incorporates the British word for spear. However, its true identity is Trapain Law, a hillfort of the Gododdin. In this campaign, Geoffrey wrongly guesses that Lincoln is the British Kaerluitcoit, which is actually Wall-by-Lichfield.

Missing out the battle on the Bassas, Geoffrey has Arthur pursue the Saxons to the Caledonian wood. There is no certainty that Geoffrey understands this as in Scotland (his name for Scotland is Albania). He may imagine that it is nearer to Lincoln. Arthur blockades the Saxons in the wood until they are forced to make peace, surrendering hostages and tribute. But the Saxons, instead of returning to Germany as promised, turn back to land at Totnes, ravage the West Country and besiege Badon.

The Saxons land at Totnes, a recurring feature in Geoffrey. Brutus, Vespasian, Constantine and later Ambrosius and Uther land at this obscure spot. Although peculiar as a point of arrival for Saxons from the north aiming at Bath, the location makes sense if we assume a Breton perspective on the most obvious 'gateway to Britain'.

Now comes the great battle of Badon. The Saxons raid up to the Severn until they reach the country of Badon (*pagum Badonis*), where they besiege the town. As we hear later that Badon is in the province of Somerset, we know Geoffrey equates Badon with Bath. He made this clear when he related the establishment of the baths of Kaer Badum 'which is now called Bado' (Geoffrey's actual nominative form. I have kept Badon for ease of reference).

The Saxons thus provide the siege. The Britons drive them back to a neighbouring hill (Gildas's Mons Badonicus) after a day of fighting. On the second day the Britons fight their way up the hill, defeating with great slaughter the Saxons who flee eastwards to the Isle of Thanet.

The action of the battle could easily be spun out from evidence available to Geoffrey. The first indication that he has another source is the fact that his siege and battle last at least three days, which seems to be the import of the entry in *Annales Cambriae*. Geoffrey, however, had not read the *Annales*, but probably has that information from a related source.

Interestingly, Arthur is the lone named participant. Hoel is left behind 'ill' in Alclud and Cador does not appear until the mopping-up process. Geoffrey seems to have arrived at the same conclusion as we have, that 'no-one slew them save him alone' did not mean that Arthur acted single-handedly, but that he won the battle without his allies. He also has no support from the famous champions who feature prominently in his later campaigns.

Aside from conventional scenes and speeches inspired by the crusading rhetoric of the twelfth century, only one element of the battle sticks out as externally derived – a description of Arthur's arms and equipment: 'Arthur himself put on a breast-plate (*lorica*) worthy of so great a king. On his head he placed a golden helmet, with a crest carved in the shape of a dragon, and across his shoulders a circular shield (*clipeus*) called Pridwen, on which there was painted a likeness of the Blessed Mary, Mother of God, which forced him to be thinking perpetually of her. He girded on his peerless sword (*gladius*), called Caliburnus, which was forged in the Isle of Avallon. A spear (*lancea*) called Ron graced his right hand.' Geoffrey ends this tour de force with a line of poetry (of his own composition?) 'this spear was strong and broad and ready for slaughter' (HRB IX.4).

Geoffrey interprets the phrase from the *Historia* battle-list about Arthur carrying the image of the Virgin Mary on his shoulders without difficulty '*humeris . . . suis clipeum . . . in quo . . . imago sancte Marie . . . impicta*' – 'On his shoulders a shield painted with the image of St Mary'. It is not true that the line can only be understood with recourse to a lost Welsh original. Geoffrey's explanation may not be the right one, but it is still based on the Latin text as its stands. William of Malmesbury, incidentally, interprets *Historia Brittonum* by saying the image is 'sewn upon his armour' (White 1997).

Even if the Roman-style descriptions of Arthur's equipment may be inspired by classical epics rather than preserved fifth-century descriptions, the fact remains that Geoffrey knows some very archaic names for them. Both Caliburnus and Ron are earlier versions of the Welsh names given in *Culhwch and Olwen*. Geoffrey's naming of Arthur's shield, rather than his ship, as Pridwen, seems the earlier tradition. Further, these names have come to Geoffrey in written form. One possibility is that he has a Latin poem which contains the names, with the surviving hexameter line as proof. Other lines or half lines of poetry crop up through the work, and one small section near the beginning is entirely in verse. I am inclined to view these as Geoffrey's own experiments with verse forms. His next work, the *Vita Merlini*, was entirely in verse.

The only source for Arthur's equipment must be a very ancient book in the British language, pre-dating *Culhwch and Olwen*. From this fragment we cannot deduce that it was an orderly and consecutive narrative of the kings of Britain. We cannot even tell whether the context was Arthur's battle of Mount Badon. Geoffrey has added to it the description of Arthur at Castellum Guinnion, at least, and the only place-name associated with it is Avallon, of which more later. Nevertheless, the passage gives us unequivocal evidence of earlier British source-material being used in *Historia Regum Britanniae*. A list of Arthur's named equipment, however, seems unlikely to derive from a strictly historical source.

AFTER BADON

Gildas had described the siege of Mount Badon as *almost* the last victory, and this is how Geoffrey presents it. Cador is sent to harry the retreating Saxons as far as Thanet by land and sea. He swiftly corners and kills Cheldric.

Meanwhile, Arthur returns north to raise the siege of Alclud where Hoel is trapped by the Picts and Scots. Defeating them, Arthur advances on Mureis (Moray?). Having seen off an Irish invasion fleet, he treats the Picts and Scots 'with unparalleled severity, sparing no one who fell into his hands. As a result all the bishops of this pitiful country, with all the clergy under their command, their feet bare and in their hands the relics of their saints . . . fell on their knees and besought him to have mercy' (HRB IX.6; Thorpe 1966:219).

This scene is similar to the saints' *Lives*. Arthur is cruel and rapacious and the clergy have to bring him to heel. Geoffrey has simply recast this to justify Arthur's essentially defensive and patriotic functions, and to stress that the clergy are powerless and subordinate petitioners. There is an affinity with

Culhwch and Olwen, which also includes an episode of clergy humbly begging Arthur for clemency.

Like Ambrosius, Arthur completes his British triumphs by re-establishing the churches and monasteries and by restoring lands to those disinherited by the Saxons. Prime among these disinherited are three brothers from Scotland: Urianus of Murefensium, Loth of Lodonesia and Auguselus of Albany.

The section ends with Arthur's marriage to Guanhuvara/Gwanhumara, a woman of Roman descent, brought up in the household of Duke Cador – the most beautiful woman in the whole island. She is of course Queen Guenevere, the Gwenhwyvar of the Welsh sources. Arthur's wife is found in Welsh material and Caradoc's *Life of Gildas* so, clearly, Geoffrey has her from a pre-existing British source. This will be reinforced later when we analyse the role she plays in the story.

Up to this point, the story of Arthur offers nothing particularly un-expected. Now Geoffrey launches into what appears to be an extreme flight of fancy, Arthur's continental wars. Arthur fights against King Gilmaurius of Ireland, conquering the whole of his country. He then sails to Iceland and the kings of Gotland and the Orkneys submit to him. He returns to Britain for a twelve-year reign of peace, during which the kings of all the countries across the sea build castles and fortifications for dread of him.

This goads Arthur into further action and he starts his campaign by placing Loth on the throne of Norway. Loth, we hear, is the nephew and heir of the King of Norway. Arthur and Loth drive out the Norwegian pretender before devastating Norway and Denmark for good measure. These Scandinavian locations suggest a milieu no earlier than the tenth-century Viking invasions. They seem to borrow closely from eleventh-century episodes in William of Malmesbury and Henry of Huntingdon and nothing leads us to suspect any source other than Geoffrey's imagination.

Next and without provocation, Arthur invades Gaul, ruled from Paris by the gigantic tribune Frollo, a subject of Roman Emperor Leo. Arthur defeats him in single combat on an island. This bears far more affinity to the heroic Welsh legends than to the historical events previously described. This is not the last time that Geoffrey shows Arthur fighting single-handedly against a gigantic continental adversary on an island in France, which suggests some sort of source, if only folklore, for the episode.

With Frollo dead, Arthur is free to take on the rest of France. Hoel conquers Poitou and Aquitaine and ravages Gascony. After nine years of fighting, Arthur bestows Neustria (Geoffrey's pre-Norman name for Normandy) on Bedivere and Anjou on Kay. None of this is likely to pre-date Geoffrey. It seems deliberately intended to give Arthurian antecedents to the French partisans of the Empress Mathilda. Possessions of her rival King Stephen's family, Blois, Mortain and Boulogne are not mentioned.

Generally, it is thought that the continental exploits of Arthur are unique to Geoffrey. However, Ashe (1982) draws attention to the Breton *Life of St Goueznou* (Wohednovius). This is allegedly an early eleventh-century text, though it has more in common with the twelfth-century hagiographic material. The writer draws on *Historia Brittonum* to give background to his picture of a church persecuted by diabolical Saxons. Their pride is checked for a while by 'the great Arthur, King of the Britons' who 'famously wins many battles in Britain and parts of Gaul'. If this is genuinely of such an early date, then this is the first indication that Arthur was active on both sides of the Channel, and indeed was famous for doing so. We must be careful here. It is possible that the Breton writer has nothing more than the *Historia Brittonum* battle-list and imagines that some of the battle sites are on the continent. The phrase 'kings of the Britons' could easily, for him, have evoked the idea that Bretons are involved, since his 'Greater Britain' has only one king.

An early eleventh-century book of Breton origin is the only tenable candidate we have come up with for the 'very ancient book in the British language'. The accounts of the wars in Gaul are the main parts of the narrative that suggest such an unknown source. The *Life of Guoeznou* does seem to have some affinity with the alleged contents of the Book of Exile, the other source Geoffrey claims to possess. It has the characteristics of a tenth-century version of *Historia Brittonum*, expanded to include Breton hagiography, we have deduced for the 'very ancient book'.

THE COURT AT CAERLEON

Geoffrey places at the heart of his Arthurian section a literary *tour-de-force*, the Plenary Court at Caerleon. Its significance is shown by the fact that it takes up as much space as the campaigns against the Saxons.

That Geoffrey's imagination is at play is obvious: Arthur's feast is pure twelfth-century, being accompanied by two innovations of the period, the tournament and heraldry. The first example of identifiable arms in English history are the gold lions of Geoffrey Plantagenet, husband of the Empress

Mathilda. The popularity of arms and tournaments owes something to the illustrious ancient origins given to them by Geoffrey. It was his imagination which showed how characters from an obscure ancient period could be presented as modern paragons.

Geoffrey's description of Caerleon is typical of his idiom. Thus he develops Gildas's brief allusion to the martyrdom of Aaron and Julius in the 'City of the Legions' to create two fantastic churches with their complements of nuns and canons in the saints' honour. Ancient Caerleon has 'a college of two hundred learned men, who were skilled in astronomy and other arts'. They prophesied for King Arthur 'any prodigies due at the time'. Soon afterwards members of Arthur's entourage interpret the prophetic message of one of his dreams. Geoffrey later alludes to the British renaissance prophesied by Merlin to Arthur, an incident which does not feature in his book.

Stripped of its twelfth-century trappings, the feast condenses to two elements. One is Arthur's position as overlord of the British Church. Dubricius, saintly Primate of Britain, resigns to become a hermit. Arthur makes his uncle, David, archbishop in his place. Tebaus (Teilo) 'the celebrated priest of Llandaff' is made Archbishop of Dol in Brittany in place of St Samson. The bishoprics of Silchester, Winchester and Alclud go to Maugannius, Diwanius and Eledenius respectively. Geoffrey knows of St Samson of Dol, but if his source tells him this much, it is not clear why Teilo succeeds him rather than his actual Breton successor. It is difficult to know what to make of the minor bishops. Diwanius looks a little like Dewi, the Welsh spelling of St David's name, but that gives us little to go on.

The other is a catalogue of Arthur's men. The list includes the vassal kings of Scotland, Murefensium, Lothian, North and South Wales, Cornwall (Cador 'promoted' to royal rank) and Brittany. One block of knights have 'Welsh-style' names, with the 'map' patronymic. They may have been invented by Geoffrey in the same way as he produces 'Irish' and 'Saxon' names. Some are found elsewhere; Peredur, for instance, has the same name as a character in *Annales Cambriae*.

Many of the characters bear names from the Harleian Genealogies. Cadwallo Laurh, in some manuscripts the King of North Wales, is given as Maelgwn's father, Run map Neton is a late sixth-century ancestor of the kings of the Isle of Man. Kymbelin is the father of Clytno Eidin, who features in the *Gododdin*. 'Mavron' Earl of Worcester could be Mermin (later spelled Mervin), one of the later kings of Man. Anarauth Earl of Salisbury appears, next to Mavron in Geoffrey's list, paralleled by Mermin's son, Anaraut, in the genealogy. Geoffrey's Artgualchar could be the son of Anaraut, Tutagual.

That these are no more than names to Geoffrey, for him to use as his narrative requires, is clear in the case of Morvid, who appears here as Consul of Gloucester. Morvid is a name which Geoffrey has already used for a son of King Ebraucus and for a pre-Roman king of Britain eaten by a sea-monster. What Geoffrey did not know was that Morvid was actually a girl's name in Welsh! Morvid, daughter of Urien, is listed among the ladies of Arthur's court in *Culhwch and Olwen*. In the list, Morvid's name is linked (unknowingly) by Geoffrey to those of her father, Urbgennius, and grandfather, Kinmarc. Geoffrey is thus using a source containing genealogical material, of whose context he is utterly ignorant.

KING ARTHUR VERSUS THE ROMANS

The feast brings us to the point where Geoffrey parts company from any previous sources, the Roman wars. Geoffrey takes as much space to cover this as he has for all the previous Arthurian episodes put together. Although the story is quite simple, Geoffrey invents long speeches, troop dispositions, battle plans and descriptions of single combat.

It has been suggested that Arthur's continental exploits derive from Geoffrey's conception of British history (Bromwich *et al.* 1991). The *Historia* begins with Brutus invading from [the future] Rome. He founds a line of British kings culminating in Brennius, who returns to conquer Rome. The second act begins with the Roman invasion of Britain and culminates in the British leader Constantine taking over the Roman Empire. The final act reaches its apogee in King Arthur. But this time he is unable to take Rome, due to the civil war and immorality of the Britons, which not only bring his downfall but that of British rule in Britain.

Thus Geoffrey need have no source suggesting that Arthur fought the Romans, only a narrative plan which makes this an essential dramatic device. However, Geoffrey had sources for all those earlier episodes. They did not spring from his imagination. If he had no information to suggest that Arthur had a continental career, he could have used Maximianus, Constantine III, Hoel or any other Breton king to make the point that a re-match against Rome would be unsuccessful. Dramatic structure does not present a prima facie case for Arthur's war against the Romans being twelfth-century fiction.

Arthur is holding his plenary court at Caerleon when envoys arrive with an unwelcome letter from 'Lucius, Procurator of the Republic'. We find out later he is the Emperor Lucius Hiberius, ruler of the Romans of the continent. His envoys accuse Arthur of insulting the Roman senate 'to which the entire world owes submission', of withholding the tribute due to Rome and of seizing Roman territory.

Arthur takes counsel and predictably decides to respond in force. The principal advisers are Cador of Cornwall, Hoel of Brittany and Auguselus of Albany. When the armies are mustered, they include men from Britain (principally England), Brittany, the recent conquests in Ireland, Scandinavia and northern France, but not Wales.

Their opponents are a Roman Empire of the mind. As with the (Holy) Roman Empire of Geoffrey's own time, the Empire is composed of vassal kings, with a few actual Romans incorporated. Contingents arrive from Greece, Africa, Spain, Parthia, Media, Libya, the Iturei, Egypt, Phrygia, Syria, Boethia and Crete. The Romans bear such classically sounding names as Marius Lepidus, Gaius Metellus Cocta and Quintus Milvius Catullus, in contrast to their vassals' more outlandish 'Mustensar', 'Echion', 'Micipsa' and so on. The presence of Aliphatima, King of Spain, shows that Spain is envisaged as being under Muslim rule, a feature probably derived from the *Chansons de Geste*, and certainly not pre-dating the eighth century. These names have no connection with any actual rulers of the fifth/sixth centuries.

Lucius Hiberius is a slightly different matter. Geoffrey ought to have known that there was no Roman emperor of this name at the time that he sets the action. This seems apparent from his references to the Emperor Leo, ruling (presumably in Constantinople?) at the same time. The only similarly named character in history was Liberius (read as L[ucius] Iberius), a general operating in the sixth century in southern France on behalf of the Eastern Emperor Justinian. Actual opponents of fifth-century Britons, like Euric King of the Goths who defeated Riothamus, or the real sub-Roman rulers Aegidius and Syagrius, are conspicuous by their absence.

If Lucius is not Liberius, he may be identified with the Lluchs of the Welsh material. One suggestion is that he is the Lluch Lleawc of *Preideu Annwfyn*. The argument runs that, although Lluch is in the otherworld in this poem, he plays an analogous role to Llenlleawc the Irishman in *Culhwch and Olwen*. If the original was called Lluch the Irishman, this might have been Latinised as

Lucius Hibernius, and read mistakenly, perhaps by Geoffrey, as Lucius Hiberius. This would imply that Geoffrey's immediate source was in Latin.

This suggested sequence of transmission and error is unduly complicated. The fact remains that, alone of the continental adversaries of Arthur, Lucius bears a name which may be connected with that in the Welsh material. In *Preideu Annwfyn*, Lluch is shown as a warrior fighting during an overseas expedition of Arthur and his men. Spain is generally seen as an otherworldly or fantastically distant location in Dark Age sources.

If this section of Geoffrey is thought of in terms of an overseas expedition to legendary locations, possibly involving a character called Lluch, then the material is much more in keeping with the Arthurian canon than a historical expedition to France. Sure enough, when Arthur arrives he is confronted by a ferocious giant from Spain which he has to defeat in single combat.

This episode is in a different idiom from the rest of the Arthurian material and its antecedents are not difficult to see. The giant has carried off Hoel's daughter Helena to what is now Mont St Michel. The Breton knights pursue him but are unable to defeat him. The newly arrived Arthur with his companions Kay and Bedivere set out to confront him. 'Being a man of outstanding courage, he had no need to lead a whole army against monsters of this sort. Not only was he himself strong enough to destroy them, but by doing so he wanted to inspire his men' (HRB X.3, Thorpe 1966:238).

The heroes arrive too late to save Helena, but Arthur kills the giant in single combat, after which Bedivere cuts off his head. Hoel has a chapel built on one of the twin peaks of Mont St Michel, 'which is called to this day Helena's tomb'.

That this giant-killing episode was a rather familiar motif is referred to directly. Arthur himself states that he has never fought anyone so strong since he took on Ritho the Giant of Mount Aravius (Snowdon), who wanted to wear Arthur's beard on his cloak of beards. Arthur beat him in single combat too, and took his beard instead.

We have seen all of these features elsewhere, and we can imagine the sort of source from which Geoffrey derived them. The beard incident involving giant Ritho recalls solving the tasks of Urnach the Giant and Dillus the Bearded in *Culhwch and Olwen*. The abduction of a royal lady to a famous ecclesiastical hill is found in Caradoc's *Life of Gildas*. The association of Arthur with Kay and Bedivere alone is familiar too from the saints' *Lives*, as is the denouement of a prince's endowment of an ecclesiastical foundation.

A seeming interpolation in William of Malmesbury's 'On the Antiquity of the Church at Glastonbury' tells of a combat between one of Arthur's knights, Ider, son of King Nut, against three giants at Brent Knoll in Somerset. Arthur turns up later, after Ider has succumbed to his wounds. He makes amends by granting the knoll to Glastonbury Abbey. Geoffrey adds 'Hyderus son of Nu' to Arthur's forces later in the Roman campaign. We might speculate that Geoffrey found the episode in a Breton source, a saint's *Life* or a charter, and recalled its similarity to Welsh tales.

With the giant-killing out of the way, Arthur marches for the River Alba (Aube) outside Augustudunum (Autun) to confront the Romans. Four Britons are named in the episode: Boso, Gerinus, Hyderus and Gualguanus. None has featured in the British wars. Boso of Oxford is unknown in any earlier source. The suspicion is that he is Geoffrey's creation, deriving his name from 'Bos' – ox. If locating Gerinus in Chartres is just Geoffrey's artifice (as Kay and Bedivere are described as of Anjou and Normandy respectively), then we have no difficulty in identifying him as Gereint. Gerennius was an acceptable Latin form, found earlier in Geoffrey and in the *Book of Llandaff*. Lands named Dumnonia and Cornwall, home of the historical Gereints, are also found in Brittany. This leaves the possibility that Geoffrey found Gerinus in a Breton source, perhaps mistakenly giving him a continental location.

Hyderus, son of Nu, appears in *Culhwch and Olwen*, in pseudo-William of Malmesbury and carved on an archivault of Modena Cathedral, built *c.* 1105, where he is called 'Isdernus'. We thus know that he is a pre-existing character.

The fourth knight would become one of the most famous in the Arthurian cycle, the king's nephew Gualguanus – Sir Gawain.

Sir Gawain

Gualguanus is the son of Loth of Lodenesia and Arthur's sister 'who Loth married in the time of Ambrosius', *Loth . . . qui tempore Aurelii Ambrosii sororem ipsius* [i.e. Arthur] *duxerat* (HRB IX.9). In fact, Loth married her in Uther's reign, and the confusion led Thorpe to make her 'sister of Ambrosius', although Gualguanus is unequivocally Arthur's nephew throughout the book. At the time of Arthur's conquest of Norway he is twelve years old and has been sent to serve in the household of Pope Sulpicius, who dubs him knight. St Sulpicius flourished in the early fifth century. However, there was no Pope of this name, the nearest being Simplicius (468–83).

Gawain joins Arthur between the Plenary Court and this battle on the River Alba. He acts as both a hot-headed envoy and a commander. At the next battle he and King Hoel command one of the king's divisions. 'No better knights than Hoel and Gawain have ever been born down the ages', Geoffrey writes. 'Gawain, fearless in his courage . . . was the bravest of all the knights'. 'Hoel was in no way less brave . . . It would be difficult to say which of these two was the braver' (HRB X.10; Thorpe 1966:254). Gawain takes on Lucius himself in single combat, and the Emperor rejoices at the opportunity of proving himself against one of whose fame he had heard so much. Gawain survives the Roman war, only to be killed by the forces of his brother Modred at Rutupi Portus (Richborough in Kent).

Geoffrey gives more information about Gawain than any of the other warriors who accompany Arthur. Unlike Kay and Bedivere, we learn about his parents and upbringing. There is more material about his exploits than about most of the kings of Britain in the book.

The most reasonable supposition is that Gawain was a famous warrior, whom Geoffrey wished to incorporate. But in what context did he find him? He might share a source with his companion Hoel or alternatively Geoffrey may be trying to reconcile competing regional claims as to who is Arthur's greatest warrior. He does not figure in Arthur's historical campaigns, whether against the Saxons or at Camblan.

The account of Gawain's childhood reads like the '*Enfances*' romances that he and many other Arthurian characters are later to figure in. At this point in the development of the legend it is unique. We have not even heard about Arthur's childhood, let alone those of his men. The nearest genre to this is hagiography. The *Life of St Kentigern*, for example, already noted as sharing some features with Geoffrey, gives Kentigern's parentage, birth and upbringing.

We have a check on Gawain, because Geoffrey is not the only person to mention him. William of Malmesbury, writing slightly earlier, says that the tomb of Walwenus had been found in the Welsh region of Ros (Pembrokeshire) in the time of William the Conqueror. It was 14 feet long and lay on the seashore. This is presumably connected with the (inland) site known since the late thirteenth century as Walwyn's Castle. Buried in this tomb was 'the noble Walwenus, who was the nephew of Arthur by his sister. He reigned in the part of Britain which is still called Walweitha (Galloway). Although a warrior most renowned for his valour, he was expelled from his kingdom by Hengist's brother and nephew . . . but not before he compensated for his exile by causing them considerable damage. He deserves to share the praise justly given to his uncle since together they delayed for many years the destruction of their collapsing country' (White 1997).

William's locating of Gawain's tomb in Pembrokeshire seems more likely than in Richborough. Assuming they both draw on a common legend, it seems unlikely that William took a tradition naming the Port of Rutupi and accidentally located it in an obscure corner of Wales, especially as he connects Gawain with Galloway. Far more likely, Geoffrey mistook or distorted a name like Ros into the only channel port beginning with R, as required by his geography of continental campaigns.

We note in passing that if Arthur's overseas campaigns derive from myth, then Ros is a good location for a return from a western expedition, to Ireland or the otherworld.

William's story, connecting Gawain with South Wales and the war against Hengist's nephew and the Saxons is much more expected than Geoffrey's wars in France. He provides two alternative endings, one that Gawain is 'wounded by his foes and cast out in a shipwreck', which has an affinity with his death during the amphibious assault in Geoffrey. The other, that he was killed by his fellow citizens at a public banquet, shows at least that more than one story of Gawain was in circulation. That he was already a famous Arthurian figure is proved by his appearance on the Modena archivault.

This discussion is muddied by the presence in the Welsh legends of the king's nephew, Gwalchmei, son of Gwyar, found in *Culhwch and Olwen*. In the Welsh translations of Geoffrey, this Gwalchmei ap Gwyar always replaces Gawain. This identification has problems. Gwalchmei came complete with a patronymic while Gawain had both parents named as Loth and Anna. Geoffrey makes Gawain and Modred brothers. It is certain that Gwalchmei and Medraut were not regarded in this way, as Medraut is never given the patronymic 'ap Gwyar'.

THE EMPEROR LUCIUS

Lucius decides to withdraw into Augustodunum (Autun) to await reinforcements from the Emperor Leo. He marches for Langres en route to Autun. Arthur, however, outmarches him, bypassing Langres to take up position in the valley of Siesia. The only location which almost fits the bill is Saussy, which is how Thorpe translates the name. The ensuing battle of Siesia is Geoffrey's *pièce-de-résistance*, taking twice as long as the battles of Badon and Camblan put together.

The deployments of the troops are recorded. Arthur sets up his command-post and field hospital under his standard of the Golden Dragon, to the rear of the main divisions. Arthur and Lucius deliver lengthy speeches to their troops. Kay and Bedivere die in the first assault, overwhelmed by Medes and Libyans. Hoel and Gawain counter-attack at great loss. Fighting with the Emperor's bodyguard, 'Three other famous leaders were killed, Riddomarcus, Bloctonius and Iaginvius of Bodloan. Had these men been rulers of kingdoms, succeeding ages would have celebrated their fame, for their courage was immense' (HRB X.10; Thorpe 1966:253).

The Britons are again forced back, but this time Arthur and his division come to their support. With his sword Caliburnus, Arthur strikes down men or horses at a single blow. Lucius joins in the combat and fate hangs in the balance, until Morvidus brings the British reserve down from the hills. Lucius is killed fighting in the midst of his men. The Romans break and are slaughtered as they flee.

Arthur spends the winter subduing the cities of the Allobroges (Geoffrey's name for the Burgundians), before preparing to march on Rome. At this point, he receives bad news from Britain: his nephew Modred has usurped the throne. He rushes back to reclaim it.

What are we to make of this? There are lists of British commanders, some, such as Cador, Gerinus, Loth, Hoel, Gawain, Kay and Bedivere, are already familiar. Others, like Urbgennius of Bath, Cursalem of Caistor and Chinmarchocus of Treguier, are relative newcomers. These last three demonstrate how unlikely it is that Geoffrey found them in a context of fighting alongside Arthur. Shorn of their territorial epithets, they are found in the Harleian Genealogies. Urbgennius is the earlier form of Urien, and Chinmarochus is his father. Cursalem is a figure in the genealogy of neighbouring Strathclyde. It looks as if Geoffrey has again been mining non-narrative sources for names.

There are three possible explanations:

1. Geoffrey is being whimsical. The battles could be anywhere, against anyone, they just happen to be in Burgundy against the Romans.
2. The dramatic structure of his work, or narrative considerations, necessitated it.
3. External considerations suggested Burgundy as a site for the action.

The first option is contrary to Geoffrey's methods of working. The exploits of his kings take place in locations we can usually explain in terms of geographical plausibility, etymology, archaeological deduction and regional or political bias. Arthur's earlier campaigns combine speculation on the *Historia* battle-list, analogy with the wars of the Viking era, and the politics of the Anglo-Normans. Geoffrey was not able to sit down and study detailed maps to invent battle plans or likely locations. Only major towns would feature on the schematic maps of his time, not obscure places like Siesia.

Geoffrey has, moreover, only a vague grasp of where these places are. Augustodunum would seem, if we knew only Geoffrey's text, fairly close to Mont St Michel, with the Aube somewhere between them. Langres would be en route from the Aube to Autun, with the valley of Siesia just outside. Burgundy would be a different place, south of Siesia, and nearer Rome. None of these things is true.

We have looked at the possible dramatic structure of *Historia Regum Britanniae* as a reason for sending Arthur to Rome. Geoffrey conceives the Lands of the Allobroges as being on the way to Rome. Brennius, king of the Allobroges by marriage, leads a combined force of Allobroges and Britons on Rome. Geoffrey intends Arthur's conquests to involve the Allobroges and mishandles their incorporation at this point. One of the charges brought by Lucius against Arthur is that he has 'seized the province of the Allobroges'. In fact, the Allobroges are only subdued after Arthur's victory at Siesia. Even if Geoffrey's narrative structure requires Arthur to follow in the footsteps of Brennius, this does not involve Autun, Langres, the Aube and Siesia. Neither possibility explains why Geoffrey has chosen these specific details of the campaign, which returns us to the suggestion that he was driven by external considerations.

Nothing we know of the life of Geoffrey of Monmouth suggests a connection with Burgundy. There is no evidence that he ever went there, nor that Walter the Archdeacon was connected to the place. Furthermore, Burgundy was not a factor in the Anarchy or the French wars of Henry I. Burgundy was on the border of France and the (Holy) Roman Empire, so Geoffrey could see it as a location for conflict between the Romans and Arthur as overlord of France, but this would not explain the exact locations chosen. They must have come to Geoffrey from a source of some sort. Whatever source he used, it is hugely unlikely that it related to the wars of King Arthur. The expeditions of Riothamus, Maximus or Constantine III, while possibly contributing to the picture, do not involve the named Burgundian locations.

One possibility is the wars of Julius Caesar. Geoffrey knew about these, writing 'It happened, as can be read in the histories of Rome, that after he had conquered Gaul, Julius Caesar came to the sea coast of the Ruteni' (HRB IV.1; Thorpe 1966:107) to prepare his invasion of Britain. These histories of Rome would have told Geoffrey how Caesar defeated the Aedui near the present site of Autun. Siesia might recall Alesia, site of Caesar's final defeat of the Gauls in the nearby lands of the Arverni.

Geoffrey's treatment of Caesar's wars is similar to this Arthurian material. Caesar and Arthur, for example, are the only characters to have named swords (Caesar's is called *Crocea Mors*, Saffron Death) and both use them to kill with single blows. Cassibellanus fights Caesar at his last battle in a valley. Caesar arrives here after landing at Rutupi Portus and is aided by Cassibellanus's treacherous nephew, features which will be revisited with Arthur. These similarities do not explain why Geoffrey specifically chose the locations he did. There are plenty of other places, including the Auvergne and Brittany, where Caesar fought the Gauls, which would be more appropriate for Arthur's major confrontation.

Historically, there was in fact a battle at about the right time (Geoffrey imagines this as happening in 541) at Autun. The city and surrounding Burgundy were assaulted and taken by the sons of Clovis. These kings were the actual overlords of the lands Geoffrey has appropriated for Arthur. We can imagine that Bretons took part in this fighting, but from the meagre evidence we cannot say why this campaign in particular should have turned up in a possible Breton source book. It may have been important in eleventh-century hagiography or in the military career of a famous Breton warrior but, if so, that has not survived in any source.

The last time Arthur could possibly have fought the Romans in northern Gaul is 486, when the Roman Kingdom of Soissons under Syagrius was conquered by Clovis of the Franks. It is possible that this has lent its name to Siesia, but otherwise Geoffrey knows nothing of this kingdom or its rulers. Another remote possibility is that Geoffrey's source is one dealing with mythical otherworld locations such as Caer Sidi and Annwfyn, and that he casts about for vaguely similar names (Siesia? Augustudunum?) to replace them.

One last possibility is that the location of Arthur's final campaign was circumscribed by knowledge that he would end up mortally wounded in

Avallon. Avallon is actually one of the major ecclesiastical centres between Autun and Langres. Geoffrey may have been working towards this location and simply have looked at other nearby cities. Avallon is practically equidistant from Langres and Autun. If Arthur were wounded in battle halfway between them and was borne away from the battlefield in the direction of Britain, he might well arrive in Avallon. If Geoffrey does have some need to end the career of Arthur near the Burgundian Avallon, however, he has to make a detour by way of a British location for Arthur's last battle, Camblan.

SHROUDED IN MYSTERY – THE END OF ARTHUR

The only part of Geoffrey's work which he specifies as coming from the ancient book is the war between Arthur and Modred. It is supported by the testimony of Walter the Archdeacon. Geoffrey tells us that while Arthur was away, his nephew Modred has assumed the crown of the kingdom through tyranny and is now living adulterously with Guanhuvara. Although not specifically in the source book, it is the assumed background to the rest of the episode. Later Guanhuvara flees from York on hearing of Arthur's victories and becomes a nun at the Church of St Julius in Caerleon, 'promising to live a chaste life'.

Arthur fights three battles against Modred, at Rutupi Portus, at Gwintonia (Winchester) and finally at Camblan, a river in Cornwall (presumably the Camel). Gualguanus is killed at the first battle. This is either because he is mentioned in the source as dying or, on the contrary, expressly because he is not among Arthur's men at Camblan in the source. Kay and Bedivere do not make it back from the continent and we must suppose that they did not figure in the Camblan tradition. This could be because the battle was associated with Arthur and Medraut before these 'brave men' came on the scene. The only named heroes on Arthur's side are Olberic, King of Norway, Aschillus King of Dacia (Denmark), who has featured briefly as a commander in the Roman war, Cador Limenic and Cassibellanus. None of the characters associated with Camlan in the Welsh sources is mentioned.

Modred's associates are a motley crew, 'some Christians, some pagans'. He has attracted Saxons from Germany, led by Chelric, with the promise of the lands between the Humber and Scotland, and the possessions in Kent that Vortigern ceded to Hengist and Horsa. This conveniently links the Kent-based

Saxons at the start of the *Historia* battle-list with the Northumbrians who follow. Modred's vassals and allies include the Saxons Elaf, Egbrict and Brunning, and the Irishmen Gillapatric, Gillasel and Gillarvus, along with unnamed Picts and Scots. These names are unattested and seem made up.

One other person is named in the section, Hiwenus, son of Urianus (Owain, son of Urien), who 'in the wars which followed . . . became famous because of the many brave deeds which he accomplished' (HRB IX.1; Thorpe 1966:258). He does not take part in the action and it is therefore quite likely he did not feature in the ancient book at this point.

Modred himself is described as 'the boldest of men and always the first to launch an attack' (HRB IX.2; Thorpe 1966:260). We have encountered him as Medraut in *Annales Cambriae*. In Geoffrey, his name is given in Cornish or Breton form, pointing either to a Breton ancient book or a Cornish legend locating Camblan on the Camel. Camblan is in an older form than we have in any other source, though I am inclined to view it as a fortunate survival, not an indication of the age of the source.

Modred falls in the battle of Camblan, as expected, but Arthur does not. Instead, he is carried off, mortally wounded, to the isle of Avallon (Insula Avallonis), so his wounds can be attended to. As Avallon was not then a known British place-name, we have to consider Geoffrey's use of it. This is as the place from whence Arthur's sword Caliburnus came. If Avallon occurs in the source book, then perhaps that is an indication that the list of Arthur's equipment shares the same provenance.

Shorn of material unlikely to derive from an earlier source, Geoffrey's account of Camblan is very slim. This, however, is to ignore the single most important fact about it – Geoffrey knows that Camblan was the last battle, between Arthur and Modred. We have lost sight of the importance of this bare fact because we already 'know' that Arthur and Medraut fell at the battle of Camlann. How did Geoffrey know this?

We know about the battle of Camlann because it appears in *Annales Cambriae*. The *Annales*, however, are not a common text. Only three copies survive, only one of which, in the Harleian Manuscript, was actually in existence when Geoffrey wrote. Geoffrey incorporates no other Arthurian material from the *Annales*, not the idea that Arthur carried the Cross of Our Lord at the battle of Badon three days and three nights, not the fact that Camlann occurred in the same year as a great plague. He specifically contradicts the *Annales'* placing of Dubricius some hundred years after Arthur.

Without the *Annales* or Geoffrey, our impression of the battle of Camlann would be very different. It does not feature in any other historical source. The Black Book poems give nothing about Medraut or Arthur's fate. In both *Culhwch and Olwen* and the *Dream of Rhonabwy*, we might think that Camlan has already been fought, in the early career of Arthur. In the *Dream*, Arthur and Medraut are paired as adversaries at the battle, but a literal reading would be that Arthur has emerged victorious. Even the triads do not make it clear that it is the battle in which Arthur and Medraut fell. Yet Geoffrey knows this important information and we have to ask again, how did he know it?

Geoffrey obligingly answers: he knows because it is in his very ancient source book, confirmed verbally by Walter the Archdeacon. Here, we have no option but to accept him at face value. The idea is of genuine antiquity, as evidenced by its appearance in *Annales Cambriae*. It is arrived at independently, since it is not accompanied by any other material from the *Annales*. The form of the name Modred is different, pointing to a Breton origin. The spelling 'Camblan' is suggestive of an old manuscript form.

Geoffrey has a narrative of Camlann which does not involve any of the 'best men in the world'. Even Arthur's companions, Kay and Bedivere, do not accompany him. *Culhwch and Olwen*'s reference to a continuing feud between Arthur and Kay, so that the latter would not help him, even when his men were being killed, could indicate a specific tradition that Kay was absent for the last battle, but there is nothing like this relative to Bedivere. Arthur's defeat is not brought about by the gradual whittling away of his followers, but by the indefatigable courage of his opponents. I would therefore deduce that Geoffrey's information on Camlann comes from that earlier stratum of historical material before the accretion of superhuman champions to the side of Arthur.

The list of the 'usual suspects' on Modred's side does not give us much confidence that this feature pre-dates Geoffrey. The four names of Arthur's slain companions, however, do not raise our suspicions so readily. They do not obviously include any of the heroes we might expect to find in a roll-call of the fallen at Arthur's last battle. Aschil and Odbricht are unknown characters. If their regional origin is in Geoffrey's source, then this points to a post-Viking date, fine for a document contemporary with the Vatican Recension or *Annales Cambriae*. If the regional attributions are Geoffrey's caprice, then the names show an impression that the battle, while essentially part of a British civil war, does involve Saxons as well. There is nothing outlandish about Geoffrey's idea that the participants are both pagans and

Christians. This could be true of an actual battle between British commanders in the early sixth century.

The two British participants offer more grounds for speculation. Neither has specifically appeared elsewhere in Geoffrey. Cador Limenic could be the same as Cador of Cornwall, last seen as a commander in the Roman Wars. His son, Constantine, succeeds Arthur as king of Britain, so we infer that something has happened to him between these two points, and death at Camblan seems a dramatically likely fate. Geoffrey may have a source where, at this point alone, Cador is given a Welsh surname.

The association between Cador and Cornwall does not seem to originate with Geoffrey. Cato, of the *Life of St Carantocus*, is located, perhaps, south of the Severn, and Cadwy, son of Gereint, was firmly linked to Devon and Cornwall.

Cassibellanus appears for the first time in the list of the casualties. The previous use of the name in the book is for Julius Caesar's adversary. The name, however, is the same as the Welsh *Caswallaun*, given by Geoffrey as Cadwallo. It may be that Geoffrey has Latinised the name here, inconsistent with his preference for its Welsh form. The Cambridge manuscript of Geoffrey does give an Arthurian period *Cadwallo*, Cadwallo Lauhr, King of the North Welsh. This Cadwallo Lauhr appears in the Harleian Genealogies as the father of Maelgwn Gwynedd. Geoffrey does not make this link explicit, but the chronology makes sense both dramatically and historically.

Intriguingly, the possible connections between the rulers of Cornwall, North Wales and the battle of Camblan provide an answer to the conundrum posed by our analysis of *Annales Cambriae*. This showed a strong presumption towards a North Welsh source on the grounds of style, with the less probable option of Cornwall. A tradition with the ruler of Cornwall falling at a North Welsh Camlann, or a North Welsh leader at a Cornish Camlann would make sense of the possible inferences from the *Annales* entry. It accords with what we know from Gildas, that the tyrants were not merely regional in their preoccupations. A source which actually specified that Arthur, Modred, Caswallaun of Gwynedd and Cador of Cornwall, called Cador Limenic, fell together is a distinct possibility.

Geoffrey is working with the assumption that adultery is involved in causing the battle, and that his audience already knows this. Although he does not say so explicitly, it seems likely that this information was in the ancient book. The evidence that it has an external source is Geoffrey's seeming reluctance to include it.

The milieu is not one of courtly romance or even another take on the folkloric abduction theme seen in *Culhwch and Olwen* or the *Life of St Gildas* (Bromwich *et al.* 1991). Gildas himself in *de Excidio* makes it clear that treachery between close relatives and adultery are features of the age in which he lives. The wives of the tyrants are 'whores and adulteresses', the men are 'adulterers and enemies of God'. A later writer could deduce from Gildas that this was the sort of thing that might have happened. Alternatively, Gildas may have had specific high-profile examples of adultery in mind, signalling a change from the admirable generation of Mount Badon to that of the tyrants.

One final point on the battle of Camblan is that Geoffrey gives it a date: 'this [occurred] in the year 542 after our Lord's Incarnation' (HRB IX.2; Thorpe 1966:261). This is one of three AD dates in the whole work, and obviously something Geoffrey sets store by. It seems rather at the end of the range of dates we would expect for Arthur. What was its provenance? Whenever we have encountered AD dates before, we have always looked in the direction of the historian who popularised the system, Bede, and Geoffrey's History is no exception. The other two dates, for King Lucius and Cadwallader, are both from Bede, and it is reasonable to suppose that 542 is as well. Bede, of course, does not mention Camlann. He does, however, date the event we know from *Historia Brittonum* closes the Arthurian period, the arrival of Ida in Bernicia: 547. Geoffrey may have given five years' grace before the Saxons start up again (Arthur's successor Constantine rules for four-plus years). It is equally possible that the date is simply five years out due to scribal error (DXLII for DXLVII).

Merlin predicted that the end of Arthur would be shrouded in mystery. Although Arthur falls at the battle of Camblan, his fate is described thus: 'But the famous King Arthur (*inclitus ille rex Arturus*) was mortally wounded. He was carried from there into the Island of Avallon for his wounds to be healed' (HRB IX.2). This proved too puzzling for some scribes, and their versions make it clear that the healing was unsuccessful. The Bern manuscript adds 'may his soul rest in peace'.

Although Arthur plays no more part in the story, and might as well have died, it is unlikely that Geoffrey intended it to be read in this way. William of Malmesbury relays the early twelfth-century view that Arthur has no grave, 'for which reason ancient fables claim that he will return again' (White 1997). Herman of Tournai, writing about ten years after Geoffrey, recorded a fund-raising trip to Devon and Cornwall early in the century, where the inhabitants 'said that this had been Arthur's land'. A man argued with Herman's party 'as the Britons are accustomed to quarrel with the French about King Arthur . . . saying that Arthur was still alive' (Coe and Young 1995). Geoffrey is not explicit about this. He follows the tradition in the poem *Armes Prydein* that a British renaissance will occur from the union of the British peoples against the English, with the heroes Cynon/Conan and Cadwallader representing them.

In *Historia Regum Britanniae*, it is not clear what Geoffrey means by Avallon. It is the place where Arthur's sword Caliburnus was forged. Though frequently described as the 'best of swords' and used for amazing martial feats, it does not have any magical or otherworldly properties. If we did not know anything else, we would probably read the passage as referring to the real Avallon, not far from Arthur's last continental battles. This Avallon is not an island, but allowance could be made for poetic licence or simple mistake. Avallon, meaning place of apples, is a not uncommon Celtic place-name. There was one in Britain, too, known to us under the Roman form Aballava – Brugh-by-Sands in Cumbria, close to the possible Camlann site of Camboglanna.

SUMMING UP

Geoffrey of Monmouth provided a template for later writers. Some of his ideas proved so potent that the question 'did Arthur really exist?' is now bound up with the image of a man who ruled Britain, wielded Excalibur, was betrayed by Queen Guenevere and was carried off to Avalon, all motifs derived from Geoffrey. A King Arthur who does not fit that template is hardly considered 'the real' King Arthur at all.

Some of the Arthurian legends are revealed by their absence from either Geoffrey or the earlier material, as being unlikely to preserve historical truths. That Arthur had to demonstrate his title to rule against rival British kings, that Merlin was 'his' magician and Morgan Le Fay an enemy enchantress, that his famous knights sat together at a round table or that questing for the Holy Grail was their chief activity, the sources not only do not say, but in some cases flatly contradict. However appealing these motifs are, we have to conclude that they are products of the imaginations of twelfth- and thirteenth-century fiction writers.

We have seen from the Welsh material that Geoffrey's was not the only interpretation of the terse early sources. Before considering if Geoffrey's model adds anything useful to the picture we have already presented of the reign of Arthur, it is worth summing up what we have deduced about his sources.

Geoffrey does indeed have written sources, perhaps a single manuscript, distinct from anything that survives. As a single manuscript confers no greater authority than a claim to possess several ancient books, we can give Geoffrey the benefit of the doubt. Geoffrey's source, by its content and language, cannot be 'very ancient' in the sense that it goes back to Arthurian times. It is a secondary source with all the limitations that implies. It is unlikely to pre-date *Historia Brittonum*. Consequently, where it contradicts the earlier sources then they are to be preferred.

We have good reason to think that the source is of Breton origin, and that it may be related to Breton hagiographic writing. The main element which suggests a source is the battles in Langres, Autun and Siesia. No ulterior motive for these is plausible. Even so, it is unlikely they represent real events of the reign of Arthur. The continental stories showcase the exploits of Arthur's famous knights, another suggestion of a later date.

Geoffrey relies on Gildas and Bede to give a chronological frame to his reign of Arthur. This suggests that, in spite of his protestations, his source is not an orderly and consecutive narrative. Material on Merlin, Stonehenge, Uther Pendragon, the conception of Arthur, Loth and Urianus form a related group, inspired by characters of the late sixth century. Their misplacing is due to Merlin being identified by Geoffrey with Ambrosius of *Historia Brittonum*.

Arthurian features in Geoffrey which suggest an additional source include some battle names, a connection with Silchester, the names of Arthur's possessions and some of his men, especially Gawain, the motif of Arthur fighting giants, Guenevere as Arthur's wife and her adultery, Camblan as the battle where Arthur and Modred fell, and Avalon as his last resting place. The closest affinity these elements have to any type of source is to the Welsh prose tales and hagiography.

The best case for Geoffrey adding to our historical knowledge is the Modred–Guenevere–Camblan sequence. We have speculated that an end to Arthur's reign caused by civil war is a distinct possibility, and that Arthur and Modred are adversaries a reasonable hypothesis. The idea that Modred was Arthur's regent while he fought abroad does not seem authentic. On the other hand, the feud caused by adultery does ring true as the kind of thing

Gildas leads us to believe wrecked the succeeding generation. Which brings us to the last significant point, a location of Camblan in Cornwall to match a conception place in Tintagel.

Nennius does not know much about Dumnonia. *Annales Cambriae* does give a possibility that Camlann is in Cornwall. On the other hand, there is likely to be a bias towards Cornwall in any Breton source Geoffrey might be using, considering the close connections between the two areas. Geoffrey's concept of the battle as between a true king and an adulterous usurper is plausible, given Gildas's view of the period. However, so is the Welsh version of Arthur and Medraut as rival British leaders, set at each other's throats by bickering wives or plotting subordinates. Geoffrey's disputed succession to the throne of a united England displays the recurring pattern of his History, influenced by the circumstances of his own time. Both views, that Arthur and Medraut are essentially opponents or that they are essentially on the same side, might be extrapolated from *Annales Cambriae*.

The historical Arthur, leader of an alliance of British rulers against the Saxons, and, crucially, victor at the siege of Badon Hill, has been distorted and marginalised by Geoffrey. He replaces this with Arthur, King of England ('Britain'), aided by British rulers of the twelfth-century Celtic periphery, Cornwall, Brittany and Scotland. The battle of Badon is not the culmination of Arthur's career, but a necessary step in domestic pacification before he moves on to greater victories in the international arena.

As with the Welsh sources, the distortion is in this direction – a mythical King of Britain has been spun out of historical materials, and not vice versa. While it is easy to see how Uther Pendragon could have been derived from a mythical Mabinogion-style source and grafted on to history, through a connection with Merlin or Arthur, this is emphatically not the case with Geoffrey's King Arthur. The bones of the Arthurian section are clearly derived from historical sources, with additions obvious from their content.

Geoffrey of Monmouth's work does not illuminate the historical fifth and sixth centuries. It has exerted a slight pull towards a Dumnonian aspect of Arthur's career, adding to the south-east Welsh dimension deduced from the earlier material. Some of the peripheral characters such as Guenevere may have had their names preserved across the centuries, but figures such as Arthur's father seem legendary accretions. It is possible that the real Arthur might have been the nephew of Ambrosius, but our evidence for thinking so is very suspect. Not the least of our grounds for suspicion is that Geoffrey tells us nothing about the relatives Gildas says Ambrosius had. His parents, remember, were slain in the Saxon revolt, something Geoffrey glosses over as he has identified them as Constantine III and his wife. He had at least one child and at least two grandchildren, but these characters do not exist in Geoffrey. And if Geoffrey does not know even these characters, what faith can we put on his assertion that Uther Pendragon is his brother and Arthur his nephew?

Geoffrey's idea that Britain (England) was a unified kingdom in the Arthurian period, even to the extent that the Saxons are generally resident in Scotland, has erased anything of value about Arthur's relationship with the *civitas* kings. We can see traces of this erasure, where Geoffrey removes Vortiporius's title, though he knew as well as we do that he was the tyrant of Dyfed. Geoffrey presents Arthur as operating primarily from Caerleon, with bases in London and York. This does not contradict anything we know from the period and, especially in the South Welsh aspects, fits our expectations. However, Geoffrey's obvious geographical bias gives more than enough reason for his linking Arthur to the region, without speculating that he found such material in an ancient source.

Over ten years after *Historia Regum Britanniae*, Geoffrey composed his verse epic, the *Vita Merlini*. In this, Merlin and Taliesin reminisce about taking Arthur to the island of Avallon to be healed of his wounds. Geoffrey makes it clear that Avallon is an actual island in the sea, presided over by Morgen and her priestesses. He uses the description of the Isle de Sein, off the north coast of Brittany, from the work of first-century geographer, Pomponius Mela. There is no reason to think that Geoffrey does not identify the two islands. Isle de Sein could be a possible place for someone wounded in Cornwall to be carried to. However, by the end of the twelfth century, this mystery would be replaced by a certainty that 'Avalon' was a real location in mainland Britain – Glastonbury.

EPILOGUE: DIGGING UP ARTHUR – GLASTONBURY 1190

Archaeology is often seen as providing 'forensic' proof for the theories of historians. No amount of text-criticism can compare with tangible evidence unearthed from a boggy trench. Whatever the written evidence, many historians will never be convinced that King Arthur was a real person until his actual grave is unearthed, complete with an unequivocal inscription testifying to his identity.

This has, in fact, already happened. In 1190, or perhaps the following year, the monks of Glastonbury were digging just outside the walls of their very ancient church. Although the wooden building had recently burned down, written records traced its existence back to the late seventh century at least.

The dig seems to have been prompted by a monk's desire to be buried between two pyramids in the graveyard. These monuments, inscribed with illegible ancient characters, were most probably what we would call obelisk-shaped – tall and thin. They could have been Celtic crosses which had lost their heads, christianised standing stones or early Christian grave-markers.

Not surprisingly, the monks soon turned up evidence of a burial. Two or three bodies were unearthed. Accounts differ as to whether each body had a coffin or two bodies shared a divided coffin. The latter version, describing the primitive coffin as being carved from an oak bole, seems the most likely, paradoxically because it is so unusual. A writer ignorant of the facts might imagine the burial conformed to normal twelfth-century practice. The description of the hollowed-out oaken coffin, divided two-thirds along its length, serves no ulterior motive and is not inherently implausible.

One of the skeletons was of a very large man. His face was broad, a palm's breadth between the eyes, the thigh bone was three inches longer than the shin of the tallest person present when, soon afterwards, Gerald of Wales examined the find. The head bore ten healed wounds and one unhealed and presumably mortal one. The bones are not unfeasibly gigantic, not dinosaur bones, they were apparently large and human. Another set was identified as female by their delicate graceful size and, according to the accounts, by a hank of long blonde hair found with them. This piece of evidence did not survive the excavation and might just be made up to prove their identification as female.

The bare fact of the excavation was confirmed by an archaeological dig at the site in 1962. This uncovered what seem to be the pyramid sites. Between then, as expected, was an area of digging dating from soon after 1184, and containing two or three disturbed slab-lined graves (Ralegh Radford in Ashe 1968).

So far, nothing particularly unlikely features in this story. Unlike details of ecclesiastical exhumations in the 'reliable' work of Bede, which usually come with a combination of uncorrupted flesh, the odour of sanctity, radiant lights and, shortly after, miraculous cures, this seems no more than the chance discovery of ancient burials in a crowded graveyard. What was significant was that this discovery was accompanied by an inscribed lead cross.

The cross read 'Here lies the famous King Arthur, buried in the Isle of Avalon' or some other combination of those words. A celebrated engraving from Camden's *Britannia* (1610) shows what, in his day, purported to be that very cross. Gerald was shown the cross soon after its discovery and reports 'We saw this and traced the inscription . . .'. Here lies buried the famous King Arthur with Guenevere his second wife in the Isle of Avalon' (White 1997), and the smaller set of bones was readily identified as Guenevere's. The Margam chronicle records that Modred's body was found as well, but that must have been guesswork, as no inscription to that effect is recorded by anyone (Barber 1984).

The various descriptions of the discovery of Arthur's grave are often treated as clues in a fiendish whodunit, that some stray observation or contradiction might expose either the monks or the king, or both, in some Piltdown-style deception. This is to mistake the nature of the evidence. The accounts were written specifically to refute any allegations of fakery. Thus Gerald was told that the cross was found under a stone slab, with its written face fixed to the underside of the stone. This is clearly to emphasise the fact that the cross is not a later intrusion into the burial. Gerald imagines this put the inscription in an unusual upside-down position, though in fact it would have faced upwards, as any inscription would be expected to.

Was this really the grave of Arthur? Although after the fact, 'the visions and revelations seen by holy men and clerks' and even King Henry II of England (died 1189) were cited as sources of information used by the monks to locate the burial, the reality is that no source predicted anything like it. Gerald testifies to the surprise the discovery caused: 'In our own lifetime Arthur's body was discovered at Glastonbury, although the legends had always encouraged us to believe that there was something otherworldly about his ending, that he had resisted death and had been spirited away to some far distant spot' (Thorpe 1978). Glastonbury was not an unknown or new location. It featured in an Arthurian context in the *Life of St Gildas*. However, it had never been described as the place of his burial. The discovery was not inspired by or intended to vindicate any known Glastonbury tradition.

It is now common to write about the discovery of Arthur's grave as an obvious fraud perpetrated by the monks to raise money after the recent fire. This cynicism is supported by a misapprehension about the money-spinning potential of the find. Medieval pilgrims, though they bear some affinity to modern tourists, did not visit religious sites just for a chance to see the graves of famous people and buy the souvenirs. They went to receive the religious benefits, usually indulgences off some time due in purgatory, bestowed on those sites by the ecclesiastical authorities, or, more immediately, to experience the healing or other miraculous powers attributed to the bones of the saints. If they were handing money over to the church, they expected a *quid pro quo*.

Churches like Glastonbury wished to have powerful men and women buried in them for prestige, certainly, but more importantly for the grants of land and other sources of revenue which accompanied them, to provide chantries for the souls of the deceased.

The grave of Arthur failed on both these counts. Glastonbury was already famous for its antiquity and claimed many important relics. All the monks had to gain was a slightly raised profile and the possibility that upper-class Arthurian enthusiasts might choose to be buried in proximity to their hero. That was a vain hope, and it does not explain why they would arbitrarily choose Arthur. There were plenty of important characters, saints like Joseph of Arimathea, for instance, the discovery of whose bones would be just as sensational. This is not to say that the discovery of Arthur's tomb was not made up or embellished by the monks, but it does cast doubt on the casual charges that it was a money-making hoax too common in modern accounts.

If the monks did not stand to benefit from the find, another culprit often singled out to gain is the King of England. The argument runs, to follow Barber (1986), among many others, 'Arthur's grave may have been inspired by Henry II himself: the hope of Arthur's return was still a political rallying point for the Welsh, and the discovery neatly destroyed a propaganda weapon used to good effect by the king's enemies.' There is absolutely nothing to support this view. The intelligentsia of whatever political persuasion saw belief of Arthur's survival as a vulgar superstition. It beggars belief how the king's enemies (who included his sons and his wife as much as Welsh nationalists) could expect to benefit from a popular superstition. Arthur was hardly likely to turn up to help them out, nor is it easy to see how they could have used the legend to mobilise support.

The belief of Arthur's survival was particularly strong in Cornwall (Coe and Young 1995), which had no noticeably anti-Plantagenet feeling, and was a *cause célèbre*, as reported earlier, between Henry's allies the Bretons and his enemies the French. Gerald reports that Henry heard the story from an aged British singer and passed on the exact location of the burial. If this is true (and there is no reason to think it is) and the king had a political agenda which involved the discovery, why did he not get the monks to 'find' it straight away? He was, remember, dead before the body turned up. Richard the Lionheart, his successor, made no political capital out of the burial. Richard's nephew and heir, Arthur of Brittany (aged three when the burial was discovered), seems to have been specifically named to hark back to the Arthurian glories, and could be readily seen by Welsh and Bretons as a potential King Arthur come again.

Even if the Plantagenets had some peculiar agenda for proving that Arthur was dead, why they would have chosen to do this by discovering his body at Glastonbury is not explained. They could, for instance, have refused to support such court writers as Wace and Layamon who, in works written for them, disseminated the idea of Arthur's survival in the vernacular languages. With the whole Angevin Empire to choose from, they could have decided to find Arthur on Isle de Sein, at Camelford, Caerleon, London, Silchester, Stonehenge or any other location which took their fancy which actually featured in Geoffrey of Monmouth's works. The choice of Glastonbury is inexplicable.

The motives of making money or political capital do not seem likely for inventing a burial. That leaves the simplest explanation the most plausible:

the monks actually thought they had discovered the body of King Arthur. Could they have been right?

Let us start with the most obvious piece of evidence, the cross. As Camden draws it, it does not have the look of a late twelfth-century object. Its shape and inscription seem earlier than this. It does not, however, look like a fifth/sixth-century memorial. Nothing like it has ever been found at any other site of the period. Monuments to Arthur's contemporaries are of carved stone. Their inscriptions are in an expansive, cursive script. We have already noted the memorial of Voteporix, but we could also add, among many others, one actually sited at Slaughter Bridge, Camelford. The metal cross was, however, found – according to Gerald – attached to a stone slab, and in association with two no-longer legible inscribed stones. It is therefore possible that its inscription might be based on an older carved one, and represent a renovation of a period between the sixth and the late twelfth centuries. Ralegh Radford (Ashe 1968) suggests that the cross was added to the burial in the middle of the tenth century, when the work of St Dunstan raised the level of the cemetery. This might have made the standing stones unreadable and necessitated a new marker.

Some have drawn sceptical attention to the phrase 'The famous King Arthur' as an unlikely one for a contemporary inscription, arguing that Arthur was not a king. As we have seen, Arthur could have at least ended his reign with the title *rex*, self-styled or granted by contemporaries. Vortiporius was almost certainly a king. However, his memorial says he was *Protector*, not *Rex*. Even the hyperbole of the description 'famous' is not unparalleled. The memorial stone to Catmanus of Gwynedd calls him 'The wisest of all kings'. Boasting was a Celtic tradition and his heirs might want to celebrate the deceased's fame. Perhaps significantly, though, the phrase is almost a direct quotation from Geoffrey of Monmouth.

The most problematic feature of the cross is that it proclaims that Arthur is 'buried in the Isle of Avalon'. While grave slabs could use a variety of words to describe who they commemorated, I cannot find a single example where the place of burial is named. By their nature, this is obvious as the memorial marks the location. The only conceivable value of the inscription giving the name of its own location was to identify Glastonbury as the Isle of Avalon.

The discovery of Arthur's body at Glastonbury was bound to raise objections from readers of Geoffrey of Monmouth that Arthur had last been seen en route to the Isle of Avalon. If he had not recovered, but had died there, it might be expected that he was buried there as well. For twelfth-century etymologists, it was clear that Glastonbury was an English name and that, if the foundation pre-dated the Saxon Conquest, it must have had an earlier British name. Caradoc of Llancarfan obligingly gives it – *Inis Guitrin*. Gerald of Wales copies this '[Glastonbury] used also to be called in British Inis Guitrin, that is the isle of glass; hence the Saxons called it Glastonbury. For in their tongue *glas* means Glass and a camp or town is called *buri*' (*de Principis Instructione* in Bromwich 1961).

Welsh sources do not know of anywhere called Avalon. The Welsh Bruts opted for *Ynis Afallach* as a translation of Geoffrey's Avalon. After the discovery of Arthur's body, this name rather than the established *Ynis Guitrin* was applied to Glastonbury. *Afallach* means orchard and Bromwich (1961) argues fiercely that this is its meaning here, following the consensus that *Avalon* means place of apples. However, an equally persuasive case can be made that the name was read as a personal one, yielding a meaning of 'Afallach's Island'. Aballac appears near the head of two of the Harleian Genealogies, and it is from a similar source that Geoffrey appears to have drawn the name Aballac, used in his History for one of the daughters of ancient King Ebraucus. Owain's mother in the Triads is named Modron, daughter of Aballach, reinforcing the idea that this is a personal name.

The Margam Chronicle explains the inscription thus: 'for that place [Glastonbury] was once surrounded by marshes, and is called the Isle of Avalon, that is the isle of apples. For Aval means in British an apple.' Gerald elaborates the same theme, saying that apples used to abound in that place. He draws on Geoffrey's *Vita Merlini* to add that 'Morgan, a noblewoman who was ruler of that region and closely related to Arthur [in a later source he says cousin] . . . carried him away to the island now called Glastonbury to be healed of his wounds' (Thorpe 1978). Gerald later berates those who made this 'Morgan le Fay' a fantastical sorceress. By this time, Gerald had heard the version deriving Avalon from a personal name, 'a certain Vallo, who used to rule over the area'. In the confusion that exists over William of Malmesbury's *de Antiquitate Glastoniensis ecclesiae*, we cannot be sure when a similar passage translating '*insula Avallonia*' as 'island of Apples' from the British *Aballa* – apple, or alternatively from 'a certain Avalloc, who used to live in this place with his daughters' was incorporated in the text (Scott 1981).

Geoffrey's Avalon is not Glastonbury, an identification he was perfectly able to make if he had considered it. It is an island in the sea and not an ancient ecclesiastical foundation. The inscription on the cross seems intended to harmonise an established idea that Arthur's last resting place was Avalon with the fact that his body had turned up at Glastonbury. That can only mean that the inscription on the cross post-dates Geoffrey and is therefore, at the most, only a generation earlier than the discovery.

Radford's mid-tenth-century explanation is implausible as we do have material from this period relating to Arthur, *Annales Cambriae* and the Vatican Recension. The latter is the closest a Saxon abbot might have been expected to come to Arthurian material. In those sources, there is no indication that Arthur is a famous king. In fact, the Vatican Recension specifically denies this. Finally, it is inconceivable that all sources between then and 1190 omitted to mention that Glastonbury was once called Avalon. This in spite of the fact that some, like Caradoc, provided a British name for the monastic centre. Radford's tenth-century cross is just as unlikely as a sixth-century one. If an inscribed cross was an original feature of Arthur's grave, it is highly unlikely to have been the one seen and described by Gerald.

The records of Glastonbury Abbey were extensively reproduced by William of Malmesbury. However, they were soon revised in the light of Geoffrey of Monmouth and increasing interest in Arthurian material, making it difficult to disentangle the various strands. Gerald confirms that by the time of his visit Arthur was 'much praised in the history of the excellent monastery of Glastonbury, of which he himself was in his time a distinguished patron and a generous endower and supporter' (Thorpe 1978), a feature to which Caradoc of Llancarfan alluded.

If we set aside for the moment the issue of the cross, could the grave have been Arthur's? One possibility, given the unusual oak coffin and the healed head wounds, which could be evidence of trepanning, is a Bronze Age burial. The lack of any concept of prehistory frequently led to extremely ancient finds and sites being associated with historical figures. Geoffrey of Monmouth's attribution of Stonehenge to a fifth/sixth-century Merlin is a case in point.

However, the absence of grave-goods, the Christian context and the seeming alignment of the grave with the wall of the ancient church all suggest that a historic and Christian burial was intended. If the inscribed 'pyramids' were associated with the grave, this would again point to a Christian inhumation. The burial has no affinity to the practice of the only other literate culture, the pagan Romans.

Arthur would certainly have been a Christian. *Historia Brittonum* and the *Annales* both associate his victories with Christian symbolism and devotion. From Gildas, there can be no doubt that the victors of Badon were Christians. We would therefore expect that, in reality, he would have been buried at a Christian site according to Christian rites.

Glastonbury was a flourishing centre of some kind in the fifth/sixth centuries. Some high-status person was living on top of Glastonbury Tor, as evidenced by the remains of the dwelling and the indicative 'Tintagel ware'. The ancient church, too, was probably in existence, given that it was 'ancient' in the early eighth century. The site is in the *civitas* of the Durotriges, close to its border with the Dobunni. This, as we have seen, was a likely site of Arthurian activity and could easily have been patronised by Arthur and his heirs. It might also be seen as the nearest major ecclesiastical site to a final battle in Cornwall, although it seems rather far to come from North Wales or Camboglanna.

If Arthur was buried in Glastonbury, it might explain the lack of a Welsh tradition of his last resting place, or at least the lack of a tradition that his tomb was in Wales. If he was buried outside this locality in an area which soon after would become a Saxon possession, it would explain why his grave became an unknown or unlocatable site.

The burial does not, therefore, stretch credulity very far. As Arthur must be buried somewhere, then outside the ancient church at Glastonbury is the kind of place, if not the very place, that we might expect to find him.

That more than one body was recovered is a common feature of all accounts. No motive has ever been advanced for anyone faking Guenevere's grave, still less Modred's. Their presence points towards an actual find of more than one body, with a sweep of likely characters to identify them. Guenevere had been associated with Glastonbury in the *Life of St Gildas*. As with Arthur, all previous sources were silent as to her burial. From Geoffrey's account, it seems that he imagined her to be buried at Caerleon.

Though there are hints in the Medieval romances of Arthur having two wives called Guenevere – the False-Guenevere story – these would not result in Arthur's burial with a 'second wife'. Similarly, although Guenevere features in abduction stories, none results in Arthur remarrying her, or any scenario where she could be called his second wife. One might argue that such stories preserve a memory of Arthur's multiple marriages, but unfortunately most were written after the evidence that the Glastonbury cross called her Arthur's second wife had been disseminated. The Triads alone give an explicit claim that Arthur had three wives, all called Guenevere.

If the Triad and the Glastonbury cross derive from the same legend, then either the Triads have inflated the number of Gueneveres, or we might imagine that the third wife, the adulterous daughter of Ogvran the Giant, would not be buried with Arthur but that Arthur might choose to lie in the same grave as a favoured earlier wife. Gerald was surprised to hear that Arthur was married twice, which suggests the monks might have added to their credibility by avoiding that single word *Secunda* from the cross inscription as Gerald saw it. We might wonder if the Isle of Avalon wording was added to a cross which formerly only included Arthur and his (second) wife.

It is not completely clear that Gerald did read an inscription on the cross. He traced the letters but, given their antiquity or poor state of preservation, may have been reliant on the monks for the transliteration he gives. He was at pains to set down that the cross was not the only proof that this was Arthur's grave. He referred to 'signs that the body had been buried here were found in the records of the place, in the letters inscribed on the pyramids (although these were almost obliterated by age) and in the visions . . . of holy men' (Thorpe 1978).

If *Annales Cambriae*, or the *Mirabilia*, for argument's sake, said that Arthur's grave was at Glastonbury, and no actual grave had been discovered there, then the information would have fitted comfortably into our theory. It seems a reasonable place for a Christian king operating in south-east Wales and the adjoining area of England to be buried. The burial itself and the circumstances of its discovery are quite believable. Even an inscription calling Arthur a famous king and saying he was buried with his second wife do not strain credulity.

If the monks had left it there, we would have been disposed to view the discovery leniently. It is the inscription identifying the site of Arthur's grave with Avalon which is unbelievable. It seems, ironically, that the monks, in trying to prove their case, fatally weakened its plausibility.

CONCLUSION: THE REIGN OF ARTHUR?

'**M**any tales are told and many legends have been invented about King Arthur and his mysterious ending. In their stupidly the British people maintain that he is still alive. Now that the truth is known, I have taken the trouble to add a few more details in this present chapter. The fairy-tales have been snuffed out, and the true and indubitable facts are made known, so that what really happened must be made crystal clear to all and separated from the myths that have accumulated on the subject.' Gerald of Wales, *Speculum Ecclesiae* 1216 (White 1997).

So, was there ever a time when a King Arthur ruled over Britain? The popular conception of Arthur as a medieval king of England, was an invention of Geoffrey of Monmouth, along with other twelfth-century writers. It is futile to trace that particular model any further back. It is not based on sources, but on assumptions arising from the era in which the authors wrote. That medieval King Arthur could not have existed in the fifth or sixth century. Yet behind that illusory image are the figures of two men with whom we have been particularly concerned, both of whom did exist.

The first was called Arthur. Sometime before the ninth century (and we have argued about 300 years before) northern Britons listened to a lament on the fallen hero Guaurthur. As the poet brought to mind his generosity with his valued horses, his prowess, the 300 men who fought around him, the slaughter before the Roman walls, the audience understood how a comparison between this man and *Arthur* strengthened the image and the poignancy of his death.

That this Arthur was a real person seems unarguable. We have no reason to think that he did not exist, and every reason to suppose that he did. This is not all we can say about him. The comparison seems most apt if we take this Arthur as being the character presented to us in *Historia Brittonum*, the soldier and general who led the kings of the Britons in the wars against the Saxons perhaps two generations before Guaurthur, fighting in the same disputed areas of the north. This seems the obvious background which the poet invokes, comparing the dead warrior to his similarly named forebear.

In order for the comparison in the *Gododdin* to make sense, the germ of the idea, that Arthur was a warleader of the Britons in the days before the sixth-century Anglian colonisation of Bernicia, must have existed before the poem. If the Guaurthur/Arthur verse genuinely dates back to the sixth century, then Arthur the warleader would have been fighting not far beyond the living memory of the audience, and must have been a real person.

Historia Brittonum does not merely describe an Arthur of the north-east, as we might expect from *Y Gododdin*. It combines Arthurian material from more than one source, including ones linking Arthur to south-east Wales. It is a work of its time. It does not present ancient documents unaltered from the distant past. What it does do, however, is testify to widespread and consistent material on Arthur the Warleader from before the early ninth century. Equally importantly, it identifies Arthur with another indisputably real person, the leader of the Britons at the battle of Mount Badon.

We know that this man existed, based on his real achievement, the victory at the siege of Badon Hill. The contemporary record is silent as to his name, and indeed the names of just about everyone else in Britain in the period, but that does not detract from the fact he must have existed.

Common sense dictates that somebody coordinated the British military response to the Saxons. He lived, it seems, at the turn of the fifth and sixth centuries and led the Britons in their united defence. For the Saxon advance to be stopped across the country, the fighting must have occurred in other areas beyond the immediate vicinity of Badon. The political reality of the period seems characterised by the growth of small kingdoms. If they combined in a united response against the Saxons, they must have enjoyed military unity on a different basis and at a higher level than the *civitas*.

Although the victor of Badon was obviously a military commander, the political realities of the time blurred the distinction between military and civil power, with warlords dominating or overthrowing provincial rulers across the western empire. The logistics of supplying and coordinating a united response across the *civitates* necessitates a higher authority, which the military commander might have dominated. This higher authority combined responsibility for the *civitates* of Britannia Prima, the wall system of Britannia

Secunda and the enclaves of Britons in the east. It is therefore not misleading to state that this authority 'reigned' over Britain.

The coincidence between the British *Magister Militum* and a supporting civil authority, waging wars against the Saxons in the generation before Gildas and Maglocunus, and Arthur the Warleader of *Historia Brittonum* and the *Gododdin* is obvious. It is likely they were one and the same person. The only counter-argument is wildly unlikely: that every British person forgot the true name of the man who led the British resistance and replaced it with that of another man who did not.

This position, at its most extreme, would make the author of *Historia Brittonum* the creator of a fictional Arthur, which somehow obliterated all traces of the real warlord. It seems impossible that a single work could ensure that among the Britons no trace of an alternative name for the victor of Badon survived.

Historia Brittonum is not the sole authority linking the names Arthur and Badon. *Annales Cambriae* present independent yet supporting material. This not only provides corroboration for Arthur's role at Badon, but also an account of his death which seems to place this in a civil war, exactly as Gildas's characterises the succeeding period. The *Gododdin*, *Historia* and *Annales* describe the same real man, the victor of the battle of Badon, and are perfectly consistent with historical reality.

It is easy to discern a faultline between this material and Welsh Arthurian legends. The historical material pre-dates these legends and does not derive from them. The legends, including the saints' *Lives*, do not see Arthur as a warleader coordinating the kings of the Britons against the Saxons. Instead, he is shown as a Dark Age Welsh king, with a similar position to the tyrants of *de Excidio*. He is shifted in time, to become a contemporary of Gildas, Maelgwn and Owain, son of Urien. Furthermore, he is assigned his own warband of fabulous heroes, rather than his actual colleagues, the kings of the Britons.

All this is a distortion of the picture presented by the historical sources. Even Arthur's victory over the Saxons at Badon, the touchstone of his existence, is missing. This eleventh-century legendary Arthur is distinct from everything which has gone before. This causes no problem for researchers into the real Cassivelaunus, the real Magnus Maximus, the real Gildas, who similarly became the focus of Welsh legendary material at the same time.

The legendary and the historical Arthurs were blended by the artifice of Geoffrey of Monmouth, producing a fictionalised picture in which the legendary aspect predominated. This has cast doubt on the historicity of Arthur, but it is relatively easy to see where Geoffrey has built on and reinterpreted existing sources. His fictionalised Arthur has no bearing on whether the real Arthur existed or not, and it is unfair to treat a refutation of the former as reflecting on the latter.

The victor of Mount Badon was a real person, and his dominating role in Britain implicit in his achievement. We have every reason to think that he is the original behind the Arthur of the *Gododdin* and *Historia Brittonum*. We have equally no reason to think that those sources are wrong in granting him the name Arthur. This man, this Arthur, commanded kings, at a time when private citizens and public officials kept to their allotted positions. In this sense, therefore, it is reasonable to say that the generation which witnessed the siege of Badon did indeed live in the 'reign of Arthur.'

BIBLIOGRAPHY

Abbreviations

DEB   Gildas's *de Excidio Britanniae*
EH   Bede's *The Ecclesiastical History of the English People*
HB   *Historia Brittonum ('Nennius')*
HRB Geoffrey of Monmouth's *Historia Regum Britanniae*
YG   *Y Gododdin*

Abrams, L. and Carley, J.P. (eds) *The Archaeology and History of Glastonbury Abbey: Essays in Honour of the Ninetieth Birthday of C.A. Ralegh Radford*, Woodbridge: Boydell Press, 1991

Adams, J.dQ. 'Sidonius and Riothamus', *Arthurian Literature 12* (1993)

Alcock, L. *By South Cadbury is that Camelot*, Thames & Hudson (1972)

——, *Arthur's Britain: History and Archaeology AD 367–634*, Harmondsworth: Penguin, 1971

Anderson, W.B. (ed. and trans.) *Sidonius Apollinaris: Poems and Letters*, 2 vols, Cambridge, Mass: Loeb Classical Library, 1936

Ashe, G. *The Quest for Arthur's Britain*, Pall Mall Press, 1968

——, *Kings and Queens of Early Britain*, Methuen, 1982

——, '"A certain very ancient book": traces of an Arthurian source in Geoffrey of Monmouth's History', *Speculum 56*

Barber, R. *Arthur Hero and Legend*, Woodbridge, Boydell Press, 1986

——, *The Figure of Arthur*, Harlow: Longman, 1972

——, 'Was Modred buried at Glastonbury? An Arthurian Tradition at Glastonbury in the Middle Ages', *Arthurian Literature 4* (1984)

Barron, W.R.J. (ed.) *The Arthur of the English*, Cardiff: University of Wales Press, 1999

Bassett, S. (ed.) *The Origins of the Anglo-Saxon Kingdoms*, Leicester: Leicester University Press, 1989

Bromwich, R. *Trioedd Ynys Prydein: The Welsh Triads*, Cardiff: University of Wales Press, 1961

Bromwich, R. and Evans, D.S. *Culhwch and Olwen: An Edition and Study of the Oldest Arthurian Text*, Cardiff: University of Wales Press, 1992

Bromwich, R., Jarman, A.O.H. and Roberts, B.F. (eds) *The Arthur of the Welsh*, Cardiff: University of Wales Press, 1991

Brooks, D.A. 'Gildas' De Excidio: Its revolutionary meaning and purpose', *Studia Celtica* 18 (1983–4)

Bryant, N. (trans.) *The High Book of the Graal*, Cambridge, D.S. Brewer, 1978

Campbell, A. *The Chronicle of Æthelweard*, Nelson Medieval Series, 1959

Campbell, J. (ed.) *The Anglo-Saxons*, Phaidon, 1982

Casey, P.J. and Jones, M.J. 'The date of the Letter of the Britons to Aetius', *Bulletin of the Board of Celtic Studies 37* (1990)

Castleden, R. *King Arthur: The Truth behind the Legend*, Routledge, 2000

Chadwick, H.M. and Chadwick, N.K. *The Growth of Literature I*, Cambridge: Cambridge University Press, 1932

Coe, J.B. and Young, S. *The Celtic Sources for the Arthurian Legend*, Felinfach, Llanerch, 1995

Collingwood, W.G. 'Arthur's Battles', *Antiquity 3* (1929)

Crawford, O.G.S. 'Arthur and his battles', *Antiquity 9* (1935)

Cunliffe, B. *Roman Bath Discovered*, Routledge, 1984

Dark, K.R. *From Civitas to Kingdom: British Political Continuity 300–800*, Leicester University Press, 1994

——, *Britain and the End of the Roman Empire*, Stroud: Tempus, 2000

Davies, W. *Wales in the Early Middle Ages*, Leicester: Leicester University Press, 1982

——, *An Early Welsh Microcosm: Studies in the Llandaff Charters*, Royal Historical Society, 1978

——, *The Llandaff Charters*, Aberystwyth: The National Library of Wales, 1979

Doel, F., Doel, G. and Lloyd, T. *Worlds of Arthur: King Arthur in History, Legend and Culture*, Stroud: Tempus, 1998

Dumville, D.N. *Histories and Pseudo-histories of the Insular Middle Ages*, Aldershot: Variorum, 1990

——, *The Historia Brittonum: The Vatican Recension*, Cambridge: Brewer, 1985

Ellis, P.B. *Celt and Saxon: The Struggle for Britain, A.D. 410–937*, Constable, 1983

Fairbairn, N. *A Traveller's Guide to the Kingdoms of Arthur*, Evans Brothers Ltd, 1983

Faral, E. *La légende Arthurienne: Etudes et documents, les plus anciens textes*, 3 vols, Paris: Librairie Ancienne Honore Champion, 1929

Field, P.J.C. 'Nennius and his History', *Studia Celtica 30* (1996)

Frere, S. *Britannia: A History of Roman Britain*, Routledge, 1987

Gantz, J. *The Mabinogion*, Harmondsworth, Penguin, 1976

Garmondsway, G.N. (ed. and trans.) *The Anglo-Saxon Chronicle*, Everyman, 1953

Gilbert, A. with Blackett, B. and Wilson, A. *The Holy Kingdom: The Quest for the Real King Arthur*, Bantam Press, 1998

Griscom, A. *The Historia Regum Britanniae of Geoffrey of Monmouth*, Longman, Green and Co., 1929

Hay, D. *The Anglica Historia of Polydore Vergil*, London: Camden Society 3rd series, 74 (1950)

Higham, N.J. *King Arthur: Myth-making and History*, Routledge, 2002

——, *The English Conquest: Gildas and Britain in the Fifth Century*, Manchester: Manchester University Press, 1994

Holmes, M. *King Arthur, a Military History*, Blandford, 1996

Hood, A.B.E. (ed.) *St Patrick, His Writings and Muirchu's Life*, London and Chichester: Phillimore, 1978

Howlett, R. (ed.) *Chronicles of the Reigns of Stephen, Henry II and Richard I*, Longman, 1885

Hughes, K. 'The Welsh Latin Chronicles; *Annales Cambriae* and related texts', *Proceedings of the British Academy 59* (1973)

——, *Celtic Britain in the Early Middle Ages: Studies in Scottish and Welsh Sources*, Woodbridge: Boydell, 1980

Jackson, K.H. 'Once again Arthur's Battles', *Modern Philology 43* (1945)

——, 'Arthur's Battle of Breguoin', *Antiquity 23* (1949)

——, *The Gododdin: The Oldest Scottish Poem*, Edinburgh: Edinburgh University Press, 1969

——, *A Celtic Miscellany*, Harmondsworth: Penguin, 1971

Jarman, A.O.H. 'The Arthurian allusions in the Book of Aneirin', *Studia Celtica 24–25* (1989–90)

——, (ed. and trans.) *Aneirin. Y Gododdin*, Llandysul: Gomer Press, 1988

Johnson, S. *Late Roman Britain*, Book Club Associates, 1980

Jones, G.D.B. and Mattingly, D. *An Atlas of Roman Britain*, Oxford: Basil Blackwell, 1990

Jones, M.E. 'The appeal to Aetius in Gildas', *Nottingham Medieval Studies 32* (1988)

Jones, T. (ed and trans.) *Brut Y Tywysogyon or the Chronicle of the Princes*, Cardiff: University of Wales Press, 1952

Jones, T. and Jones W. *The Mabinogion*, London and New York: Dent & Dutton, 1949

Kirby, D.P. and Williams, J.E.C. 'Review of the Age of Arthur, J. Morris' *Studia Celtica 10–11* (1975–6)

Koch, J.T. *The Gododdin of Aneirin. Text and Context from Dark-Age Northern Britain*, Cardiff: University of Wales Press, 1997

Lacy, N.J. (ed.) *The New Arthurian Encyclopedia*, New York and London: Garland Publishing, 1991

Lapidge, M. and Dumville, D.N. (eds) *Gildas: New Approaches*, Woodbridge: Boydell Press, 1984

Loomis, R.S. 'Edward I, Arthurian Enthusiast', *Speculum 28* (1953)

——, (ed.) *Arthurian Literature in the Middle Ages*, Oxford: Clarendon Press, 1959

MacDowall, S. *Late Roman Infantryman 236–565 AD*, London: Osprey, 1994

——, *Late Roman Cavalryman 236–565 AD*, London: Osprey, 1995

Major, A. *Early Wars of Wessex*, Poole: Blandford Press, 1978

Miller, M. 'Date-guessing and pedigrees', *Studia Celtica 10-11* (1995–6)

——, Bede's use of Gildas', *English Historical Review 90* (1975a)

——, 'Historicity and the pedigree of the North Countrymen', *Bulletin of the Board of Celtic Studies* 26 (1975b)

——, 'Starting to write history: Gildas, Bede and "Nennius"', *Welsh History Review 8* (1976–7)

——, 'Consular years in the Historia Brittonum', *Bulletin of the Board of Celtic Studies 29* (1980)

Moffat, A. *Arthur and the Lost Kingdoms*, London: Weidenfeld & Nicolson, 1999

Mommsen, T. (ed.) *Chronica Minora saec. IV, V, VI, VII*, 3 vols, Berlin: Weidmann, 1891–8

——, *Monumenta Germaniae Historica, Auctorum Antiqissimiorum, xii, 1, De Excidio et Conquestu Brittaniae*. Berlin: Weidman, 1894

Morris, J. *The Age of Arthur*, Weidenfeld & Nicolson, 1973

——, *Nennius, The British History and the Welsh Annals*, London and Chichester: Phillimore, 1980

Myres, J.N.L. *Anglo-Saxon Pottery and the Settlement of England*, Oxford: Clarendon Press, 1969

——, *The English Settlements*, Oxford: Clarendon Press, 1986

Nicolle, D. *Arthur and the Anglo-Saxon Wars*, Osprey Publishing, 1984

Ordnance Survey, *Map of Britain in the Dark Ages*, Southampton, Ordnance Survey, 1974

Phillips, G. and Keatman, M. *King Arthur: – the True Story*, Arrow, 1993

Piggott, S. 'The Sources of Geoffrey of Monmouth', *Antiquity 15* (1941)

Plummer, C. *Two of the Saxon Chronicles Parallel*, Oxford, 1892–9

——, *Venerabilis Bedae opera Historica*, 2 vols, Oxford: Clarendon Press for Oxford University Press, 1896

Rahtz, P, *English Heritage Book of Glastonbury*, London: Batsford, 1993

Reid, H. *Arthur the Dragon King: The Barbarian Roots of Britain's Greatest Legends*, Headline, 2001

Rich, J. (ed.) *The City in Late Antiquity*, Routledge, 1992

Ridley, R.T. (trans.) *Zosimus: New History*, Sydney: Australian Association for Byzantine Studies, 1982

Rivet, A.L.F. and Smith, C. *The Place-names of Roman Britain*, Batsford, 1979

Roberts, B.F. (ed.) *Early Welsh Poetry: Studies in the Book of Aneirin*, Aberystwyth: National Library of Wales, 1988

Salway, P. *Roman Britain*, Oxford: Oxford University Press, 1981

Scott, J. *The Early History of Glastonbury*, Woodbridge: Boydell & Brewer, 1981

Sherley-Price, L. (trans.) *Bede: A History of the English Church and People*, Harmondsworth: Penguin, 1955

Skene, W. *The Four Ancient Books of Wales*, Edinburgh: Edmonston and Douglas, 1868

Skene, W.F. *Arthur and the Britons in Wales and Scotland*, Felinfach, Llanerch, 1988

Smith, A.H.W. 'Gildas the poet', *Arthurian Literature 10* (1990)

——, The names on the Stone, in *Ceridwen's Cauldron 39*, Oxford: Oxford Arthurian Society, 1998

Snyder, C. *An Age of Tyrants: Britain and the Britons* A.D. *400–600*, Stroud: Sutton Publishing, 1998

——, *Exploring the World of King Arthur*, London: Thames & Hudson, 2000

Tatlock, J.S.P. *The Legendary History of Britain*, New York: Gordian Press, 1950

Thomas, C. *Tintagel: Arthur and Archaeology*, Batsford/English Heritage, 1993

Thompson, E.A. 'Gildas and the history of Britain', *Britannia 10* (1979)

——, *Saint Germanus of Auxerre and the End of Roman Britain*, Woodbridge: Boydell Press, 1984

Thorpe, L. (ed. and trans.) *Geoffrey of Monmouth, The History of the Kings of Britain*, Harmondsworth: Penguin, 1966

——, *Gerald of Wales: Description of Wales*, Harmondsworth: Penguin, 1983

Thorpe, L. (trans.) *Gregory of Tours: History of the Franks*, Harmondsworth: Penguin, 1974

Vinaver, E. *Malory, Works*, Oxford: Oxford University Press, 1971

Wacher, J.S. *The Towns of Roman Britain*, Routledge, 1995

Wade-Evans, A.W. *Nennius's 'History of the Britons' together with 'The Annals of the Britons' and 'Court Pedigrees of Hywel the Good'*, London: Society for Promoting Christian Knowledge, 1938

——, *Vitae Sanctorum Britanniae et Genealogiae*, Cardiff: University of Wales Press Board, 1944

Walsh, P.G. and Kennedy, M.J. (ed. and trans.) *William of Newburgh, Historia Rerum Anglicarum*, Warminster, Aris & Phillips, 1988

White, R. *King Arthur in Legend and History*, J.M. Dent, Orion Publishing, 1997

Whitelock, D. (ed.) *English Historical Documents c. 500–1042*, Eyre & Spottiswoode, 1955

Williams, H. *Two Lives of Gildas by a Monk of Rys and Caradoc of Llancarfan*, Cymmrodorion Record Series, 1899

Williams, I. *The Beginnings of Welsh Poetry*, ed. R. Bromwich, Cardiff: University of Wales Press, 1972

Williams, I. and Williams J.E. Caerwyn, ed. and trans. *The Poems of Taliesin*, Dublin: Institute for Advanced Studies, 1968

Winterbottom, M. *Gildas: The Ruin of Britain and other Documents*, Chichester: Phillimore, 1978

Wood, M. *In Search of the Dark Ages*, BBC, 1981

Wright, N. 'Geoffrey of Monmouth and Gildas', *Arthurian Literature 2* (1982)

——, 'Geoffrey of Monmouth and Gildas Revisited', *Arthurian Literature 4* (1985)

——, 'Did Gildas read Orosius?' *Cambridge Medieval Celtic Studies 9* (1985)

——, *The Historia Regum Britanniae of Geoffrey of Monmouth*, Cambridge: D.S. Brewer, 1985

——, 'Geoffrey of Monmouth and Bede', *Arthurian Literature 6* (1986)

INDEX